Intru
in the

The Australian Quest for Identity

Intruders in the Bush

The Australian Quest for Identity

Edited by John Carroll

DAMAGED

DAMAGED

Melbourne
Oxford University Press
Oxford   New York   Auckland

OXFORD UNIVERSITY PRESS
Oxford London Glasgow New York Toronto
Delhi Bombay Calcutta Madras Karachi
Kuala Lumpur Singapore Hong Kong Tokyo
Nairobi Dar Es Salaam Cape Town
Melbourne Auckland

and associate companies in

Beirut Berlin Ibadan Mexico City

National Library of Australia
Cataloguing in Publication Data:

Carroll, John
Intruders in the Bush
ISBN 0 19 554308 4
1. National characteristics. Australian—Addresses,
essays, lectures. I. Carroll, John, 1944
155.8'9'94

Designed by Steve Dunbar
Computer photocomposed at Griffin Press Limited
Printed in Hong Kong
Published by Oxford University Press, 7 Bowen Crescent, Melbourne

To arrive in a new and alien land, to build houses and towns, to join them with roads, even to clear the land and start to farm it, all this—the physical inhabiting—is much easier than the psychological settling of the country. This book is about the attempt to find a psychological, even a spiritual, home in Australia. What was at stake in such an endeavour, which is far from complete, was the development of a feeling of attachment to the new land: that this was home, that this was where we belonged. Such a settling of the mind takes many generations, and even when great progress has been made the attachment, the bond, is a precarious one for each new generation to take up and maintain, never mind strengthen. For such bonds to develop, kith and kin need to have been buried in the soil; young men and women need to have grown up under the skies, to have tested their dreams of intimacy and family, of work and citizenship; they need to have suffered and triumphed, to have strained and failed, and in many different ways; institutions of government and law, of education and religion, have to be built and occupied; communal and national crises, whether of drought, fire, economic depression or war, have to be experienced and withstood. Only then the great restlessless, the feverish insecurity, that comes from being homeless, may start to calm.

Many do now feel a little at home in Australia. They look back over their shoulders to the country of their ancestors as the centre of meaning and authority less and less. They are becoming 'Australian', and if we had the insight we could show a part of their identity that has grown out of their living on this continent and among its people. Some peculiarity of experience, almost a national identity, has by now evolved.

For a hundred years there have been repeated attempts to give this peculiar experience a name, to plot its identity. It has become a national obsession, which suggests that nobody among the commentators and myth-makers has really succeeded in reaching the truth. Many have tried to portray identity in terms of a typical character, a special sort of man who grew up in Australian conditions. Others have attempted to enshrine rites and events that are uniquely Australian. This book will look at the more important and influential attempts to generate a national myth, it will consider the drawbacks of the resulting myths—whether they are plausible—and finally it will turn to recent attempts at a different vision of Australia.

I am indebted to the journal, *Historical Studies*. Its October 1978 issue, devoted to the Australian Legend, gave me the idea for this book. The editors have kindly allowed me to use three articles from that issue; they appear here as chapters 2, 6 and 7, the first and last partly amended. I wish also to acknowledge the splendid editorial work of Valerie Haye, at Oxford University Press in Melbourne, whose suggestions led to great improvements in both the structure and content of this book.

John Carroll

Part I
The Classical Legends of Australian Identity

One legend from the nineteenth century has dominated Australia's thinking about itself, that of the bushman, of his egalitarian temper, and the value he placed on mateship. In this part, Eleanor Hodges summarizes the most thorough and influential presentation of the bushman legend, that given by Russel Ward in his book *The Australian Legend*. John Hirst outlines the alternative nineteenth-century legend, also from the bush, that of the pioneer. Ned Kelly has an obvious place among the classical myths, as the one figure in Australian history to become a legend himself: Angus McIntyre tells the story of this folk hero. Finally Bill Gammage tells of the type of heroism and fellow feeling that made the Anzacs the one group in our history to have caught the national imagination. Both Kelly and Anzac amplify the bushman tradition.

1. The Bushman Legend

Eleanor Hodges

The Australian Legend[1] presents the results of Dr Russel Ward's research into the historical origins and development of the national self-image. Its thesis is that a specifically Australian out-look emerged first and most clearly among the early bush workers in the pastoral industry . . . 'and that this group has had an influence, completely disproportionate to its numerical and economic strength, on the attitudes of the whole community'.[2] The author claims that the myth of the 'typical'—not average— Australian, although exaggerated and romanticized, has reality, not only because it is rooted in a nation's real past, but because it influences present-day ideas of how Australians ought 'typically' to behave.

In Ward's view, the stereotype of the myth is commonly regarded as

. . . a practical man, rough and ready in his manners, and quick to decry affectation. . . . He is a great improviser . . . willing to 'have a go' at anything, but . . . content with a task done in a way which is 'near enough'. Though capable of great exertion in an emergency, he normally feels no impulse to work hard. . . . He swears hard and consistently, gambles heavily and often, and drinks deeply on occasion. . . . He is usually taciturn . . . stoical . . . and sceptical about the value of religion, and of intellectual and cultural pursuits generally. He believes that Jack is not only as good as his master, but

... probably a good deal better, and so he is a great 'knocker' of eminent people, unless, as in the case of his sporting heroes, they are distinguished by physical prowess. He is a fiercely independent person who hates officiousness and authority—especially when ... embodied in military officers and policemen. Yet he is very hospitable and, above all, will stick to his mates through thick and thin. . . . He tends to be a rolling stone, highly suspect if he should chance to gather much moss.[3]

Ward maintains these characteristics were widely attributed to the pastoral workers of last century: a group described by Anthony Trollope in the 1870s as 'a nomad tribe'. Drawing upon historical documents, literary writings, and folk ballads, the author traces the process by which the distinctive ethos of the bush worker spread upwards through Australian society, and outwards from the interior, to influence subtly the manners and mores of the whole population.

The aim of this chapter is to present a condensed version of Ward's major arguments in support of his thesis. The sub-headings used throughout replicate the chapter titles of *The Australian Legend* from Chapter Two onwards.

The Founding Fathers

The national 'mystique' of this country owes more to the convict influence than is generally supposed or acknowledged. For almost the first half-century of its existence, White Australia was primarily an extensive gaol, with 'Old Australians'—convicts, ex-convicts, and native-born people (Currency)—outnumbering free settlers and officials by seven to one in 1828, and remaining a majority of the population until the discovery of gold in 1851.

The lack of an established aristocracy in Australian society encouraged many of the more respectable free settlers and officials to strive towards attaining upper-class exclusiveness, chiefly through the maintenance of English attitudes and connections. This meant that not only the native-born, but poor immigrants generally, aligned themselves with the emancipist class, and tended to adopt the manners and mores of the ex-convicts. The result was a disproportionately weighted lower-class in pre-Gold Rush Australia, which greatly intensified the erosion of traditional beliefs and attitudes occurring in all English-speaking societies in the nineteenth century.

Class divisions and hostility were further reinforced by the labouring class in Australia initially being almost entirely composed of assigned men or ex-convicts. Nevertheless, the perennial labour shortage, and the necessity to adapt to the difficult conditions of life in the colony produced attitudes among the workers which were variously described as 'manly independence' or 'insolent insubordination' according to the view-point of the observer.

If the convict influence was strong in early Australia, what was its particular nature? Undoubtedly the brutality of the prison system and harshness of life in the colony reinforced many vicious aspects of convict behaviour, but the same conditions also fostered traits usually regarded as characteristic of the convict in this country: a collectivist anti-authoritarian morality, physical endurance, and resourcefulness. Added to these germinal elements of the Australian mystique was the greater degree of social mobility occurring in comparison with older societies which, combined with the insatiable demand for labour, tended to have a generally levelling effect without diminishing class consciousness and hostility.

Celts and Currency

While convicts had a disproportionately strong influence upon the nascent Australian ethos of the working class, within this class, Irishmen and native-born similarly exerted a disproportionately strong and increasing influence.

In the 1840s, there were three times as many people of Irish descent in New South Wales as in the British Isles, and more than half of the assisted immigrants reaching the mother colony were Irish. Most were extremely poor working people who brought with them a strong antipathy to British rule; an antipathy already present among the political prisoners transported after the 1798 rebellion in Ireland. This anti-British feeling aided the growth of nationalism by weakening attachment to England and Empire, while the Irish–Catholic outlook in general played an important role in shaping the developing nationalist feeling among the working class in pre-Gold Rush Australia.

Among the Currency population, nationalism found its main expression in a pride based upon a high valuation of the 'practical' virtues, and consequent contempt for the 'new chum' middle-class Englishman. Currency Lads were famous—or infamous—for their precocity, rough behaviour, dislike of authority, independence, and thorough-going egalitarianism based on a relative economic security. Convicts, emancipists, native-born, and immigrant workers alike shared the conviction that, morally, Australia was 'their' country, and resented that so much of it should be given by the government to rich new-comers. This resentment was to find its clearest expression in the elevation of the bushranger to the role of folk hero.

'Up the Country'

It has been seen that many of the principal ingredients of the Australian myth—a collectivist morality, an anti-authoritarian egalitarian outlook, independence, toughness, resourcefulness and adaptability—sprang from convict, Irish and native-born sources in early Australian society. After the crossing of the Blue Mountains in 1813, these streams were to converge and coalesce beyond the Great Dividing Range, where the particular conditions of the Australian interior would transmute them '. . . into something new, which yet included them all'.[4] What was the nature of this distinctive ethos?

Unlike the American West which promoted small farm settle-ment and therefore the ethic of individualism, the nature of the Australian interior and the economic conditions of the nine-teenth century created large single properties employing many casual hands. This brought into being a semi-nomadic rural proletariat, overwhelmingly masculine in composition, and strongly collectivist in outlook. The hazards, hardships, and extreme loneliness of bush life made the practice of 'mateship' not only essential for survival but, in the absence of white women and organized religion, virtually the only vehicle for emotional release, altruism, and commitment. Several bush songs and stories suggest the extent to which mateship became for many bushmen a substitute for religion.

A further necessity for survival in a nomadic lifestyle is a free and easy hospitality, and this, too, became a tradition of life in the outback, although operating always on the two levels of 'house' and 'hut'. Toughness and adaptability were similarly essential abilities for bush workers, with stringy-bark and green-hide coming to symbolize the outback Australian's capacity for improvisation.

The lack of white women and the practice of paying off workers at the end of a season helped establish the custom of 'work and bust': the drunken spree which became a ritual of outback life. The custom probably also had its roots in the wide-spread belief among the workers that Australia's land laws made it impossibly difficult for a poor man ever to become a land owner.

Nevertheless, the wages offered by the squatters on the stations were high, and this, together with the promise of a free, vagabond way of life, attracted many 'old Australians' to the bush. Newer immigrants to New South Wales were generally repelled by the strangeness, hardships, and isolation of bush life, and preferred to remain in or around Sydney. Hence, Australians came to be viewed by newcomers as typically men of the outback complete with stockwhip and cabbage-tree hat, because, relative to the rest of the population, that was where most were to be found.

The particular ethos which emerged as a result of these social, geographic, and economic conditions therefore had as its major elements a comradely independence based on group solidarity and relative economic plenty, an intense loyalty to one's 'mate', a capacity for improvisation, physical endurance and physical prowess, a reckless improvidence, and the conviction that the working bushman was the 'real' Australian.

The Gold Rush

The germinal nationalist feeling which developed among the working people of Australia in the first half of the nineteenth century found its clearest expression in the bush ethos described above. What, however, was the effect of the gold discoveries upon the men of the outback and the growing spirit of nationalism?

Although the Gold Rush brought many dramatic changes to Australian society and greatly strengthened the middle class in the cities, its influence upon 'up-country' life was small. For a start, its impact was felt less in New South Wales than in Victoria, for although the population of Victoria increased six-fold during the 'golden decade', that of the mother colony merely doubled, and more than half this number were ex-convicts or native-born. Nevertheless, the gold-fields were a natural attraction for the adventurous and vagabond pastoral worker, and many more were encountered on the diggings by newcomers than would have been the case had the immigrants remained in or near the cities.

It is certain that the 'old Australians' influenced the gold-seekers more than they were influenced by them. On the diggings, only the Chinese remained a distinct group; the British tended to merge with the existing population and learn their ways as quickly as possible. In the words of one observer '. . . it is a constant ambition among the "new-chums" to be taken for old hands in the colony'.[5] Later arrivals on the gold-fields were to find their predecessors already strongly influenced by the indigenous outlook.

Mateship, and an anti-authoritarian, collective morality were two important elements of the bushman's ethos taken over by the diggers. The first aspect was evident among the small groups of men who worked the mines, and who were universally known as 'mates', while group solidarity was reinforced by the miners shared antagonism to the licence-hunting officials.

The diggings were also forcing grounds for other outback traits such as adaptability, physical endurance, independence, and egalitarian relationships. The presence of the Chinese injected a new element, that of racism, into the developing ethos. Another new element came with the increased literacy of many of the newcomers in comparison with the pre-Gold Rush inhabitants. Before this time, the sentiments of the bushmen had largely been embodied in song and speech, but increasingly what was felt to be distinctively Australian was captured in prose and verse. The result was to make the 'nomad tribe' more self-conscious, and aware of its distinctive ethos.

It is clear that the flood of immigrants during the decade 1851–61 did not have the effect of swamping the existing social mores of the Australian working class as is often supposed. Some elements were reinforced by the conditions of life on the diggings. Neither was the developing spirit of nationalism destroyed by the influx of newcomers; at most, it was temporarily delayed and superficially overlaid. The sentiment re-emerged powerfully in the last decades of the century to deeply influence and colour the political and literary outlook of the middle class.

The Bushrangers

One reason for the importance of the bushranger in the Australian legend has already been noted, but there were other reasons why bushrangers enjoyed such great prestige during the convict period.

Apart from the fact that the romantic aura surrounding the highwayman in European society was at its height at the end of the eighteenth century, bushrangers in Australia gained prestige in the eyes of many colonists simply by being professional opponents of the police. Originally, nearly all the New South Wales police force were convicts or ex-convicts, who were detested by their fellows for breaking the first principle of the 'government man': loyalty to one's mates. Throughout the nineteenth century there is evidence of constant complaints against police brutality, stupidity and corruption. Even in Victoria—a state which prided itself on its lack of convict ancestry—anti-authoritarian feeling was quick to flair up whenever a bush-ranger embarrassed the forces of law and order.

Most bushrangers were runaway convicts, and many were Irish. The convict system 'manufactured' bushrangers, not only because of its brutality, but because the chronic shortage of labour was a constant temptation to free settlers to prolong an assigned servant's sentence, particularly of those who worked hard and behaved well. What began, however, as an alternative to despair, continued for so long because of the widespread popular sympathy and admiration the outlaws enjoyed. The bushranger exemplified the outback ethos in its most extreme form, being more completely independent, anti-authoritarian, tough, resourceful, and loyal to his mates, than the most thoroughly acclimatized bush worker. To lower-class people generally—and usually to themselves also—bushrangers were the 'wild colonial boys': Australians *par excellence*. In a newly developing society which lacked war heroes it was not surprising that '. . . folk tradition clothed their crimes in nationalist garb'.[6]

The Bushman Comes of Age

Before being enshrined in the national self-image, the bushman had to reach full stature in his up-country life.

Although the influence of the Gold Rush had been felt more in the cities than in the interior of Australia, some changes had taken place in the outback as a result of the gold discoveries.

One important development was a great strengthening of nationalist feeling as a consequence of the anti-Chinese agitations on the gold-fields, and contempt for the English 'new-chum'.

Another effect of the Gold Rush had been the fencing of sheep runs as a result of the shortage of labour in the inland. This did away with the need for shepherding, considered by most outback workers to be a degrading occupation, and the virtual disappearance of the despised 'crawler' greatly enhanced the *esprit de corps* among the bushmen. Nevertheless, hierarchical levels of prestige among shearers, overlanders, cattle-men, and sheepmen were still evident.

The pattern of 'work and bust' continued, but in the later part of the century there appears to have been some moderation in the bushman's drinking habits. This was possibly due not only to the increasing presence of white women in the outback, but to the outback workers growing self-respect and self-awareness.

Although class lines were almost as sharply drawn as in convict days, squatters and men were united in their antipathy towards the selector. Most small farmers were desperately poor and over-worked, and could neither afford to pay the migratory bushman the high wages offered by the squatters, nor provide the traditional bush hospitality obtainable on the stations. The term 'cocky' applied by the pastoral worker to the small farmer was synonomous in the 1880s with meanness and stupidity.

In spite of these changes, however, the most striking thing about the manners and mores of the bush lay in their continuity: the later bushman exhibiting even more clearly than his predecessor the 'manly independence' and egalitarian collectiv-ism whose sum was comprised in the concept of mateship. By the end of the 1880s, mateship in the outback had become such a powerful institution that contemporary writings imply it could be perilous to refuse an invitation to drink. Bush songs and stories of the period clearly underline the predominant values: the greatest good was to stand by one's mates; the greatest evil, to desert them. The fictional characterizations of bushmen by Furphy, Lawson, and Paterson, the great nationalist writers of the nineties, clearly reveal the prototype at the turn of the century; a prototype which is supported by many of the more factual writings of the time.

Apotheosis of the Nomad Tribe

The process by which the romanticized figure of the 'noble bushman' became the core of a nation's self-image culminated in the surge of nationalist sentiment towards the end of the nineteenth century, the ideal giving strength and cohesion to the dominant, but disparate social forces at work in Australian society during this period.

Underlying the surfacing of this powerful current and the emergence of the symbol was the newly predominant influence of the native-born, and the decreasing isolation of the bush. Railways and other forms of communication had not only brought the bush closer to the city, but had made city dwellers aware as never before of the old up-country ethos. As the nomad tribe of pastoral workers disappeared from the real world, their distinctive outlook and lifestyle became embalmed in the national consciousness as myth.

The myth-making process was greatly accelerated by two events in particular: the rapid growth of the trade union movement, and the discovery of the bush by literary men. Trade unionism was shaped and coloured by the pre-existent bush ethos and drew much of its early strength from the Amalgamated Shearers' Union, but although the movement helped spread the ethos widely through the whole community, it was probably literature, being less class-bound and operating at a deeper level of consciousness, which was the more important force in the osmotic process. As Vance Palmer states:

It is hard to realize now the excitement caused by such ballads as Paterson's 'Clancy of the Overflow', or such stories as Lawson's, 'The Drover's Wife' but to the people who read them they seemed to open up new vistas.[7]

By the time of Federation, the extinct bushman of the writers of the nineties was firmly enshrined in both the literary and popular imagination as the culture-hero upon whose characteristics many Australians tended—consciously or unconsciously —to model their attitudes to life. The myth was to become particularly potent in wartime, when so many of the conditions of active service reproduced the conditions of life among the nomad tribe.

Two Noble Frontiersmen

The steps have been traced by which the distinctive ethos of the Australian pastoral workers of last century came to have a quite disproportionate influence on the Australian mystique. There remains the question of why this should have happened.

A partial answer is suggested in the 'frontier theory' put forward in 1893 by the American historian, F. J. Turner. Before this time, American historians had tended to explain successive developments in American history by reference to European influences, but Turner argued that indigenous influences—and in particular the frontier influence—were no less important to an understanding of American history, the two most important effects of the frontier being the promotion of national unity and sentiment, and the promotion of democracy.

It has been argued that the Australian outback has been a similar kind of forcing ground, although important differences exist between the two nations' concepts of democracy. To the pioneer of the American West democracy meant freedom to get to the top; to the Australian pastoral worker it meant freedom to resist authority by combining with one's mates against the wealthy squatter, an attitude epitomized in 'Waltzing Matilda', Australia's most popular folk ballad.

Australia, like America, has needed to develop national cohesion and identity through differentiation from its origins. In the nineteenth century's partly unconscious search for a culture-hero to symbolize the nation, the interior offered a candidate whose outlook and lifestyle least resembled those of his British or European ancestors. While it is true, therefore, that the Australian frontier has promoted the growth of nationalism, it is also true that nationalism has promoted the romanticization of the frontier.

2. The Pioneer Legend

J. B. Hirst

Schools have been the most influential purveyors of the pioneer legend and in literature for children it occurs in its purest form. The first item in the Fifth Grade *Victorian School Reader*, in use for two generations or more earlier this century, was the poem 'Pioneers' by Frank Hudson:[1]

> We are the old world people,
>> Ours were the hearts to dare;
> But our youth is spent, and our backs are bent,
>> And the snow is on our hair . . .
> We wrought with a will unceasing,
>> We moulded, and fashioned, and planned,
> And we fought with the black, and we blazed the track,
>> That ye might inherit the land . . .
> Take now the fruit of our labour,
>> Nourish and guard it with care,
> For our youth is spent, and our backs are bent,
>> And the snow is on our hair.

This legend, it need scarcely be said, is very different from the one discussed by Russel Ward. It celebrates courage, enterprise, hard work, and perseverance; it usually applies to the people who first settled the land, whether as pastoralists or farmers, and not to those they employed, although these were never specifically excluded. It is a nationalist legend which deals in an heroic way with the central experience of European settlement in Australia: the taming of the new environment to man's use. The qualities with which it invests the pioneers—courage, enterprise and so on—perhaps do not strain too much at the truth, although it assumes wrongly that owners always did their own pioneering. Its legendary aspect lies more clearly in the claim that these people were not working merely for themselves or their families, but for us, 'That ye might inherit the land.' The pioneer story can also be described as legendary because of what it leaves out: there is usually no mention of the social, legal or economic determinants of land settlement. The pioneers are depicted in a world limited by the boundaries of their proper-ties, subduing the land, and battling the elements. Their enemies are drought, flood, fire, sometimes Aborigines; never low prices, middle-men, lack of capital, or other pioneers.

The pioneer legend can scarcely help being conservative in its political implications. It encourages reverence for the past, it celebrates individual rather than collective or state enterprise, and it provides a classless view of society since all social and economic differences are obliterated by the generous applica-tion of the 'pioneer' label. In claiming that the pioneers were working for us, it puts on later generations a special obligation not to tamper with the world which the pioneers made. One of the first of the epic pioneer poems was written in 1898 by Robert Caldwell, a conservative politician in South Australia. It concluded with an attack on land reformers and socialists for wanting to deprive the pioneers of their rightful heritage.[2] During the 1890 Maritime Strike, the *Argus* declared 'this country should remain what the pioneers intended it to be—a land free for every man who is willing to work, no matter whether he belongs to a union or not'.[3] The travelling lecturer of the Victorian Employers Federation used the same theme to keep the country safe from socialism,[4] and it has remained a minor strand in conservative rhetoric since.

Although the pioneer legend is very different from the other legend, in its origins it is quite closely linked to it: it began at the same time—in the 1880s and 1890s—and was celebrated by the same people. It owes much to Paterson and Lawson.

The term 'pioneer' came into common use in Victoria and South Australia sooner than in New South Wales.[5] It was applied to those immigrants who had come to the colonies in their early years and so was not limited to those who had settled and worked the land. These pioneers were much honoured at the jubilee of South Australia in 1886 and during the Melbourne Centennial Exhibition of 1888.[6] New South Wales could not look back with similar confidence to its origins or so readily identify its 'pioneers'. In Victoria the members of the Australian Natives Association, looking towards the future of the coming Australian race, showed only a formal respect for the pioneers and were seeking genuinely national symbols and causes.[7] The honouring of early colonists as pioneers reflected the growth of colonial and local patriotisms; they clearly could not serve as heroes for the new nation.

'Pioneers' acquired its present primary meaning—that is, those who first settled and worked the land—in the 1890s. The older meaning survived, and still survives, but it now took second place. The shifting of meaning is nicely illustrated in the special Old Colonist numbers of the Melbourne *Tatler* in 1898.[8] Under the heading 'The Pioneers of Victoria' appeared bio- graphies of many early colonists, including bishops, officials, merchants, professional men, as well as settlers on the land. These were pioneers according to the earlier meaning of the word. But the cover illustration depicted a settler pushing his way through the bush and carried two lines from a woeful poem, 'The Pioneers', which appeared in full inside: 'Can you not follow them forth/Through the black treacherous bush.' This was the new meaning of the term, but it was not well deserved by many of the worthies featured inside who had moved straight from the ship to Melbourne and had never pioneered in the bush. The pioneers as settlers on the land were a much more anonymous group than pioneers as early colonists, who always had an establishment, who's-who air about them. They were not identified with a particular colony and were much more closely connected with the land itself. The pioneers as immigrants had been first identified and honoured by the old colonists themselves. Pioneers as settlers and national heroes were the creation of poets and writers. It is to their work we now turn.

Ken Inglis in *The Australian Colonists* has outlined the largely unsuccessful search for national heroes in the years before 1870 We can see the difficulties facing a nationalist writer of this period in the work of Henry Kendall, the native-born poet who, like his friend Harpur, knew that poets can make a nation, and saw that as one of his tasks, but who never found the words or the audience to succeed. At the last, however, he touched on the pioneer theme which was left to others to develop. Kendall's views of what a proper hero should be were heavily influenced by the classical tradition of Greece and Rome. Heroes had to be statesmen or soldiers, preferably those who died for their country. For statesmen Kendall offered Governor Phillip, Wentworth, Bland, Lang, and other politicians of the 1840s and 1850s. This civic theme was extended by the celebration of those who built the Australian cities; this rather than the settlement of the land was the great triumph of colonization, and one that could be described in classical terms. Melbourne is 'Like a dream of Athens, or of Rome'; Sydney is 'this Troy'. Australia had no great warriors, but the explorers in their bravery and in their deaths were acceptable substitutes. Kendall frequently celebrates Cook, Leichhardt, Burke and Wills. In a later poem 'Blue Mountain Pioneers' (1880) he moves away from the more heroic big-name explorers and celebrates the work of Blaxland, Lawson, and Wentworth in crossing the Blue Mountains in 1817.[9] This was a short expedition and it didn't end in death, but it could be linked much more closely than other expeditions to the settlement of the land.

> Behind them were the conquered hills—they faced
> The vast green West, with glad, strange beauty graced;

> And every tone of every cave and tree
> Was a voice of splended prophecy.

What that conquest foretold was the settlement of the western lands, but Kendall was tied so closely to the notion of the heroic as public and civic, that he never celebrated the coming of the settlers themselves. For him 'pioneers' was reserved for the explorers.

This poem was published posthumously in collected editions of Kendall's work in 1886 and 1890. Paterson must have read it there for it forms the basis of the historical section in his poem 'Song of the Future' which is the classic statement of the pioneer legend, frequently reproduced in anthologies and school magazines.[10] This poem is much more ambitious than his usual ballad or bush-yarn work. It calls for a new response to landscape and nature in Australia, and to the history of European man in the continent. Paterson begins by criticizing Adam Lindsay Gordon, Marcus Clarke, and others who had written in gloomy terms about the Australian scene, and he rejects the stock claims that Australian birds were songless and its flowers scentless. On Australian history he acknowledges that there has been no 'hot blood spilt'—a commonly held prerequisite for worthwhile history—but Australians do have something to celebrate: 'honest toil and valiant life'. This introduces the historical section of the poem. The treatment of the crossing of the Blue Mountains is more extensive than Kendall's, and it is told as a great saga of the people, rather than as a celebration of individual heroes. The names of the explorers, significantly, are not mentioned, and the poem is more concerned with the achievements of those who came after them.

> The mountains saw them marching by:
> They faced the all-consuming drought,
> They would not rest in settled land:
> But, taking each his life in hand,
> Their faces ever westward bent
> Beyond the farthest settlement,

> Responding to the challenge cry
> Of 'better country farther out'.

Paterson measures the extent of this achievement by dealing with a sceptic who declares 'it was not much' since the resistance to expansion was slight and—the stock objection—'not much blood was spilt':

> It was not much! but we who know
> The strange capricious land they trod—
> At times a stricken, parching sod,
> At times with raging floods beset—
> Through which they found their lonely way,
> Are quite content that you should say
> It was not much, while we can feel
> That nothing in the ages old,
> In song or story written yet
> On Grecian urn or Roman arch,
> Though it should ring with clash of steel,
> Could braver histories unfold
> Than this bush story, yet untold—
> The story of their westward march.

This poem, more than any other single piece, did bring about that new perception of Australia's past which Paterson sought. He still had to defend his heroes against those of Greece and Rome, but soon the heroism of the pioneers was accepted without question, and the references to the classical tradition ceased.

Lawson was more consistently preoccupied with Australia's past than Paterson. In a contribution to the *Republican* in 1888, he called for much more Australian history to be taught in schools.[11] As a nationalist, he wanted to give his country a past to be proud of. In the early stories and poems Lawson follows the orthodox line of dating Australia's greatness from the gold rushes, and so he accords heroic status to the diggers. These were the men 'who gave our country birth'.[12] He rates their achievements higher than those of the explorers, the ranking heroes of the time: 'Talk about the heroic struggles of early explorers in a hostile country; but for dogged determination and courage in the face of poverty, illness, and distance, commend me to the old-time digger—the truest soldier Hope every had!'[13] For the settlers on the land and particularly the selectors, Lawson in his early years had scant respect. He criticizes the selectors for their slovenliness, dirt, and ignorance, and depicts settling on the land not as an heroic endeavour, but as a madness. But this attitude changed with time. His early emphasis on the wretchedness of the selector's life had had a political purpose, since he wanted to discredit those who saw small holdings as the cure for Australia's social ills. He never abandons the view that the life of small settlers could be wretched and narrow, but he becomes more willing to celebrate their powers of endurance and the co-operation between them and, in the Joe Wilson series, the satisfactions and pleasures which their small successes gave them, although here Mrs Spicer, 'watering them geraniums', is still present as counterpoint being worn literally to death. In his verse, where he always wrote at a higher level of generality and usually with disastrous results, he came to see the settling of the land as the central theme of the nation's history, which could comprehend much more than the coming of the diggers. 'How the land was won' (1899) is a complete statement of this theme, and is the counterpart to Paterson's 'Song of the Future'.[14] The settlers are described firstly as immigrants leaving the old world, and the poem tells of the variety of hardships and deprivations which they experienced in Australia. These two verses give the flavour of the whole, perhaps too favourable a view, since six verses of hardships become a little tedious, although the quality of the verse is better than Lawson's average:

> With God, or a dog, to watch, they slept
>   By the camp-fires' ghastly glow,
> Where the scrubs were dark as the blacks that crept
>   With 'nulla' and spear held low;

Death was hidden amongst the trees,
    And bare on the glaring sand
They fought and perished by twos and threes
    And that's how they won the land!

They toiled and they fought through the shame of it—
    Through wilderness, flood, and drought;
They worked, in the struggles of early days,
    Their sons' salvation out.
The white girl–wife in the hut alone,
    The man on the boundless run,
The miseries suffered, unvoiced, unknown—
    And that's how the land was won.

In the early twentieth century scores of pioneer poems by many hands rang the changes on these hardships. Two important aspects of the legend are embodied in 'How the land was won': in the first verse (not quoted here) we are told that the land was won 'for us'; secondly, there is no differentiation of the settlers—they are all simply 'they'. This conflation is the more noticeable in Lawson since elsewhere he gives such particular detail about social conflict on the land. Nor can the co-operation among the settlers—in the stories he describes young men putting in crops for sick men and widows, and women caring for bereaved neighbours—find a mention here, since the pioneer legend prefers to see hardships overcome, if at all, by further individual effort. It is a sign of the attractiveness of the pioneer legend to nationalists that Lawson was ready to abandon so much to produce his simple compelling saga. Of course the Lawson of 1899 had abandoned much of his early radicalism, and in his disillusionment the struggle on the land took on an elemental, purifying quality, but changing personal views will not wholly explain 'How the land was won'. The pioneer legend is a literary mode or a type of history which shapes material in its own way. Writing on a different assignment in the same year he composed 'How the land was won', Lawson highlighted the gossip and bitchiness of country towns and hinted broadly that incest was frequently practised in the isolated selectors' huts.[15] That would never do for the pioneers.

In Lawson's prose there is little explicit glorification of the pioneers, but here Lawson made his most powerful contribution to the pioneer legend with his description of bush women. 'The Drover's Wife' occupies an important place in the pioneer canon. There is a sense in which all his bush women are heroines because, as he insists time and again, the bush is no place for women. When her husband had money, the drover's wife was taken to the city by train—in a sleeping compartment—and put up at the best hotel. For Lawson, women deserve the attention and comfort which this signifies, and which bush life denied them. While she waits for the snake, the drover's wife reads the *Young Ladies Journal*, but Lawson does not use the hard life of a country woman to deride the artificiality of the woman's journal world; rather, he accepts that as legitimate, and so emphasizes the sacrifices of the women who are obliged to live a different life, and in many cases do the work of men. The theme of women as pioneers was taken up by G. Essex Evans, a Queensland poet of the nineties, in his 'Women of the West'—'The Hearts that made the Nation were the Women of the West'. This, together with his other pioneer piece 'The Nation Builders', have frequently been reprinted in children's literature and anthologies.[16]

The work of Paterson and Lawson is described by Ward as the chief vehicle for spreading a democratic, collectivist, national mystique. How was it that these writers also celebrated the pioneers which meant frequently the squatters, who had been, and were still, the enemy of democrats and radicals? In *The Australian Tradition*, A. A. Phillips has noted how sympathetic writers of the nineties were in their description of individual squatters, despite the squatters being the class enemy. Phillips offers a number of explanations for this. He wonders first whether 'the triumph of human sympathy over social prejudice' reflected the breadth of feeling one would expect in any good writer. Scarcely so, he concludes, since in other areas, notably the description of Englishmen, the writers reveal severe limitations and create caricatures. The writers knew some squatters personally and this no doubt helped them to write individualized, sympathetic portraits. But more importantly, according to Phillips, the squatter was a bushman too, and had shared with his men 'the pride and expansiveness' that came with the escape from 'fetid slums and the tight little hedgerow squares' of the old world, into the cast spaces of the new continent where the strength of individual character as a man determined success or failure. He concludes that the democratic tradition embodied in the literature reaches deep back into the pastoral age.[17] But we must remember that what squatters had felt, or others had felt about them, may well be different from their depiction in imaginative literature. The tradition of the pastoral age did not flow automatically to the pages of Lawson and Paterson. The writers were making a tradition as well as reflecting one—how much they created and how much they reported has been one of the matters debated in the argument over *The Australian Legend*. We can extend Phillips's analysis and come closer to understanding these writers' attitude to the squatter–pioneer if we examine what influenced their view of the pastoral age.

Both men were disturbed and angry at the new harshness and poverty which drought, depression, and strikes brought to the colonies in the 1880s and 1890s. They were cast into a world they did not like and, like many others before and since in this predicament, they began to exaggerate the virtues of the world they had lost. Lawson's poem 'Freedom on the Wallaby' is well known.[18] It was written in Brisbane in 1891 to support the shearers' strike, and its last verse contains the much-quoted threat of violence: 'If blood should stain the wattle'. Less well known is the previous verse:

> Our parents toiled to make a home,
>   Hard grubbin' 'twas an' clearin',
> They wasn't troubled much with lords
>   When they was pioneerin'.
> But now that we have made the land
>   A garden full of promise,

> Old Greed must crook his dirty hand
> And come ter take it from us.

Those who know Lawson's usual description of the Australian country—unyielding, desolate, drought-ridden—will scarcely credit that he could describe it as a garden: domestic, fruitful, a symbol of paradise. Lawson's explanation for the lowering of wages and the assault on the unions is that Greed has invaded this garden. It was a theme he used many times. Sometimes Greed had invaded the countryside from the cities; on other occasions it was an unwelcome import from the old world into the new. In the poems the particular forms which Greed assumed were not always defined. The stories identified the process more explicitly. In the countryside it meant the increasing ownership of pastoral properties by banks and companies, and the replacement of resident proprietors by managers. Before this process began were the good times, and squatters of that time, or who have survived from it, are described as squatters of the 'old school'. In describing Black, the squatter who employed Joe Wilson, Lawson outlines their virtues: 'He was a good sort, was Black the squatter; a squatter of the old school, who'd shared the early hardships with his men, and couldn't see why he should not shake hands and have a smoke and a yarn over old times with any of his old station hands that happened to come along.'[19] A. A. Phillips errs when he says Black is Lawson's only portrait in any detail of a squatter. There were several other good squatters—Baldy Thompson, Job Falconer, Jimmy's boss[20]—and their goodness is carefully explained: they are resident proprietors of long standing, not managers for absentees. Job Falconer, for instance, was 'Boss of the Talbragar sheep station up country in New South Wales in the early Eighties—when there were still runs in the Dingo-Scrubs out of the hands of the banks, and yet squatters who lived on their stations'. Lawson's one detailed portrait of a bad squatter is that of Wall, the man who, until it was almost too late, refused to send his employees to fight the fire on Ross's farm. Until this last-minute repentance, Wall was a hard man who had done all he could to make the selector Ross's life impossible. But he had not always been so: 'Men remembered Wall as a grand boss and a good fellow, but that was in the days before rabbits and banks, and syndicates and "pastoralists", or pastoral companies instead of good squatters.'[21] The pattern is clear: it is not only that managers for absentees are mean: all resident proprietors of the old days were good.[22]

In Paterson's work there was much less overt social commentary than in Lawson's, but briefly around 1890 Paterson was a committed reformer, and in his poem 'On Kiley's Run', published in December 1890, he gives a clear picture of the world which Greed had disrupted and the new world it was making.[23] The poem describes the 'good old station life' on Kiley's run. The squatter was resident, swagmen were welcome, there was plenty of good fellowship and horse racing with neighbouring stations, and relations between squatter and his men were excellent.

> The station-hands were friends, I wot,
>   On Kiley's Run,
> A reckless, merry-hearted lot—
> All splendid riders, and they knew
> The boss was kindness through and through.
> Old Kiley always stood their friend,
> And so they served him to the end
>   On Kiley's Run.

But droughts and losses forced the squatter into the hands of the bank, which finally took possession of the stock and sold the station. The new owner is an English absentee; a half-paid overseer runs the place, shearers wages and all other expenses are cut, swagmen and drovers receive short-shrift—and the name of the run has been changed to Chandos Park Estate. Paterson felt this transformation very keenly, for at the end of the poem he adds, for him, a rare call to arms:

> I cannot guess what fate will bring
>   To Kiley's Run—

> For chances come and changes ring—
> I scarcely think 'twill always be
> Locked up to suit an absentee;
> And if he lets it out in farms
> His tenants soon will carry arms
>   On Kiley's run.

'The Song of the Future', Paterson's classic pioneer piece, in its last section contains a similar lament for the old bush life and urges that the land be thrown open to all to reduce poverty and unemployment.

Men live by myth, and golden ages have frequently been created. What is odd about this one is that it was placed in the very recent past. The democrats and land reformers of the 1850s had denounced the squatters as monopolists and tyrants: they were the lords who would make everyone else serfs if they could. In their defence the squatters had actually attempted, fruitlessly, to attach to themselves the name of 'pioneers' and so justify their claim to retain their lands.[24] Thirty years after their political defeat, they were accorded that title, among others by the poets of democracy. How could they overlook the denunciations made so recently? A large part of the answer is simply that Lawson and Paterson, like most other people in the 1890s, knew very little of the struggles of the 1850s. John Robertson had given his name to the Selection Acts and had achieved legendary status, but he was not seen as part of a wider movement. The Australian-born certainly did not learn of the land reform movement in school. Those who had survived from that era, like Robertson himself and Parkes, did not talk freely of their early struggles, chiefly because, one supposes, the bitter social and economic divisions of those years and the whiff of republicanism which hung around the reform movement were no longer apt for their present political purposes.

The Sydney *Bulletin* was republican, a constant derider of British aristocrats and Australians who fawned on them, and it had no qualms about disturbing the liberal consensus over which Parkes and Robertson had presided, but it too did little to inform its readers—among whom were Paterson and

Lawson—of the democratic movement of the 1850s or to celebrate its triumphs. The *Bulletin* ran a very crude line on New
South Wales history: it insisted that very little had changed in the
colony since the convict days.[25] The British had created an
abomination in the convict system, and since its influence was
still potent, New South Wales could never establish a truly
democratic society until the British connection was severed. It
wrongly attributed the flogging of criminals and other evils to
the survival of the spirit of earlier times. Victoria, by contrast,
had managed something of a fresh start with its gold rushes and
the Eureka rebellion, whose anniversary the *Bulletin* wanted to
celebrate as Australia's national day. Such a view of the past
could not allow that there had been genuine and far-reaching
reforms in New South Wales in the 1850s and 1860s. The
history which the *Bulletin* promoted was Price Warung's *Tales of
the Convict System*. This was the stick to beat the British with. The
triumphs of Robertson over the landowners and squatters
would not have suited its purpose.

We are now in a position to understand better why Paterson
and Lawson were among the founders of the pioneer legend.
Their work is suffused with a generalized nostalgia—"'Twas a
better land to live in, in the days o' long ago'[26]—but they also
created a highly specific past which was free from the social evils
of the present. Before Greed invaded the land there were
humane employers and decent class relations in Australia.
Having made that past, and as they made it, they elevated the
early settlers into pioneers. That they could create this past so
freely gives new meaning to the dictum that Australia had no
history. For Paterson and Lawson, the 1840s and 1850s, when
the squatters were the popular political enemy, might never
have existed. No democratic tradition had survived from these
years.

In broad terms, the creation of the pioneer legend can be
explained by the growth of nationalism in the 1880s and the
1890s and the need to find new national heroes and symbols.
Paterson and Lawson were attracted to the pioneers as nationalists, but also as radicals. They used the past to condemn the
present. However, the pioneer legend quickly shed its radical

overtones. Paterson's classic statement 'Song of the Future' is very simply rendered innocuous in anthologies and school readers by the omission of the last section which urges that the land be thrown open to all. In any case, the golden age of pioneering was, in some respects, rather uncertain in its political implications. Paterson's claim, though false, that there had been a time when land was freely available to all did relate clearly to the current radical demand for land taxes and breaking up of large estates. But the depiction of the old station life of hard work and mutuality between boss and men can serve the conservative cause, for clearly there were no unions or industrial arbitration or parliamentary limitations on hours worked on Kiley's Run. Reform movements which aim to purify and simplify government can appeal with some chance of success to golden ages; once radicalism is associated with state regulation and ownership, as it was in Australia from the 1890s, the ideal society needs to be placed in the future rather than the past. In finding a glorious past for Australia, Paterson and Lawson ultimately did more to help the conservative cause than their own. Once there is a valued past, the future is more confined. 'She is not yet' Brunton Stephens had written of the Australian nation in 1877. Because we are nationalists as they made us, we still enjoy the celebrations of Lawson and Paterson, and we forget that as well as being an affirmation, their work marked also a retreat: the nation was no longer yet to be, it had arrived, and, more amazing still, its best days were already passed.

In 1904 Frederick McCubbin painted 'The Pioneers', a massive work in three panels which is the classic embodiment in art of the pioneer legend. The first panel shows a settler and his wife on first arriving at their selection in the forest; the second shows the selection established; and in the third, the 'triumphal stanza' as the *Age* described it:

A country youth, with reverent fingers, clears away the undergrowth from the rough wooden cross marking the last resting place of the gallant couple. In the distance the spires and bridges of a glorious young city and the stooks of a rich harvest field tell of the joys that another generation is reaping from the toil of the once lusty pioneers now gone to dust.

The painting was, and is, enormously popular, and the *Age* successfully urged that it be purchased for the National Gallery. It described the work as a 'poem of democracy'.[27]

The conservative implications of the legend have already been noted; in what sense is the legend, nevertheless, a democratic one? In the first place it accords heroic status to the ordinary man—frequently the pioneers were squatters, but small settlers were also honoured with the title. The pioneer legend transforms the low-status selector of the nineteenth century into a nation builder. The legend also proclaims that success is open to all since all may possess the requisite qualities of diligence, courage, and perseverance. Secondly, the legend provides a simple, unofficial, popular history of the nation. When it was formed the standard histories were still organized by the terms of office of the various governors to parallel the British histories which dealt with monarchs, the dates of their accession and death, and the chief events of their reign. Governors made some sense as organizing principles for the period before responsible government, but in some works their comings and goings continued to be crucial events even after responsible government. In contrast to history as high politics and administration, the pioneer legend offered social (and economic) history and declared that the people had made the nation. The 'people' in the pioneer legend have always included women. Feminists may object that too often they are seen merely as helpmeets for men, but their complaint that women have been omitted altogether from Australian history is not true of the popular history fostered by the pioneer legend. There are pioneer-women gardens and memorials in Melbourne, Adelaide, and Perth. In the celebration of state and national anniversaries, pioneer women have been honoured in special ceremonies and commemorative histories.[28] The pioneer legend is a people's legend; in this sense it is democratic. Its conservatism is not the conservatism of deference, but of communal pride in what the people have achieved.

Of democracy in the sense of a system of government, the legend has nothing to say, since it implies that politics were unnecessary or irrelevant to the work of pioneering. It is a further instance, then, of the Australian tendency to isolate politics from the heroic or the good. Paterson claimed his pioneers as worthy of Greece and Rome, but in fact he had abandoned the classical tradition which found its heroes in those who served the state. Kendall, true to that tradition, thought that an Australian democracy would want democratic statesmen for its heroes, but he was wrong, and he worked in vain on Deniehy and Lang.

The pioneer legend had a significant influence on the writing of formal history. It solved the problem which formal historians could never overcome satisfactorily: the embarrassment of the convict origins of the nation. The pioneer legend, by proclaiming the settlement of the land as the chief theme in Australia's history, found it easy not to mention the convicts at all. If you begin Australia's history with Governor Phillip, it is very difficult to avoid the convicts, although some histories for children managed it. The first formal history to reflect the influence of the pioneer legend was James Collier's *The Pastoral Age in Australasia* (1911). This dated Australia's freedom from the opening of the pastoral lands west of the mountains and rejected the traditional view that the gold rushes marked the divide from the convict origins. Collier described the old society to the east of the mountains as static, unfree, with the settlers relying on government for land, labour, stock, and markets. The new pastoral society was dynamic, independent, a wild free life that 'lifted the community to a higher plain, and started it on a new career'. He conceded that convicts were still employed but in a 'radically different' way, which was never explained.[29] Stephen Roberts in *The Pastoral Age in Australia* (1935) celebrated the pastoral expansion in a similar way and from Collier borrowed the image of the protoplasm of the nation, long lying dormant, and in the magic year 1835 showing at last what form it was going to take.[30] The theme is present too at the opening of Hancock's *Australia*: 'Wool made Australia a solvent nation, and, in the end, a free one.'[31] The concentration on the pastoral expansion meant that Sydney's merchants and trades went unexamined. So it was only recently that historians rediscovered the importance of the whale fishery and the Pacific trade, which had been known to the older historians like Rusden (1883) and Jose (1899) whose approach was strictly chronological and who wrote uninfluenced by the pioneer legend. The pioneer legend, having first excluded convicts, eventually enabled them to be rehabilitated and given a place in the nation's history. Convicts could be regarded as pioneers. In this role Mary Gilmore depicts them in 'Old Botany Bay':[32]

> I was the conscript
> Sent to hell
> To make in the desert
> The living well;
>
> I split the rock;
> I felled the tree:
> The nation was—
> Because of me.

By the early twentieth century a new meaning of 'pioneer' had come into common use. It was now also applied to people who were at present at work on the land, and particularly on new farms or at the edge of settlement. This extension of meaning occurred at a time of heightened concern for racial strength and purity and a new awareness of the vulnerability of the nation. Cities were now seen as dangers to national and racial health, and further development of the land was considered on all sides as essential for the nation's survival. The pioneer's struggle with the elements and the nation's struggle to survive in a more hostile world became fused. 'The people in the bush were fighting the battle of Australia every day and every year', said George Reid in 1909 at the foundation of the Bush Nursing Association which was formed to bring medical help to remote country areas. 'From a national point of view,' the Association declared, 'the lives of pioneers and their children are of the utmost value to the State.'[33] G. Essex Evans, one of the important makers of the legend, caught these new concerns in 'The Man Upon The Land':[34]

> The City calls, its streets are gay,
>   Its pleasures well supplied,
> So of its life-blood every day
>   It robs the countryside.
>
> How shall we make Australia great
>   And strong when danger calls
> If half the people of the State
>   Are crammed in city walls . . . ?

The concluding lines of the poem are its refrain:

> And the men that made the Nation are
>   The men upon the land.

The change of tense here illustrates nicely how the men upon the land gained in glory from the heroic status of their predecessors. Well before the Country Party was formed, its ideology had been made—by no means solely by country people—and the pioneer legend gave it added force.

After the landing at Gallipoli, Australians acquired a legend more powerful than either those of the bushmen or the pioneers. In *The Australian Legend*, Russel Ward has outlined the way in which the legend of the digger embodied aspects of the bushmen's legend. A similar process occurred with the pioneer legend. *The Anzac Memorial*, published in 1917, carried a poem by Dorothy McCrae, 'The First Brigade', reproduced subsequently in the Victorian *School Paper* with the sub-title 'The Pioneers of Australia':[35]

> They cleared the earth, and felled the trees,
> And built the towns and colonies;

> Then, to their land, their sons they gave,
> And reared them hardy, pure, and brave.
>
> They made Australia's past: to them
> We owe the present diadem;
> For, in their sons, they fight again,
> And ANZAC proved their hero strain.

The first celebration of Anzac Day in 1916 posed a problem for the compilers of the Victorian school calendar. Since 1911, 19 April had been set aside as Discovery Day. This was the anniversary of Cook's sighting of the Australian coast and was devoted to the celebration of explorers and pioneers. Since it fell so close to Anzac Day, it was suspended in 1916, but on Anzac Day teachers were encouraged to link diggers, explorers, and pioneers together: 'The lessons and addresses on Anzac Day will, no doubt, include matter appropriate to Discovery Day, such as reference to the discovery, settlement, and development of Australia.'[36] The connection between 'settlement and development' and the Anzac spirit took substantial form after the war in the soldier settlement schemes. Diggers were to become pioneers.

The subsequent history of 'pioneer' and the legend cannot be fully traced here. The legend still survives, although its foundations are not as firm as they were in the early twentieth century. It has suffered inevitably from the waning of faith in progress and the virtues of European civilization. No one now writes of the pioneers as Paterson did, although his pioneer verse is still collected in anthologies.[37] Historians have for a long time escaped the romanticism of Roberts's *Squatting Age* and have emphasized the clash between squatters' interests and those of the rest of the community. Paterson's golden age has received no help from them. The legend, which was made by creative writers, was eventually attacked by them. Brian Penton in *Land-takers* (1934) overturned the view that the squatter's life was exhilarating and free. His theme was the coarsening and hardening of a well-bred English emigrant as he coped with life in a 'gaolyard' and then on the frontier, with 'the grind and ugliness and shame of Australia'. Xavier Herbert's *Capricornia* (1938) is still the most devastating anti-pioneer piece in our literature. It confronts the legend explicitly. Herbert's Northern Territory society is brutal, chaotic, hypocritical, and drunken. The book is an indictment of the white settlers of the Territory for the destruction which they brought to Aboriginal society and for their continuing exploitation of Aborigines and half-castes. 'The Coming of the Dingoes' is how Herbert describes the arrival of the white man in the Territory. Herbert was the first to write black history in this country. Pioneers were the enemy to the original inhabitants of the land, and as sympathy with Aborigines grows and the brutalities of the frontier continues to be highlighted, the pioneers' reputation will suffer more. The growing concern with the environment will damage the pioneers still further as their ruthless exploitation of the land comes under closer scrutiny. And yet, sympathetic accounts of pioneering men and women continue to be written. Among the most notable are Margaret Kiddle's *Men of Yesterday*, Patrick White's *Tree of Man*, and Judith Wright's *Generations of Men*. While not endorsing the crudities of the pioneer legend, these works nevertheless depict the pioneers as a creative, ordering force, whose work gives their lives a certain nobility and completeness. *The Tree of Man* describes in its first pages the arrival of Stan Parker at his uncleared land in a forest, a similar scene to that McCubbin depicted in the first panel of 'The Pioneers':

Then the man took an axe and struck at the side of a hairy tree, more to hear the sound than for any other reason. And the sound was cold and loud. The man struck at the tree, and struck, till several white chips had fallen. He looked at the scar in the side of the tree. The silence was immense. It was the first time anything like this had happened in that part of the bush. . . .

The man made a lean-to with bags and a few saplings. He built a fire. He sighed at last, because the lighting of his small fire had kindled in him the first warmth of content. Of being somewhere. That particular part of the bush had been made his by the entwining fire. It licked at and swallowed the loneliness.

We may come at last to see Stan Parker merely as a destroyer of the natural environment or as a labourer transforming himself into a small property holder, but so long as our spirit stirs in other ways at this scene, the pioneer legend will not be without its force.

Popular history is still very much pioneer history, embodied in new forms now in the reconstructed pioneer villages and settlements which have proliferated throughout the country in recent years. What is conveyed by these is in some ways rather different from the classic pioneer statements in literature. The concentration is much less on the struggle on the land, partly because the encounter with the elements, which was central to the drama, cannot be reproduced. But the buildings and their fittings strike the visitor with a sense of the pioneers' achieve-ment, in making their homes or farms or businesses where nothing was before, and with a sense of the pioneers' hardships in contrast to his own life. We noted earlier how the legend confines pioneers to their land and ignores their wider society. The pioneer villages carry this tendency to its ultimate by leav-ing out people altogether. We are shown empty buildings, disembodied achievement, and are told nothing of the social and economic factors which determined who had the chance to achieve what. Buildings cannot speak readily of social conflict; these pioneer villages are powerful contributors to the consen-sus view of Australia's past.

Early immigrants generally, as distinct from the first settlers on the land, are still honoured as pioneers. In New South Wales there is a Pioneers' Club, formed in 1910, and in South Australia a Pioneers' Association, formed in 1935, to keep their memory alive.[38] These organizations define categories of membership by year of arrival of ancestor, construct genealogies and exercise a declining influence on the edge of the old state establishments. The pioneer–immigrants continued to be associated more with state than national loyalty. They were also honoured more frequently by those who wished to stress the British identity of Australia, and who saw its history as the winning of new areas for the Empire. The British heritage these pioneers brought with them was as important as their accomplishments here. At some times in the twentieth century—particularly in South Australia with its clear and clean foundation—pioneers as first immigrants may have had greater standing than pioneers as settlers on the land, but there is no doubt now of the latter's primacy. The two groups of pioneers are, of course, not totally distinct. The pioneer poem at the beginning of the Fifth Grade *Victorian Reader*, quoted earlier, is concerned chiefly with the struggle on the land, but the pioneers are identified clearly as British immigrants—'We are the old world people'—and this is part of their virtue—'Ours were the hearts to dare'. The pioneer legend has served local, Australian, and imperial patriotisms.

The survival of the word 'pioneer' itself means much. The word originally applied to those in an army who went as pioneers before the main body to prepare the way by clearing roads and making bridges and so on. It was then extended to the initiator of any new enterprise or new undertaking who 'showed the way' for those who came after. In this sense it could well be used as Kendall used it in 'Blue Mountain Pioneers' for the explorers. In the new world, first in North America and then in Australia, the meaning was again extended to refer to first settlers on the land. But to whom or in what were the first settlers showing the way? Their aim was to occupy the land for their own use and to keep others out. The metaphor of showing or preparing the way was now being stretched further to make them pioneers in a very general sense; they showed the way to the generations or the nation which came after them, and benefited from their labours. In this way the word itself obscures the private interests which they had in acquiring the land and depicts it as a service, as something for which we should be grateful, thus embodying a central concept of the legend. Let any who doubt the significance of the word consider what would have to change before we consistently referred to the first settlers as, say, landtakers, which was Penton's term.

I have shared here Russel Ward's assumption about the significance of a nation's legends, or its dreaming: 'The dreams of nations, as of individuals, are important, because they not only reflect, as in a distorting mirror, the real world, but may some-times react upon and influence it.'[39] That the legend which Ward describes exists is unquestionable; he is misleading, how-ever, when he implies that this was the only national legend. Ward claimed with very little analysis that Lawson and Paterson embodied the legend which he had described; what they embodied was a great deal more complex and varied. We have already noted their favourable view of the squatters, which A. A. Phillips identified. Ward takes too little account of this in his attempt to stress the radical collectivist aspect of the legend. Phillips is closer to the literature in writing of 'The Democratic Theme'. The anti-police aspect of the legend is not well reflected in Lawson, who nearly always makes his policemen good cops, sympathetic to the poor and outcast, and who wrote a poem celebrating the bravery of a police trooper.[40] And both writers fostered the development of the pioneer legend.

Some of Ward's critics, over-reacting perhaps to his less-guarded claims for the legend's influence, have attempted to deny its existence or force by citing social behaviour which runs counter to the legend. This is, of course, very easy to do, but when faced with this criticism Ward can retreat to very safe ground and declare that he was merely tracing the origins of the national legend which is not fully founded in fact, nor vastly influential.[41] Those who feel that Australia has not been made according to the legend would be better advised to establish the other legends, stereotypes, and symbols Australians have made or adopted. The pioneer legend is one such. It is a national rural myth, democratic in its social bearing, conservative in its political implications.

3. Ned Kelly, a Folk Hero

Angus McIntyre

Ned Kelly, (1855–80), that 'loud-mouthed, law-breaking, swaggering, son of an Irish convict' stood head and shoulders above the other bushrangers. Partly, this was because the selectors of north-eastern Victoria, discerning a theme of social protest in his actions, viewed him more as a noble robber or Robin Hood than as a common criminal. But Kelly was not the only bushranger to occupy such a role. Matthew Brady enjoyed a similar position among the Vandemonian agriculturalists as did Ben Hall in the case of the Wheogo's small landowners. Yet, Ned defined this role in a far more grandiose fashion than the other two. For while it is true that all three of them bailed up towns at one time or another, it is also true that only Ned Kelly appeared in armour at a shoot-out with the police.[2]

This grandiosity also manifested itself in other forms. Ned issued threats against the authorities so dire in their implications that they clearly implied an elevated conception of his powers. Moreover, he regarded other people as important only insofar as they confirmed this self-image, and sometimes even viewed them as likenesses or extensions of himself. He frequently boasted about his various skills, such as his horsemanship, and occasionally showed them off. Such exhibitionism was not always so soundly based.

The Fitzpatrick Affair

On 15 April 1878, an incident occurred, which in the opinion of the 1881 Royal Commission of Enquiry into the Victorian Police, precipitated the outbreak of the Kelly Gang. This was the attempt by Constable Fitzpatrick to arrest Ned's younger brother, Dan, at his mother's hut at Eleven Mile Creek near Greta on a charge of horse stealing. A fracas ensued. Later that night, Fitzpatrick turned up in Benalla with what he claimed was a bullet wound in the wrist which, he said, had been inflicted on him by Ned Kelly. On the strength of this and related claims by Fitzpatrick, warrants were issued against Ned Kelly for shooting with intent to murder, and against Dan Kelly, Mrs Kelly, her neighbour, Williamson, and son-in-law, Skillion, for aiding and abetting this shooting.

When the police arrived to enforce these warrants, the Kelly brothers were nowhere to be found. They had to be content, therefore, with the arrest of Mrs Kelly, Skillion, and Williamson. One month later, on 17 May, Mrs Kelly was granted bail. Then, on 9 October, at the Beechworth Assizes, a jury found Mrs Kelly and the two men guilty of the abovementioned charges. On 14 October, the presiding judge, Sir Redmond Barry, sentenced her to three years jail and Skillion and Williamson to six years each.

It was a harsh judgment. At least, that was the opinion of Mr Alfred Wyatt, a police magistrate. In his evidence before the 1881 Royal Commission, he stated: 'I thought the sentence upon that old woman, Mrs Kelly, a very severe one.' As to Ned's feelings about his mother's sentence, there is one ominous clue. Mrs Kelly told a fellow prisoner, named Williams, in the jail at Beechworth 'that they [Ned and Dan] would play up, that there would be murder now'. Also, a relative and an acquaintance of Ned's—Quinn and Isaiah ('Wild') Wright—offered to bring in the Kelly brothers if Mrs Kelly was allowed to go free. Mr Alfred Wyatt, to whom the offer was made by Quinn, told the Royal Commission: 'Quinn's and Wright's feeling was that it would be better for the men themselves to be brought in. It was not a feeling of treachery towards them, but that they could not hold

out, and that it was better for them themselves to bring them in.'
Presumably, they feared what would happen if the police tried
to bring them in.[3]

Stringybark Creek

On the morning of 25 October 1878, Sergeant Kennedy and
Constables Lonigan, Scanlan, and McIntyre, dressed in plain
clothes, set out from Mansfield to do just that. Like Ned, they
were of Irish Catholic descent, with the exception of McIntyre
who was an Ulsterman. That night, they camped at Stringybark
Creek near Mt Wombat.

The following morning, Kennedy and Scanlan set out to scout
around the area. McIntyre and Lonigan remained at the camp
site. A little after five o'clock in the afternoon, some voices in the
bush cried out: 'Bail up! Hold up your hands!' McIntyre turned
around and saw four men, two of whom he later recognized as
the Kelly brothers, covering Lonigan and himself with guns. He
raised his hands. Lonigan reached for his revolver while slip-
ping down for cover behind the log on which he had been
sitting. He then took aim over the top of the log but was shot
through the head by Ned Kelly. He fell to the ground, exclaim-
ing: 'Oh Christ I am shot.' A few minutes later he died. 'Keep
your hands up! Keep your hands up!' Ned warned McIntyre.

Then Ned and Dan and the two other men entered the camp.
They searched McIntyre and removed the firearms from the
policeman's tent. Dan produced a pair of handcuffs. 'We will put
these on the Bugger,' he said. McIntyre appealed to Ned who
turned to Dan: 'All right, don't put them on him.' 'This,' he
added, tapping his rifle, 'is better than handcuffs.' Turning to
McIntyre, he warned: 'Mind you don't try to go away, because if
you do, I will shoot you, if I had to track you to the police station
to shoot you there.' This was an extraordinary stance for Kelly to
adopt. McIntyre was the only witness to Lonigan's shooting.
Apparently, Ned's grandiose idea of himself led him to believe
that he would be able to do just as he threatened, namely, track
McIntyre down and shoot him.

Ned then boasted to McIntyre about his firearm: 'This is a curious old gun,' he said, 'for a man to carry about the country with him.' 'It is. Perhaps it is better than it looks,' McIntyre obliged. 'You might say that,' Kelly said. 'I will back it against any gun in the country. I can shoot a kangaroo at 100 yards with every shot from it.' Afterwards, when it looked as if McIntyre was about to jump Ned, the latter warned him off with still another boast: 'You had better not mate because if you do you will soon find your match for you know there are not three men in the police force a match for me.'

On this occasion, Ned's boasts were consistent with his ability for he was, in fact, a crack shot and something of a prize fighter. Formidable as his talents were, however, they could not always match the vainglory of his inflated self-image for, in the final analysis, this view of himself was—as the Glenrowan affair will make clear—unrealistic.

It was now between half past five and six o'clock. The other two policemen were expected back at the camp any minute. Ned ordered McIntyre to persuade them to surrender. 'We don't want their lives, only their horses and firearms,' he said. When Kennedy and Scanlan appeared, McIntyre stepped towards them. He said to Kennedy: 'Oh sergeant you had better dismount and surrender for you are surrounded.' At the same time, Kelly shouted: 'Bail up! hold up your hands!' Evidently, Kennedy thought McIntyre was joking. Scanlan, grasping the true situation, unslung his rifle, threw himself from the saddle and took a step or two towards a tree, when he was shot. Kennedy, quickly disabused of his error, had by this time dismounted on the off side of his horse and returned fire. McIntyre caught hold of Kennedy's horse, mounted it and escaped. Ned then exchanged shots with Kennedy, eventually killing him.[4]

Euroa Bank Robbery

Six weeks after the Stringybark shootings, on Monday, 8 December 1878, Ned and Dan Kelly and their two companions, all now outlawed by the Victorian government, bailed up Younghusband's Station, 4 miles north-east of Euroa. On this occasion, Ned went incognito for the most part in order, it seems, to set the stage for the attention grabbing unveiling of his true identity. However, he did not withhold his name from James Gloster, a hawker, whom he stuck up at the station on the Monday evening. 'I am Ned Kelly,' he said, 'the son of Red Kelly and a better man never stood in two shoes.' This strident declaration was one of Ned's few references to his father in these years.

Of his mother, he always had much more to say, usually of an effusive nature. According to James Gloster, he told the people whom he bailed up at Younghusband's 'that his mother had seen better days and had struggled up with a large family and he felt very keenly her being sent to jail with a baby at the breast by the perjured statement of Fitzpatrick'. It is apparent from this statement that Ned's attitude towards his mother was one of deep reverence. Something of its extravagant, sentimental quality became evident when Mr McDougall told Ned that the watch which he had taken from him was a keepsake from his mother. '. . . [Ned] shivered and said, "No; we'll never take that" and he returned it, taking, however, a watch from Mr Macauley instead.'

Kelly added, Gloster claimed, 'that if his mother did not get justice and was released soon he would possibly overturn the train'. The child-like anger evident in this statement suggests, perhaps, that such threats by Ned and the inflated sense of himself on which they were based, had roots, far deeper than the Fitzpatrick affair, in his early childhood experience.

His antipathy to the police, on the other hand, seems to have been a direct consequence of the way in which they treated his mother. On this point, the Royal Commissioners stated that the 'alleged severity of the punishment inflicted upon the mother of the outlaws has been the subject of comment in the course of the inquiry, and Captain Standish [the police commissioner] considers that it formed one of the many causes which assisted to bring about the Kelly outrages'. James Gloster reached a similar conclusion to Standish. He declared: 'the impression left on me was that he [Ned Kelly] shot the police through revengeful feelings against those who swore in the case against his mother'.

On the Tuesday afternoon, the Kelly brothers and one of their Stringybark accomplices went into Euroa in order to rob the National Bank. The other accomplice stayed behind to guard the people who had been stuck up at the station over the previous twenty-four hours. Having robbed the bank of over £2000 and the mortgage deeds of local selectors, Ned returned to Younghusband's, bringing with him the bank manager, his wife, Mrs Scott, her mother, seven children, and two servants. Mrs Scott's mother had been very nervous at first, but Ned calmed her by saying: 'Don't be frightened, nothing will happen to you. I have a mother of my own.'

Ned, Dan, and their two companions then prepared to leave. Before doing so, however, they showed off before their captives. Mr McDougall described the situation: 'Having then mounted on their horses (three of which were bays, and that ridden by Edward Kelly an iron grey—all being good animals, and in excellent condition), the men began to ride up and down in a boastful and braggadocio fashion.' Ned then issued a parting threat to his prisoners, as self-inflated as his earlier very similar threat to McIntyre. '"If one of you leaves this spot," he said, "within three hours I will shoot that man dead. You can't any of you escape me in this country; I can track you anywhere, and I'll keep my word."'

After the Euroa raid the police were able to identify the Kelly brothers' two accomplices. They were Steve Hart and Joe Byrne. The four of them—soon known as the Kelly Gang—were selectors' sons who had all served jail sentences for stock theft or related offences.[5]

The Cameron Letter

The day after the Euroa bank robbery, the wife of a station hand at Younghusband's, Mrs Fitzgerald, posted a letter which Ned

Kelly had entrusted to her. It was addressed to Mr Cameron, MLA, and subsequently became known as the Cameron Letter. In it, Kelly criticized Whitty and Burns, two squatters, for mistreating the 'poor men of the district'. Also, he argued that the shooting of Lonigan, Scanlan, and Kennedy 'cannot be called wilful murder for I was compelled to shoot them in my own defence or lie down like a cur and die'. And he again made reference to Mrs Kelly having been sent to jail with a baby at the breast.

This sentimental attitude towards his mother coloured his language. He claimed, for example, that his mother, his brother-in-law, Skillion, and his neighbour, Williamson, were as 'innocent as the child unborn' of having committed any offences against Fitzpatrick. Also, he described the police, whom he accused of terrorizing his younger brothers and sisters, as never having had 'any relation or a mother or must have forgot them'.

Ned concluded the letter with a monstrous threat. He wrote:

. . . but I wish to give timely warning that if my people do not get justice and those innocents released from prison and the Police wear their uniforms I shall be forced to seek revenge of everything of the human race for the future.

With no offence (remember your railroads) and a sweet goodbye

from

EDWARD KELLY
a forced outlaw[6]

The Jerilderie Raid

Although such an elevated self-conception may, and in the case of Ned Kelly eventually did, drive its owner towards impossible goals, it can also act as a spur to singular achievements. It is, perhaps, in this light that one should assess the extraordinarily successful raid on the town of Jerilderie in southern New South

Wales by Ned and his gang. At midnight on Saturday, 8 February 1879, just two months after the Euroa robbery, they stuck up Constables Richards and Devine at the Jerildeiie police barracks and imprisoned them there. In the morning, Dan Kelly, in policeman's uniform, accompanied Mrs Devine while she carried out her usual Sunday task of preparing the courthouse for mass.

On the Monday, Joe Byrne, also in policeman's uniform, had two of the gang's horses shod at the expense of the New South Wales police force. About 10 a.m. Ned and Dan took Constable Richards with them to the Royal Mail Hotel. Richards introduced his captors to Cox, the landlord. Ned said they wanted rooms at the hotel as they intended to rob the Bank of New South Wales next door. Byrne rode to the back of the hotel and entered the bank through the rear door. He introduced himself to Mr Living, the teller, as Kelly, pointed a gun at him and ordered him to hand over his firearms. Later, Ned entered the bank and helped Joe rob it of about £2000 and, as at Euroa, of mortgage documents.

About two o'clock that afternoon Joe Byrne stuck up Mr Jefferson, the telegraph master. 'I am Kelly, walk inside,' he said, using the same form of introduction that he had used earlier in the day with Living. Obviously, it made sense for Joe to introduce himself by the name of the gang's best known member. Nevertheless, one may properly wonder whether Byrne also viewed himself if not as Kelly then as an extension of him and—more pertinent to our purposes—whether Ned viewed him in this way. Douglas Stewart thinks he did. His play, *Ned Kelly*, contains the following exchange:

LIVING: Your assistant here said he was Kelly when he held me up.
NED: Did you, Joe?

> He is Ned Kelly; he's the brains I plan with,
> And Dan and Steve, with the guns out there in the pub,
> Are the boots and fists I fight with.
> You're Ned Kelly (shouting) Jump!

> (Living starts). There you are, you jump just as my hand jumps when I tell it to.

One thing at least is certain. Joe revered Ned. In a letter to his friend Aaron Sherritt, dated 26 June 1879, he wrote: 'Neddy and I have come to the conclusion to get you to join us. I was advised to turn traitor, but I said I would die at Ned's side first.' Clearly, the Kelly Gang was held together by the personal prestige of its leader.

While he was in Jerilderie, Kelly tried to get a letter printed in the local newspaper. After he had failed to find its proprietor, he entrusted the manuscript to Living, saying: 'Get it printed, it's a bit of my life.' Living replied: 'All right, I'll see it's done.' Instead, however, he handed the manuscript over to the police upon his arrival in Melbourne on Tuesday, 11 February. It has subsequently become known as the Jerilderie Letter.[7]

The Jerilderie Letter

In this letter Ned dwelled for a second time on the malfeasance of Whitty and Burns and the shootings at Stringybark Creek. Moreover, he again made his by now familiar reference to Mrs Kelly as 'the mother of twelve children one an infant on her breast'. And again this sentimental attitude towards his mother influenced his language. He wrote, for example, that 'a Policeman is a disgrace to his country [Ireland] not alone to the mother that suckled him'.

The Jerilderie Letter, like its predecessor, also contains some monstrous threats. Particularly striking was his threat to outlaw persons helping the police and his promise to reward those who assisted him to capture such people, implying as it does that his writ was as extensive and as legitimate as that of the Colony of Victoria. The language in which he delivered the threat was a bizarre parody of official government style:

> . . . any person aiding or harbouring or assisting the Police in any way whatever or employing any person whom they know to be a detective

or cad or those who would be so deprived as to take blood money will be outlawed and declared unfit to be allowed human buriel [sic] their property either consumed or confiscated and them theirs and all belonging to them exterminated off the face of the earth, the enemy I cannot catch myself I shall give a payable reward for . . .

Another threat concludes the letter:

I give fair warning to all those who has reason to fear me to sell out and give £10 out of every hundred towards the widow and orphan fund and do not attempt to reside in Victoria but as short a time as possible after reading this notice, neglect this and abide by the conse-quences, which shall be worse than the rust in the wheat in Victoria or the druth of a dry season to the grasshoppers in New South Wales I do not wish to give the order full force without giving timely warning but I am a widows son outlawed and my orders must be obeyed.[8]

It is noteworthy that of all the people Ned might have singled out for his concern on this occasion, he chose those people who most resembled his mother and himself, namely, widows and orphans. This suggests that his relationships with others were essentially self-centred. This impression is reinforced when it is recalled that he probably regarded Joe Byrne and, perhaps, others close to him, as continuations of himself. These, then, are examples of that other manifestation of Ned's grandiose self-image, namely, his tendency to regard others as extensions or likenesses of himself. Finally, Ned's reference to himself in the last sentence as 'a widow's son outlawed whose orders must be obeyed' suggests a link between his exalted commands on the one hand and his relationship with his mother on the other.

Glenrowan

Within months of the Jerilderie affair, songs celebrating Ned Kelly began to appear. He had already become a legend. And, extraordinary as it may sound, one of the legendary qualities friends and sympathizers assigned to him was invulnerability.

For example, Aaron Sherritt, a childhood friend of Joe Byrne turned police informer, told Superintendent Hare:

I can beat all the others; I am a better man than Joe Byrne, and I am a better man than Dan Kelly, and I am a better man than Steve Hart. I can lick those two youngsters to fits; I have always beaten Joe, but I look upon Ned Kelly as an extraordinary man; there is no man in the world like him, he is superhuman. . . . I look upon him as invulnerable, you can do nothing with him.

According to Hare:

. . . that was the opinion of all his agents; nearly every one in the district thought him invincible. When the police had a row with any of the sympathizers they would always finish off by saying 'I will tell Ned about you; he will make it hot for you some day', never speaking about the others [in the gang] at all.

Douglas Stewart expresses well this view of Ned by having Joe Byrne say: 'He [Ned] talks of wearing armour next time he tackles the traps, but he doesn't need it.'

A year after the Jerilderie raid, the Kelly gang had all but exhausted their funds. Some of their sympathizers apparently suggested that the gang should rob another bank. Then, in May 1880, the police received a letter from one of their secret agents indicating that something was afoot—something decidedly unusual. The letter read in part:

Nothing definite re the diseased stock of this locality. . . . Missing portions of cultivators described as jackets are now being worked, and fit splendidly. Tested previous to using, and proof at 10 yards. . . . A break out may be anticipated, as feed is getting very scarce.

'Diseased stock' was a code word for the outlaws. And 'missing portions of cultivators' referred to a number of mould boards which had been stolen from ploughs in the neighbourhood of Greta and Oxley earlier in the year. They had now, according to the letter, been turned into armoured jackets which were bullet proof at 10 yards.

A short time after the receipt of this letter, Superintendent Hare received further news that 'the outlaws are going to do something that will not only astonish Australia, but the whole world'. The information came from Joe's mother, Mrs Byrne. It appeared that Ned Kelly was going to try and give substance to the view of himself as invulnerable.

On the evening of Saturday, 26 June, Joe Byrne, accompanied by Dan Kelly, shot Aaron Sherritt dead in his hut near Beechworth. Superintendents Hare and Sadlier received news of the murder in Benalla on the Sunday afternoon. They immediately arranged for the dispatch of black trackers to Beechworth by special train. They also decided to run a pilot engine ahead of the special between Benalla and Beechworth for, apart from Kelly's ominous reference to the railroads in the Cameron letter, the police in Benalla had received information from some of their agents that the Kellys intended to blow up a train.

The Kelly Gang had planned on a train carrying police and black trackers proceeding to Beechworth. They had not bargained, however, on the use of a pilot engine. Indeed, early on that Sunday morning, Ned Kelly and Steve Hart forced some railway labourers at gun point to break the line immediately north east of the town of Glenrowan. Ned told one of the workers: 'I expect a train from Benalla with a lot of police and blackfellows, and I am going to kill all the ——'

After the break was made, Ned and Steve not only secured the fettlers but also bailed up the inhabitants of Glenrowan and held them captive in Mrs Jones's hotel. There, Thomas Curnow talked to Joe Byrne and Dan Kelly who had ridden overnight from Beechworth. He expressed surprise that they had stuck up Glenrowan. Joe and Dan replied that they had come there to wreck a special train of inspectors, police, and black trackers which would pass through Glenrowan to take up their trail. They had torn up the line at a dangerous part, they said, and were going to send the train and its occupants to hell.

Curnow was appalled. He determined to gain the gang's confidence in the hope that they would allow him to go home, in which case he planned to alert the Benalla police. He told Ned and Dan that one of the other prisoners, Mr Stanistreet, the station master, had a revolver in his possession. 'They thanked me,' Curnow wrote, 'and I perceived that I had in a great measure obtained their confidence by telling them this.' About dusk, Curnow asked Ned to allow him and his family to go home. He added that Ned had no reason to fear him as he was with him heart and soul. Kelly replied: 'I know that, and can see it.' Finally, between eleven and midnight, Ned told Curnow that he and his family could go home. 'Go quietly to bed, and not to dream too loud', he directed them. But Curnow ran down to the railway line on the south west or Benalla side of Glenrowan just in time to signal the pilot engine, which was preceding the special police train, to stop. He informed the guard that the line was pulled up a short distance north-east of the town and that the Kelly Gang was in Glenrowan.

The pilot engine and the police train proceeded slowly to the Glenrowan railway station. The local constable, who had just escaped from the Kellys, told Superintendent Hare that the outlaws were in Mrs Jones's hotel. The police made a dash in that direction. When they were about fifteen paces away from the hotel, Hare saw a man standing in an exposed position on the verandah. He was quickly joined by three others. It was the outlaws who, now clad in their armour, appeared to regard themselves as invulnerable. They opened fire on the police. Hare was shot in the wrist. But he was still able to join the other police in returning the fire. In the middle of this firing, or soon after it stopped, one of the outlaws cried out: 'Fire away, you ——; you can do us no harm.' But, of course, the armour could not render them invulnerable. It is not surprising, therefore, that Ned Kelly was soon hurt with bullet wounds in the hand and foot.

Indeed, far from making the Kelly Gang invulnerable, the armour appeared even unable to measure up to more modest goals. For example, Senior Constable Johnston claimed that the outlaws 'could not get proper sight by the weight of armour'. He also stated that it would have been safer for the police to rush the outlaws 'with the armour on than off'. And, if Constable Phillips is to be believed, then he actually overheard Joe Byrne say to Ned Kelly at the rear of the hotel: 'Well, it's your fault; I always said this bloody armour would bring us to grief.' It seems plausible, therefore, that Ned's decision to wear the armour sprang from a personal need rather than a rational considera- tion of its utility. This need, it was suggested above, was to substantiate the claims which had been made about his invulnerability.

Not long after the first clash with the police, Ned Kelly left the hotel by the back and selected his horse, which he led away into the bush at the rear. On the way he apparently dropped his rifle and the skull cap which he wore inside his iron headpiece. He tried, it seems, to take off his armour but was unable to do so. Then he attempted to break through the police cordon in order to rejoin his comrades in the hotel.

What followed moved even the Royal Commissioners to eloquence:

As the tall figure of the outlaw, encased in iron, appeared in the indistinct light of the dawn, the police for a time were somewhat disconcerted. To some it seemed like an apparition; others thought it was a black man who had donned a nail can for a joke, but as the shots from Martini–Henry rifles, at short range, were found to have no effect, the sensation created seemed to have been akin to superstitious awe. One man described it as the 'devil', another as the 'bunyip'. Ned Kelly advanced until within a stone's throw of the hotel, when, in the vernacular of the bush, he defied the police, and called on the other members of the gang to come out of the hotel and assist him.

Sergeant Steele finally brought Ned down with a shot which hit him beneath his armoured covering. He then rushed forward and grappled with him. Others ran to his assistance and, together, they removed Kelly's armour and carried him to the railway station.

It was later learned that Joe Byrne had been shot dead early in the morning while toasting the gang's prosperity at the bar of the hotel. And Dan and Steve, it seems, took off their armour and committed suicide later in the day. This action suggests that they could not envisage themselves apart from Ned. Like Joe, conceivably, they viewed themselves as extensions of him. The date was Monday, 28 June 1880. It was a little over two years since the arrest of Mrs Kelly.[9]

Murder Trial

Ned Kelly's trial commenced in the Central Criminal Court in Melbourne on 18 October 1880. The presiding judge was Mr Justice Sir Redmond Barry, who had previously sentenced Mrs Kelly to three years imprisonment. After an adjournment, the trial resumed on 28 October. The following evening, the jury found Ned guilty of the wilful murder of Thomas Lonigan. Barry then sentenced the prisoner to death, ending with the usual words: 'May the Lord have mercy on your soul.' 'I will go a little further than that,' Kelly replied, 'and say I will see you there where I go.' He was hanged in the Melbourne jail on 11 November. Twelve days later, Sir Redmond Barry died.[10]

Conclusion

It was Ned's grandiose style of behaviour which explains his appeal, for once he aspired to invulnerability he became the hero of the small farmers of north-eastern Victoria, vulnerable men enduring hardship and often failure as selectors, while blaming the squatters for their plight. But Kelly's popularity, like that of other noble robbers, was by no means confined to his native environment. The citizens of Melbourne, although unaffected by the selectors' particular grievances, also found sustenance in Kelly's grand defiance, or so it would seem judging by the fact that 700 people waited outside the Melbourne jail for a glimpse of him when he was transferred there after the Glenrowan shoot-out. And 8000 people, meeting at the Hippodrome on 5 November, passed a resolution calling for his reprieve. Moreover, a petition to the same effect attracted 32 000 signatures. And even today, people far removed from the world of the selectors and colonial Melbourne, but who have acquired the forms of subservience appropriate to the twentieth century, continue to draw strength from Ned's story. He has become a folk hero.[10]

4. Anzac

Bill Gammage

At dawn on 25 April 1915, the four battalions of the Third Australian Brigade, the bush battalions, made a daring landing on the rugged coast of the Gallipoli Peninsula, a narrow strip of ground shielding the Dardanelles. Australians were not the only troops to land, and they were always a minority of the Allied force, but at Anzac they and the New Zealanders carved from the hills their own battle arena, and there fought a brave opponent for eight months, until ordered to withdraw.

They fought a kind of war not possible anywhere else during the Great War. There was no artillery of consequence, no gas, no tanks, virtually no aeroplanes. Despite the terrible effectiveness of machine guns, Gallipoli was in many ways the last campaign fought without twentieth-century technology, the last battlefield on which the courage and determination of individual soldiers might alone have been decisive.

Strategically, the landing itself was a failure. Almost everywhere the Turk commanded the key positions, and that night the Australian leaders, Birdwood and Bridges, requested permission to withdraw. Snipers shot at the men from every direction, shrapnel showered upon them, thirst and exhaustion wore them down. But the soldiers were content, for they thought they had triumphed, and they never considered retreat. They made ready to stay, and they stayed.

In most respects they had won a great victory. They were landed on an unexpected coast, which unhinged their orders, and they found themselves amid a tangle of steep hills and scrubby gullies, country difficult to cross in peace time, and now shielding an unknown number of enemy. Many were in doubt, many were leaderless, but most remembered what they had learnt in training—to advance always, to find and follow an officer, to inform the rear of the trend of battle. With excellent discipline, they obeyed. They went forward; when the scrub divided them, they went forward still; when most had been shot, the rest went on, or clung grimly to the ground they held. They were not experienced soldiers, they were too precipitate, and they made too many errors to be that. They were ardent, eager, brave men, naive about military strategy, but proud of their heritage and confident of their supremacy. Despite their mistakes, they did what few could have done.

Through the war the fatalism of the Australians, their courage, their manhood, and their sheer dogged determination sustained them and made so many of their attitudes possible. They fought for their own prestige because that would probably be their last cause, they took greatest comfort from their mates because their mates were all they had, they accepted the sight and spectre of death because they were themselves to die, they adjusted to the daily routine of war because they did not expect to know another. They lived in a world apart, a new world, scarcely remembering their homes and country, and grieving little at the deaths of mates they loved more than anything on this earth, because they knew that only time kept them from the 'great majority' who had already died, and they believed that fate would overtake time, and bring most of them to the last parade. So they continued, grim, mocking, defiant, brave and careless, free from common toils and woes, into a perpetual present, until they should meet the fate of so many who had marched before them down the great road of peace and sorrow into eternity.

The circumstances of a national army, an arena, a brave enemy, and the chance that individuals might assert themselves against mass technology led three nations, Australia, New Zealand, and Turkey, to create national traditions from the Gallipoli campaign. Each tradition showed how the qualities of individuals might make nations great, each proclaimed national distinctiveness, each had a rural bias, and each saw war as a test of men. Each was pre-industrial, looking back to the days of chivalry rather than forward to those of the atom bomb, and each was to struggle in later years against rapidly changing conditions in the countries that upheld them.

Yet each appealed powerfully. Among Australians, to have been an 'original Anzac', a man who had been at the famous landing, even to be entitled to wear on his colour patches the special 'A' showing that a man had simply been on Anzac, conferred forever a special distinction. Not all the mud and slaughter of France and the far greater number of Australians who fought and died there nor all the years of peace ever altered that, among those who knew, and in the 1980s the titles 'original' or 'Anzac' still distinguish old soldiers who fought in that last great gladiatorial contest. After it ended hundreds of thousands of Australians, men who fought in France and Palestine, and men not born in 1915 who in their turn went to fight in almost every part of the globe, understood by their service what Anzac was about, and accepted it as epitomizing the military and national traditions of their country. In the twentieth century, no Australian, for or against Anzac, has ever discerned or proposed a stronger national tradition.

This strength cannot be explained simply by stating what happened. Other nations fought at Gallipoli, and do not particularly remember it. Even in New Zealand Anzac, although as important as in Australia in commemorating courage and sacrifice, has never been as important as a nation-building symbol. Australia itself has fought other battles—Second Bullecourt, Alamein, Kokoda, Sattelberg, Kapyong—in which the arena has been as obvious, the conditions as tough, the enemy as determined, as at Gallipoli. Why did the landing at Anzac shape and epitomize a tradition?

It was not the first battle. There had been the Soudan and China, and in the South Africa there had been Eland's River, as clear an arena as ever brave men defended against odds. It was not a great victory or a great defeat, and if it was bloodier than anything before it, it was less bloody than what came after. It did not produce a great leader or a great hero, and it did not increase Australia's independence or add to the liberties of its citizens. It had about it the air of the Charge of the Light Brigade, or Nelson at Trafalgar, or Wolfe at Quebec, but none of those had made national traditions. What made Anzac different?

It happened at the right time. Almost six months before, on 9 November 1914, the Australian cruiser *Sydney* had driven aground the German light cruiser *Emden*. The smaller ship had had no chance, and she went to her end bravely, but Australians celebrated the victory joyously. They spoke of the action as conferring adulthood on their navy, and some edged towards declaring that it had made Australia a nation. Most held back, waiting for a more substantial basis for nationhood, waiting anxiously, wondering when and where their soldiers would fight, and how they would fare. The time was awaiting the event.

On 29 April 1915, news came. Australians were not told what had happened. They learnt only that their men were ashore in Turkey, and that the earliest cables from England were congratulating them. That was enough. Cheers, rejoicing, and editorials on nationhood swept aside the waiting months, anxiety gave way to exultation: Australia was on the stage of the world. In fact very few Australians learnt, then or later, what their soldiers did on that stage, and not many ever acquired more than a vague notion of their country's part in the Great War. But what happened was irrelevant. The praise and the success were what mattered, for they made Australia a nation, and a partner to Empire. Australians could walk among men.

This floodburst of emotion was the high water mark of ideas and attitudes which had built up steadily in Australia during the thirty years or so before 1914. It is often said that before that year 98 per cent of Australians either were born in Britain, or came of British forebears. An increasing proportion were Australian-born, which may have weakened the ancient hostility between English and Irish and the old memories of convict hulk and immigrant ship and cold and hunger in an English slum or a Scottish famine. Yet among native and immigrant alike there grew a strengthening affection for their British heritage, to which they were linked partly by the romance of green fields and ancient custom, and partly by what Henry Parkes called 'the crimson thread of kinship'—the tie of blood and race. Australians were no longer English or Scots or Welsh or Irish, but increasingly they were British, a word becoming used to describe white men of the Empire wherever they were. Like 'Empire', 'Britain' and 'British' were also words which enabled Australians to claim difference or commonality as it suited them: thus British institutions and values set Australian standards, but Australians played the English at cricket, or mocked the English class system. They were, in short, different members of the same family; they were Imperial in outlook.

Englishmen and white Australians had lived in Australia since 1788. Why did Empire sentiment take such wing only a century later? Partly it was because the Imperial idea took hold in England itself only after the 1870s, and partly because antipodean circumstances pushed Australians towards Imperial affection. In the 1870s, important changes occurred in Australia. First, the last British troops were withdrawn in 1870, which made it easier both to be nostalgic about the Motherland, and fearful for Australia's defences. Second, the overland telegraph was completed in 1872, bringing Australians for the first time the very latest European news and opinion and making it impossible to think of the world as distant and irrelevant. Forty-three years later the telegraph was to bring Australians the first news of the landing at Anzac. Third, the spread of the telegraph and the railways within Australia brought people and ideas closer together, smoothing out differences between local communities and attitudes. Henry Lawson, one of Australia's great sons, described this:

The flaunting flag of progress
Is in the West unfurled
The mighty Bush with iron rails
Is tethered to the world.

Fourth, high British prices for Australian wool in the early 1870s and heavy British investment in Australian development for most of the 1870s and 1880s seemed irrevocably to tie Australia's prosperity to Britain. Fifth, and most importantly, in the 1870s, free and compulsory education was introduced. People who could read and write could circulate information and opinion quickly, and they became more vulnerable to ideas and emotions propagated by the press, which grew rapidly with universal education, and the state. Popular education made widespread national and Imperial sentiment possible.

All these changes brought Australians closer to Europe; at the same time Europe was moving closer to them. From the 1870s, European powers began moving into the Pacific: Germany to Samoa and New Guinea, France to the New Hebrides and New Caledonia, the United States to Samoa and the Philippines. About the same time, the power of Russia, China, and Japan grew, challenging Australian isolation. Japan seemed to threaten most, defeating China in 1895 and Russia in 1905, and in 1902 becoming an ally of Britain. To Australians these were all calamities, convincing them that one day the Japanese would attempt to invade their country.

They knew that by themselves they could do little to resist Japan. They would not tolerate Asians as fellow citizens, because that offended their notions of blood and race. They assumed that to exclude Asians made them enemies, the Yellow Peril, which Australia could not defeat unaided. So they turned to Britain, or more exactly to the Royal Navy, pointing to that crimson thread of kinship, and seemingly making Australian Imperial sentiment rational.

In thus relating the Empire to the defence of their country, Australians infused Imperial sentiment with assumptions not only about blood and race, but about war. Wars had won the

Empire, and a readiness for war defended the Empire and hence defended Australia. Defensive wars could thus be considered just—indeed even today armies are commonly called 'defence' forces, in deference to this thinking. Yet it only needed a leader to declare the Empire threatened for the consequent war to be thought both just, and necessary to Australia's defence. So Australians went gladly to fight in places they had never heard of, in the Soudan, China, South Africa, and Turkey.

If wars were just, then soldiers were virtuous. Soldiers defended race and Empire, and how well they did so depended upon their moral and physical qualities. In all citizens the most important qualities were those valuable in war—strength, courage, patriotism, honour, sacrifice, endurance, and so on. These virtues could be taught to some extent, but essentially they were inherent in the race. Anglo–Saxons possessed them *par excellence* and so were the superior race, which explained their possession of the largest Empire the world had seen. The maintenance of this superiority depended on military preparedness and the willingness of individual citizens, particularly soldiers, to maintain the moral and physical excellence which made races and Empires great. War therefore tested individual virtue as well as racial superiority and Imperial might, so that by 1914, assumptions about war, race, Empire, and their own self-esteem were thoroughly intertwined in Australian hearts and minds.

The problem was, how much and how well could Australians contribute to an Imperial war? Theirs was a large country and a small population—in future wars Britain seemed likely to help them far more than they could hope to help Britain. They therefore determined, in effect, to stockpile credit—to help Britain in any war, wherever fought, even if Australia was not menaced. That led to another problem—what if Australians were not good soldiers, what if they could not earn credit? There were those who believed that the British race had degenerated in the antipodes, and in 1914, some were saying that the men of the A.I.F. would never make soldiers, and would be used better as labourers.

Wondering whether the race had degenerated in Australia was essentially to ask how significant the differences were that had evolved between Australians and Englishmen. Did these differences matter? If they did, did they point to improvement or degeneration?

The dominant tradition in Australia before 1914 was that of the bush. It was made by the last generation which could remember the days before the mighty bush was tethered to the world, and the first generation in which literacy was widespread and which could travel and communicate rapidly. Although often given expression by English writers visiting Australia, it was championed by literate Australians who had moved from the country to the city—by men looking backward, just as Anzac would be, just as all great traditions are. At a popular level, it alone asked seriously how a manifestly different physical environment might be affecting Europeans in Australia.

The bush spokesmen were certain that Australian conditions improved the old stock. They saw the bush as revitalizing basic- ally British virtues, and as did imperial traditions they used the qualities of individuals to define an ideal, and to inspire their countrymen towards it. At the same time they emphasized difference. Mateship, self-reliance, hardihood, stoicism, and so on took on peculiarly Australian conformations, and the bush- man was seen as a unique type, more competent than anyone else in the Australian environment (the Aborigines being over- looked), a man to be admired and imitated. Yet although the bush tradition could show that in Australia Australians were superior to Englishmen, it could not say how Australians might rank in world terms. Perhaps, some Australians wondered, their environment did not truly test them; perhaps by world stan- dards they had degenerated? The more alarming the inter- national situation grew after 1890, and the more world powers pressed into the Pacific, the more disturbing this doubt became.

By 1914, Australians were troubled whether they could help Britain in war as much as they expected Britain to help them, and whether in becoming different they had degenerated. They had to ask whether they could ever be worthy partners to Empire.

Their answer came in 1915. On 29 April an English cable praised the 'magnificent achievement' of Australian soldiers, and on 8 May an English war correspondent, Ellis Ashmead–Bartlett, told the world that Australians had excelled in war, and had upheld the finest traditions of their race. 'These raw colonial troops . . .', he wrote, 'proved worthy to fight side by side with the heroes of Mons, the Aisne, Ypres, and Neuve Chapelle.' It was exactly what Australians wanted to read. It made them partners to Empire. They were all right.

Immediately they were freer to make their own myths, and they made two from the war: that generated in Australia, and that forged by the A.I.F.

In Australia the war shattered that left-wing radical idealism which had uplifted the bush tradition. Even in 1914, bush radicalism could still best define what a real Australian was. He was not an Empire man, for example, he was for Australia. He was not an employer, or even an employee, he was a worker. He was not a city man, he was a bushman. The war gave Australian conservatives an opportunity to overturn this stereotype, and within a year they had done so. The great issue of the war was loyalty—whether a man was loyal to the Empire, to the men who had been killed, to mates struggling valiantly for civiliza-tion. Empire men were much more likely than bush radicals to be enthusiastic about loyalty, the most extreme Empire men were conservatives, and so the bush lost its hold on Australian national emotion, and became conservative, middle-class domi-nated, and urban. By 1916 these influences were deciding what Australian nationalism was, and who the real Australians were, and bush radicals opposed to the war were being abused publicly as un-Australian.

Within the A.I.F., however, the real Australians were not fund-raising jingoists, but men who had passed the test of the trenches. Empire loyalty mattered, but the conditions of battle produced a great reflowering of the bush tradition. The bush and the war demanded similar qualities in individuals—for example, resource, initiative, endurance, reliability, courage, and mateship. Like the bushmen, the Anzacs wanted to show

how they were different. They made a distinctive tradition—brave and tough in battle, excelling at any task to which they set their hands, careless of authority, hostile to most convention, proud of their distinctiveness and their country. For them the real Australian was the Anzac, the bushman on the stage of the world.

Both the soldiers and the civilians had their spokesmen after the war. For the soldiers spoke C. E. W. Bean, Australia's official historian, whose magnificent history was essentially about the character of the men of the A.I.F. Bean's writing reflected common A.I.F. thinking, but he, more than anyone, gave the Anzac tradition substance and direction. He wrote it down, he was the inspiration behind the Australian War Memorial, he wrote or chose much of what is said on Anzac Day. Yet few read what he wrote, and his work was too late. By the time he and his A.I.F. comrades returned from the war, the celebration of Anzac was run by civilian orthodoxy. Soldiers were to amend it, making it more distinctly Anzac, but by 1916 it was already a forum for stating such conservative values as the necessity for loyalty, conformity to the state, and acceptance of middle-class quiescence, and it has remained so ever since.

Many returning soldiers accepted the place civilians made ready for them, for it recognized their effort and sacrifices during the war, and it shared their conviction that the war to end all wars had been necessary, and had been fought for Australia by the real Australians. Yet Anzac Day rhetoric masked rather than ended that difference between how civilians and soldiers perceived Australia's part in the war. A common sense of pride and loss and a common acceptance of Anzac as nation-making did not conceal that Anzac, in the end, was a dividing rather than a unifying experience. It separated those who had fought in the war from those who had not, and one generation of Australians from all those that went before or came after, for no returned soldier could pass on the enormity of his war experience to those who had not been there. This affected the young particularly, and as the years passed Anzac Day became more and more a day on which the young were expected to accept on trust that Anzac was worth celebrating, even though it was run by those same headmasters and mayors and politicians so much associated with the less pleasant or more boring aspects of everyday life. There was nothing of the bush tradition in what they said, no romance, no questioning of convention, little of that distinctive Australianism which the Anzacs themselves valued so much. Instead the day was authoritarian, conventional, didactic, and dull. To Australians who could not remember the war, it was a day, except for the emotion of their parents, much like other holidays, admittedly more important than any save Christmas, but not really of special distinction, and certainly not epitomizing Australian identity. Had not Australians fought in later wars, and there realized what moved the first Anzacs, Anzac would probably have waned much sooner than it did.

In short, the Anzac tradition derived its impetus from a sense of national insecurity, its strength from its A.I.F. origins, and its form from a conservative Australian hierarchy. As memories of its origins wane and its form persists, Anzac seems bound to be questioned more and more as an adequate national tradition. It is not nation-forming, not so much because it excludes those who were not there—many traditions do that—but because it does not admit change in a country and a century in which times are changing rapidly. All great traditions look back, but they must also show the way forward.

Yet during and after two world wars, Anzac came closer than anything else to entrenching itself permanently as Australia's national tradition, and its failure suggests that perhaps Australians cannot find satisfying traditions for reasons running deeper than any so far stated. At the end of his first volume on the Australians at Gallipoli, C. E. W. Bean asked what motives sustained the men of the A.I.F., inducing them to risk and suffer so much. It was not, he decided, love of a fight. Nor was it hatred of the Turk, or a desire for fame, or a love of country or Empire. It was because of the mettle of the men themselves. They would not abandon their own high standards, or let down their mates, or fall short of their idea of Australian manhood. For these reasons, in the hour of greatest trial, when death confronted them, they fought on.

Bean did not suggest that the men on Anzac might have been sustained by religious conviction, and this omission demon-strates a most striking characteristic of Australian society. It is secular—it is not ruled by God. As did people in some other post-industrial frontier societies, Australians quickly decided that it was possible to live without God. The question was, was it possible to live without faith? If people believed in nothing, how could they say what was good, or brave, or honourable, or anything?

Both the bush and Anzac stemmed from a conviction of the brotherhood of man. Each painted the vision splendid, reaching for the heights of what man might do. Each can be seen as a quest for faith, but in the end each offered a creed which pro-posed a hierarchy of excellence, and which did not embrace all men as brothers. As well, both failed to convert a significant number of outsiders. They were too fixed in their time and place, and particularly as times changed they could not show how what they stood for might guide or inspire others. In 1918 Bean wrote *In Your Hands Australians*, a pamphlet which urged the men of the A.I.F. to carry into peace the qualities they had displayed so well in war, and so build a better Australia. It was not to be, for the war set the Anzacs apart from their society, rather than fitting them to be its prophets.

It may be that any search for a faith in Australia is doomed, for the lack of it does not trouble all Australians equally. Middle-class idealists like Bean have responded largely to the conditions of their own class, seeing their fellows as makers of grey, to whom wealth and liberty have brought comfort but not consola-tion. They have been anxious to find something which might replace God in inspiring men towards leaving the world better than they found it, so the traditions they have described have always had about them a schoolmasterly inclination to judge and prescribe.

Of course, faiths are often didactic, and traditions rarely truly embrace everyone in a society. But neither the bushmen nor the

Anzacs were willing to accept all the demands middle-class idealists made on them as objects of national traditions. They were
ready to compare and to judge, but they were not ready to lead.
Indeed, it was part of the essence of both traditions to be hostile
to any notion of a faith which tried to inspire men in any
direction spiritually, for both believed that man was not master
of his destiny, but a victim of chance. Both had been nurtured by
an environment which loomed harsh and huge above every
thought and action, ready capriciously to lift men up or strike
them down. The Australian land taught the bushman stoic
acceptance; war taught the Anzacs that guns were greater than
men, and men must accept fatalistically what the guns might do.
For both there was no better way, there was no faith, there was
only acceptance and endurance.

Yet if the bush and Anzac are not faiths which explain our
purpose on earth, they can teach that how we live matters. Man
may be frail, but his example can inspire his fellows, and set
standards and ideals for them to follow. For while individuals
must suffer doubt and travail all their days, those who conduct
themselves well pass on a torch to all the generations, showing
the human spirit shining unquenchable, forever.

Part II
The Problems with the Classical Legends

We turn in this part of the book to historical and sociological evidence that makes it difficult to take the classical legends seriously as representing the truth about Australia. Alan Frost shows that conditions of settlement during the first fifty years in New South Wales were far from being those presupposed by the bush legends, arduous and thanklessly hostile in a harsh and alien land. The Schedvins argue that the typical convict in early Australia came from the vagrant sub-culture of ragged and delinquent poor of urban Britain, and that he brought with him a number of traits to be later associated with the bushman, but traits that turn out to be far less attractive than the legend has it, and ones that do not include a capacity for trusting and friendly mateship. Graeme Davison shows that the legend of the bush-man was the product of discontented city intellectuals in the 1890s who romanticized a rural simplicity that was very distant from their own experience. Kenneth Dempsey shows what mateship really means in a fairly typical country town—the place today where we might expect bushman values to have survived, if anywhere. Finally, John Carroll questions the whole mythology surrounding the values of mateship and egalitarian-ism, arguing that it is rather certain oddities about the upper middle class that give the clue to any singularity in Australian culture.

5. The Conditions of Early Settlement: New South Wales, 1788–1840

Alan Frost

The classical legends of Australian identity possess an innate integrity, for their very existence bears witness to the profundity and endurance of the imaginative needs they satisfy. It would be a particularly foolhardy commentator who would seriously question the historical efficacy of these legends. All of us know, as equally from childhood experience as from adult enquiry, that Bush and Pioneer, Ned Kelly and Anzac, have provided us with means to order our experience in emotionally and imaginatively satisfying ways, and have therefore been central to how we have seen ourselves as a people in time and space.

Neither the question of whether or not these legends have reality, nor that of their potency, is one of serious enquiry. Clearly, these legends have existed, and exist still. Just as clearly, they have had a very considerable currency. And since that they have had a great imaginative impact and cultural influence cannot be denied; rather, the questions that commentators must concern themselves with are these: out of what did these legends begin? and why did we as a people make them central to our conception of ourselves?

The first point to note in the search for answers to these questions is that the legends share a common, *rural*, basis. The bush legend is the fundamental one. It developed first; its notes of distance, isolation, drought, fire, flood, skill in coping with limited means, and companionship in adversity, resonate through the others which, from one point of view at least, are merely overlays or extensions of it. How this is true of the pioneer legend is immediately obvious, and the same holds for Ned Kelly and the Anzacs.

The second point is that almost all those who have described the bush legend either wholly or in part have located its beginning in the first decades of European settlement of the continent. Russel Ward makes this point most fully. Holding it wrong for the purpose of differentiating between city and country (Sydney was at first only a 'raw frontier town' where '"bush" values grew up among the lower orders just as naturally, indeed inevitably, as they did in the bush itself'), he asserts that 'the traditionally accepted Australian pattern of behaviour' appeared first among the convicts, ex-convicts, and native-born on the Cumberland Plain, and were then reinforced and developed when settlement moved 'up-country'.[1]

From this, we may suppose that life in the County of Cumberland (to which the British settlement of continental Australia was largely confined until the late 1820s) was arduous and oppressive, a struggle for existence in a region offering little physical or emotional comfort, and that it was out of these circumstances that our progenitors forged our historical character.

Although the cultural commentators do not usually explain them, this view of life on the Cumberland Plain, like the world in Hindu cosmography, rests on a series of premises of increasingly antediluvian character: that Europeans felt alien in early Australia; that the first European inhabitants took no aesthetic pleasure in the Australian environment; that life here was a savage struggle for survival; that in a desolate land, the threat of starvation was only slowly overcome; that the first colonists were ill-equipped for the tasks of settlement; and that the European settlement began in a fit of absence of mind.

I would like to sketch what more extensive investigation shows or would likely show to be the opposing realities to indicate the grounds on which I think discussion of the origin and growth of the legends of Australian identity must proceed.

A Fit of Absence of Mind?

The view that the British colonized Australia in a fit of absence of mind is built around an assumption about the Pitt Administration—that it was inert and incompetent, incapable of planning to meet present needs adequately, or to provide for future ones, and hence, in despair of doing anything else with them, it dumped the convicts as far away as possible, with no thought for their well-being or for the colony's future development.

This view is false. A number of Pitt's ministers were certainly incapable, but the young Prime Minister was not; and he and a close group of advisers developed a far-reaching policy designed to meet the nation's present and future Imperial needs. As I have shown in *Convicts and Empire*,[2] the colonization of New South Wales was one element in this policy.

A Ragged Party?

The mounting and sailing of the First Fleet have never been adequately examined. To date, all comments about these matters have been based on the evidence of a very incomplete documentary record—some 100 pieces in *Historical Records of New South Wales*, which constitute no more than a fifth of those extant.

The probability is that detailed investigation will show that the Pitt Administration took great pains in the mounting the First Fleet, and in equipping the colonists for the tasks before them.

Certainly a number of contemporary observers well placed to judge believed this to be so. Arthur Bowes Smyth, for example, the surgeon on the *Lady Penrhyn*, commented in December 1787:

The Provisions for the Convicts was also very good of their kind, the Beef and Pork in particular were excellent—A retrospective view of these different Articles may serve to justifie the observation . . . that I believe few Marines or Soldiers going out on a foreign Service under

Government were ever better, if so well provided for as these Convicts are.[3]

And the impressively low morbidity and mortality rates on the ships testify to the great care with diet and hygiene that Phillip and his captains and surgeons took, that is, their concern for the welfare of the crews, marines, and especially, the convicts, and therefore, also the Pitt Administration's concern.

Desolation and Starvation?

It is perfectly true that Phillip and his party found the area about Botany Bay and Port Jackson not nearly as fertile as Cook and Banks's reports had led the British to expect it would be. It is also true that they experienced many other serious setbacks in the first four years, including the lack of fish; the failure of seeds to germinate and plants to flourish; the loss of stock; the failure of shovels and axes to cope with rocky ground and hardwood; the recalcitrance of the marines and convicts; and the losses of the ships *Guardian* and *Sirius*. Moreover it is true that in these circumstances the colonists went on short rations for about three years, during which there was some danger of their starving.

But Phillip came closer than modern historians have to describing the reality of their situation when he observed that many of these difficulties 'could not have been guarded against, as they never could have been expected', when he commented that 'the Chapter of *accidents* does not yet open in our favour'.[4]

Historians who have focussed their accounts on the untoward circumstances have failed to give due attention to two other important aspects of Australian settlement in its first years. First, the increased fertility of the women convicts, and the initial party's general healthiness in comparison to that of those on the Second Fleet, indicate that, even given the short rations, the First Fleeters were healthier in New South Wales than they had been in England. Second, no matter how slow progress may have seemed at the time, in any realistic view, the colonists altered their initial circumstances very rapidly. As Wentworth was later to describe, while the country immediately behind the coast was generally barren, from about 16 miles inland it improved rapidly, with open forest lands suitable for grazing, and a 'rich loam resting on a substratum of fat red clay', beyond which were the fertile flood plains of the Nepean and Hawkesbury rivers.[5]

Phillip began settling the Parramatta district in the second half of 1788 and intensified his efforts in 1790. He quickly had results. At the end of 1791, Tench observed:

Vines of every sort seem to flourish: melons, cucumbers, and pumpkins, run with unbounded luxuriancy; and I am convinced that the grapes of New South Wales will, in a few years, equal those of any other country. . . . Other fruits are yet in their infancy; but oranges, lemons, and figs . . . will, I dare believe, in a few years become plentiful. Apples, and the fruits of colder climes, also promise to gratify expectation. The banana-tree has been introduced from Norfolk Island.[6]

John Macarthur began farming at Parramatta in November 1793, and within a year he could write:

The changes that we have undergone since the departure of Governor Phillip are so great and extraordinary that to recite them all might create some suspicion of their truth. From a state of desponding poverty and threatened famine that this settlement should be raised to its present aspect in so short a time is scarcely credible. As to myself, I have a farm containing nearly 250 acres, of which upwards of 100 are under cultivation, and the greater part of the remainder is cleared of the timber which grows upon it. Of this year's produce I have sold £400 worth, and I have now remaining in my Granaries upwards of 1,800 bushels of corn. I have at this moment 20 acres of fine wheat growing, and 80 acres prepared for Indian corn and potatoes, with which it will be planted in less than a month.

My stock consists of a horse, 2 mares, 2 cows, 130 goats, upwards of 100 hogs. Poultry of all kinds I have in the greatest abundance.[7]

This process accelerated with the occupation of the Hawkesbury River valley, which Grose began in 1794. The next year, Paterson reported to Banks that 'Grapes and Figs are here in great abundance and thrive equally as well as at the Cape', and that the colony might become self-sufficient in animal food in about three years.

It took a little longer than Paterson hoped, but in 1803–04, King was able to report that he had three years' salted supply of meat (with the thousands of wild cattle on the cow pastures as an additional resource), and eleven months' supply of wheat and flour in store, with a further 11 000 bushels of wheat and 7000 of maize 'in stacks'—and these amounts were of course only the government ones, not the totals in the colony. King pointed out that the resources in grain would 'be sufficient to preclude the necessity of any being ever sent here again; for let what will happen, those supplies could not arrive before the effect of such unforeseen accidents would be replaced by the next crop of maize or wheat'. And he added that in the previous two years the colonists had 'attended more than they ever have done before' to the 'general cultivation of potatoes', so that they had 'added greatly to their general comfort'.[8]

Elizabeth Macarthur's description of their microcosm in 1815–16 indicates what the colonists had by then achieved at large in the County of Cumberland:

In their large garden ... they grew an abundance of fruits of many varieties. There was such a profusion of peaches, apricots and melons that the pigs were fed upon them when they were in season; loquats had been brought from China and did well, but so far there had been no success with gooseberries and currants. On the farm they grew wheat, barley, oats and [made hay]. ... They kept a dairy, fed hogs, fattened beef and mutton and exported fine wool.[9]

The majority of the colonists did not live in the circumstances of a Macarthur, but all benefited from New South Wales's bounty.[10]

A Struggle for Existence?

Life was not an undisturbed idyll for the early settlers of New South Wales. These Europeans encountered difficulties, including the barbarities of the convict system; short rations in the first years; periodic droughts, insect plagues, fires, and inundations of the coastal flood-plains; the lack of the capital or skill necessary to succeed on small allotments; and the rum traffic.

But were they worse off in New South Wales than they would have been in Britain? There, at the turn of the nineteenth century, rural workers (whose wages were historically low anyway) and small farmers had their ways of life greatly disrupted by the enclosure movement. Losing their traditional means of livelihood, great numbers of them moved to the new industrial centres; but given the wages and working conditions of the factories, and the temptation of gin, this was only to exchange one kind of misery for another. Scarcities of food resulting from periodic crop failures, war, and changing modes of agriculture, and the lack of money to buy what food was available, made for a low level of general health, which the crowded and unsanitary conditions of the cities further diminished—scurvy, for example, was endemic in London in the winters; and there were frequent outbreaks of typhus.

By comparison, New South Wales offered many advantages. As numerous contemporary commentators pointed out, the climate was 'salubrious', and its benefit was not diminished by crowded conditions. In the first years, colonists enjoyed the support of the government store. Quickly, they produced a considerable variety of food. Equally as important, they generally had the means of obtaining this food, whether by growing it individually on the freely available land, or by working for wages which the consistent shortage of labour made high, or by working for a combination of money and food. Instructive of the general experience in New South Wales in this period is that of one W.D., who arrived in 1841 without money:

was engaged as farm servant nine days after my arrival, at the following wages; £20 a year, and a weekly ration of 12 lbs. flour, 10 lbs.

meat, 2 lbs. sugar, 1/4 lb. tea. I have now [1845] eight head of cattle, and am worth in cash £30; the highest wages I ever received before I emigrated to this Colony was £3 10s. a year; I am well known to——and to——. I subscribe to a school, and the Colonial Observer; since in this Colony, I was out of employment about three months, but I must say it was nearly my own fault. I refused, as Mrs Chisholm knows, £15 a year, and rations; I am now receiving 20s. a week, and board myself; have a nice house, free of rent . . .[11]

Songless Bright Birds and Scentless Bright Flowers?

Just as wrong is the notion that, with its strange fauna and flora, and its reversal of seasons, the Australian environment was alien for those so disposed to derive aesthetic pleasure from it. Barron Field presented this view when he wrote that New South Wales was a place where 'Nature is prosaic/Unpicturesque, unmusical;'[12] Marcus Clarke offered its most famous formulation when, in reviewing Buvelot's 'Waterpool Near Coleraine,' he said: 'Some see no beauty in our trees without shade, our flowers without perfume, our birds who cannot fly, and our beasts who have not yet learned to walk on all fours', and a host of commentators has repeated it since.

Again, there is a considerable discrepancy between the modern image and the historical reality for, against the historians, the first European colonists did find pleasing features in the environment. In 1788, for example, Phillip reported that the 'heaths' about Sydney 'that are free from timber are covered with a variety of the most beautiful flowering shrubs'.[13] Interestingly, these were scented. Tench wrote that 'a variety of flowering shrubs abound, most of them entirely new to an European, and surpassing in beauty, fragrance, and number, all I ever saw in an uncultivated state: among these a tall shrub, bearing an elegant white flower, which smells like English May, is particularly delightful, and perfumes the air around to a great distance'. And these colonists did not find the Australian birds were songless, but rather, that their calls were not as striking as those of European species, which is a rather different matter.

As against Field, the words 'picturesque' and 'romantic' appear very frequently in early descriptions of New South Wales. The terms then carried specific aesthetic connotations,[14] so that their presence in early descriptions shows conclusively that the first European settlers did find the New South Wales environment to have pleasing features. This response grew with the progressive re-creation of English country life in the County of Cumberland. The bush image sits oddly with the evident success of the colonists in this endeavour, as the following descriptions from the time show.

Of Sydney's environs: On a slope at the eastern side of a very snug sunny little bay, with a lawn of English meadow-like verdure in front, stands the handsome mansion of Mr. W. McLeay.[15]

Here and there, on some fine lawny promontory or rocky mount, white villas and handsome cottages appeared, encircled with gardens and shrubberies, looking like the pretty 'cottages ornées' near some fashionable English watering-place.[16]

Of the country estates: I have passed a most delightful day at [Camden]; a more agreeable English-looking place I have not seen. The house, the park, the water, the gardens, the style of everything and of every person, master and servants, resembled so much what one meets with in the old country, that I could scarcely believe myself sixteen thousand miles from it.[17]

Of the ethos: A stranger has remarked, that old English hospitality expands itself throughout the colony. . . . In Sydney, he says, he was entertained with ceremonious politeness: In Parramatta, with friendly affability; and at Hawkesbury, as one of the family; but everywhere with equal liberality.[18]

As the colonists on the Cumberland Plain re-created the life they had either known or aspired to in England—that is, as they raised houses and towns, made roads, delineated holdings, raised stock and crops—so did they take progressively greater pleasure in their total environment. This description of the Emu Plains typifies their response:

The appearance of these fertile plains, situated at the base of the commencement of the Blue Mountain range, was very beautiful. The weather had been stormy and showery, but, at this time, the squall having passed away, the sun shone with brightness upon the green fields on and about the Nepean river; and the neat houses, scattered profusely about this charming spot, produced a very pleasing landscape.[19]

Among Alien Corn?

Did early settlers on the Cumberland Plain feel themselves to be in alien land and, like Ruth, weep for that which they had left? Well, some did; but for every John White ('a country and place so forbidding and so hateful as only to merit execration and curses'[20]), there were several Macarthurs, Eagars, Wentworths, and others now anonymous who felt otherwise. What is surprising is not that some of the first colonists should have felt desolate in New South Wales, but that so many should so quickly have felt at home there. Elizabeth Macarthur expressed early what became a widespread view, when she wrote home, 'Nothing induces me to wish for a change but the difficulty of educating our children, and were it otherwise, it would be unjust towards them to confine them to so narrow a society. My desire is that they should see a little more of the world, and better learn to appreciate this retirement.'[21]

There were many who came to this view in the early decades. William Charles Wentworth, for example, wrote in 1817:

It is . . . by no means my intention in becoming a member of the Law to abandon the Country that gave me birth. . . . In withdrawing myself . . . for a time from that country I am actuated by a desire of better qualifying myself for the performance of those duties, that my Birth has imposed—and, in selecting the profession of the Law, I calculate upon acquainting myself with all the excellence of the British Constitution, and hope at some future period, to advocate successfully the right of my country to a participation in its advantages.[22]

Eagar told Bigge, 'I am a Colonist, and have a Young Family growing up whose Country this is.'[23] And as a consequence of such assertion, Bigge reported that 'of the older inhabitants there are very few who do not regard the colony as their future home'.[24]

Informing this feeling of New South Wales as 'home' was the recognition that most colonists, whether in the situation of a Macarthur or an emancipist labourer, found many more favourable opportunities in New South Wales for economic and social prosperity than in England. James Henty really only elaborated the perception that then prevailed among the colonists when he told his brother in 1828:

New South Wales will do more for our family than England ever will. . . . At the expiration of 10 years [there] I shall be much disappointed if we individually are not worth [twice what we are now] . . . immediately we get there we shall be placed in the first Rank in Society.[25]

A Bush Ethos in the County of Cumberland?

Did the bush ethos develop out of life in the County of Cumberland in the first decades of settlement?

The images of that life which I have offered constitute an impressionistic history, but I believe there is a good deal more justification for the total picture they offer than for that deriving from the bush legend. Against the premises of this legend—chiefly that life in early Australia was a desperate struggle, in which people banded together the better to survive—we may say that, in general, those who inhabited the County of Cumberland between 1788 and 1840 found a pleasant climate, benign air, relative plenty, convenient access, welcoming mien, a rapidly prosperous urban centre, frequent beauty, and difficulties less than those in England.

There is also another factor to be considered here. In this period, the New South Wales colony was predominantly a maritime one, which looked outwards to the extensive ocean on whose shores it rested, rather than backwards to the vast interior. As Eagar told Bigge:

This Colony is naturally a Maritime one, and might with great advantage be extensively engaged in small Shipping, calculated for the trade with the South Sea Islands—We have an abundant supply of Timber fit for Ship Building, Our rising Generation is almost naturalized to the Sea and capable of becoming excellent Seamen, while we can supply every Article of provisions in abundance.[26]

Not until the mid 1830s did the products of the interior (specifically, wool) play a greater part in the colony's exports than those of the ocean and shoreline (seal skins, whale and seal oil, timber).

We must conclude, I think, that no matter in what lesser ways life on the Cumberland Plain between 1788 and 1840 may have foreshadowed that of the bush, its predominant character was not of such. On the other hand, it is certainly true that, from the mid 1830s onwards, as pastoralists pushed into the districts beyond the Dividing Range, and as increasing numbers of emigrants needed to go 'up the country' to find land or work, the bush of classical legend became the experience of some colonists. Gipps evoked many of the tenets of the legend when he wrote in 1844 of the pastoral expansion:

We here see a British Population spread over an immense territory, beyond the influence of civilization, and almost beyond the restraints of Law. Within this wide extent, a Minister of Religion is very rarely to be found. There is not a place of Worship, nor even a School. So utter indeed is the destitution of all means of instruction, that it may perhaps be considered fortunate that the population has hitherto been one almost exclusively male. But Women are beginning to follow into the Bush; and a race of Englishmen must speedily be springing up in a state approaching to that of untutored barbarism.[27]

But those for whom Australia has been the bush have always been a minority of the population. By the 1830s, the classical pattern of our demography had emerged in which we have been from very early times a distinctly urban nation, where a majority has gathered in or clustered about the large coastal cities. This was true in the County of Cumberland between 1788 and 1840; in 1821, for example, the 27 931 people on the Cumberland Plain constituted some 93.8 per cent of the population of New South Wales; and of these some 11 000 or 37 per cent, lived in Sydney, with another 11 000 in Parramatta, Windsor, and Liverpool. It was true of Australia at Federation, when some 1 334 000 people, or 35 per cent of the total population, lived in Sydney, Melbourne, Brisbane, Perth, and Hobart. It is true today, when more than 70 per cent of Australians live in large urban centres on the coastal fringe.

How was it, then, that we found the modes of bushman, pioneer, rebel, and Anzac to express our being as a people, when these reflect the actual experience of only a small minority of us?

It may be wrong to look for a direct correlation between fable of identity and general experience. Perhaps it was precisely because the life that developed on the Cumberland Plain in the first decades of Australian settlement was not distinctive compared to the British one that, when it came time for us to see ourselves as a people apart from those from whom we sprang, we adopted the bush identity, because it was distinctive.

But if this is so, another point arises: why did our progenitors on the Cumberland Plain not find their life on the edge of the great ocean distinctive enough to offer a separate identity? Why did we develop no legend of Pacific identity? The origins and causes of the classical legends of Australian identity remain obscure.

6. The Nomadic Tribes of Urban Britain: A Prelude to Botany Bay

M. B. and C. B. Schedvin

The nomadic races of England are of many distinct kinds—from the habitual vagrant—half-beggar, half-thief—sleeping in barns, tents, and casual wards—to the mechanic or tramp, obtaining his bed and supper from the trade societies in the different towns, on his way to seek work ... there are the urban and suburban wanderers, or those who follow some itinerant occupation in and round about the large towns ... they are more or less distinguished ... for their use of a slang language—for their lax ideas of property—for their general improvidence—their repugnance to continuous labour—their disregard of female honour—their love of cruelty—their pugnacity—and their utter want of religion.

Henry Mayhew

Australian historiography on the origins of the convicts transported to eastern Australia has passed through two distinct phases. The first, exemplified by the writings of Eris O'Brien[1] and Arnold Wood,[2] depicted the convicts as 'victims of circumstance'. The convicts were typified as English agricultural labourers or Irish peasants who had been forced into criminality by a harsh and unjust social system and tried before unforgiving magistrates who administered a penal code of exceptional inhumanity. The emergence of this interpretation may be attributed to inadequate empirical research, but it also served an important purpose during an early and sensitive phase of national self-awareness. The cultural consequences of Australia's unique origins could be left out of count: the convict system was regarded as having curiosity and antiquarian interest, but it was believed to have had no lasting influence on the culture, its institutions, and organizations. In other words, the 'victims of circumstance' were assumed to have returned to existential 'normality' on reaching Australian soil. By this means, any possible conflict in conscious perception was removed: Australians could take their full place among the British peoples and within the Empire without the taint of inferior ancestry.

The second phase encompasses the revisions of Manning Clark,[3] Lloyd Robson[4] and A. G. L. Shaw[5] based on extensive empirical research. As a result those characteristics capable of quantification have been established beyond reasonable doubt. The typical British convict may be portrayed as a man or woman of about twenty-six years of age who had never married and had been convicted of a form of larceny following a sequence of similar offences spread over several years. He was an urban dweller, most probably born in London or one of the other larger cities, and had a tendency to move about from one place to another. He was from the labouring class or from the itinerant working groups who lived in the countryside. The Irish convict was, typically, older than his British counterpart, married, of peasant stock, unskilled, and had frequently been in trouble with the police. Robson and Shaw restrict their work to enumeration, but Manning Clark interposes an important interpretative element. The social characteristics of the convicts contained an essential component of the Australian 'creed':

... the reformed town thief had one invaluable gift for his adopted country. These London thieves were deeply aware of their dependence on each other. ... Remove one cause of this fraternity—the fear of punishment—and substitute another—the need to work together in the Australian bush: then you have not a metamorphosis of the communion of sinners into the communion of saints, but a sense of loyalty and dependence between men cemented not by fear of the gallows, but by an awareness of the value of association to offset physical dangers and the great Australian loneliness.[6]

This belief in 'honour among thieves' was taken up by Russel Ward and made a building-block of *The Australian Legend.*

We would agree with Clark and Ward that the characteristics of social interaction within the convict community mediated an important component of the nascent Australian culture. But there is serious doubt about whether the quality of the interaction has been delineated accurately. Neither Clark nor Ward provides any theoretical support or empirical verification for their view that the convicts tended to forge close interpersonal bonds as distinct from defensive and expedient exchanges between peers. Indeed, theory and evidence point in the other direction: convicts because of their experiences and self-perceptions found extreme difficulty in forging any close interpersonal links.

In order to explore this proposition, we have examined qualitative evidence on the behavioural characteristics and self-perceptions prevalent within social groups from which the convicts were largely drawn using a theoretical framework derived from the human sciences. We hope this will add a useful qualitative dimension to the work of Clark, Robson, and Shaw, as well as describing systematically one of the foundation components of this nation's culture.

The perspective that underlies this approach has been derived from the work of psychoanalysts and sociologists who have emphasized the inter-relationships between the individual and society, following the pioneering work of Freud. We would agree with Melaine Klein that 'understanding of personality is the foundation for the understanding of social life'. At the same time, the need 'to define the growth of the person in a cultural milieu' is inescapable, so that the study of past or present social situations and processes cannot overlook the mutual inter-relationships of personality and culture.

The family has been seen as a microcosm of society which mediates values, symbols, expectations, and definitions of the social world to the individual. In doing so, that world is modified by selection of aspects of it 'in accord with their own location in the social structures and also by virtue of their individual, bio-graphically rooted idiosyncracies'. Dollard makes a similar point in stressing the significance of the family:

early transmission of opportunities and limitations characteristic of the wider culture is done by the family, or rather by the father, mother, and siblings; for the maturing child these persons *are* the culture. Most of the culture appears to the young child as something mother wants the child to do or will not allow or that father insists on or disapproves. It is no accident that during the rest of the life of the child the culture forms will carry plus and minus signs of specific parental character.

Such formative childhood experiences, particularly those within the intimate social world of the family, have been seen by many writers as crucial in shaping personality and the basic images of self and the world.[7]

We have mentioned that our task has been to use qualitative evidence to depict and interpret the world-images and self-perceptions of the group from which the convicts were pre-dominantly drawn. For qualitative evidence we have relied heavily (although not exclusively) on Henry Mayhew's four-volume *London Labour and the London Poor*. Mayhew collected his evidence at the end of the 1840s when transportation to eastern Australia was in its final phase. A brief assessment needs to be made of Mayhew and his evidence, and of the typicality of London and the 1840s to indicate the degree of distortion in the evidence we have used. The Irish are excluded from all that follows, for it is clear that the familial, religious, and environ-mental background of the Irish convicts produced an identifi-ably different behavioural pattern.

Himmelfarb has made the point that the title of Mayhew's study is misleading and that he selected his evidence from the bottom end of the social scale to the exclusion of most ordinary working people.[8] Settled workers were passed over in favour of the 'wandering tribes' and street folk. Himmelfarb estimated that the street people, thieves, beggars, and prostitutes constituted about 5 per cent (at the most 10 per cent) of the population of London, a large but unrepresentative component of the urban working class. But Mayhew's discrimination is an advantage to us: contemporary observers and recent historians are agreed that the 'ragged class' of London and the most disadvantaged of the working class elsewhere provided a disproportionate share of those who were convicted and transported.[9]

Mayhew's extended examination of the London poor permitted delineation of a systematic, cumulative picture comprising not only observation and statistics but also rich qualitative data, such as life histories, personal reminiscences, opinions, and fantasies culled from the street folk, itinerant labourers, beggars, thieves, and prostitutes. These subjective perceptions of self and environment reveal a great deal about their personalities and constructions of social reality; an examination of them yields insight into the life-world of the future convict.[10] While Mayhew deplored the living conditions of the poor, he was less censorious than most contemporaries and allowed informants to speak for themselves. Inevitably, however, his own values influenced his interpretations. While of middle-class background, Mayhew was hostile to aristocratic and bourgeois property values, and exasperated by the 'sticking plaster' mentality of philanthropists and sentimental do-gooders. In his view, a solution to the causes of poverty and social degradation was to be found in the protection of labour (particularly in sweated industries), and to this end he advocated combination of working men. Despite his sympathies, however, Mayhew neither varnished over the faults nor devalued the humanity of those whom he studied.

At a more general level, differences between the perceptions of middle-class observers and those of lower working-class subjects must be acknowledged. The norms and expectations of bourgeois philanthropists (including Mayhew) about home, 'family' life and sociability may appear commonplace to us, but they were not prevalent among the groups under study. Among the middle class there had been a trend towards clearer demar- cation of the family as the significant social unit distinct from broader structures of sociability and responsibility. The practice of children 'living in' with other households in order to serve and to learn declined in the seventeenth and eighteenth centur- ies, and schools and colleges were used increasingly as an alternative. For poor and working-class people, the later decline in the tradition of apprenticeship and 'service' meant that responsibility for upbringing and support of offspring devolved increasingly on parents who were often ill-equipped to fulfil it. Growth of the Ragged Schools came comparatively late, and did nothing to ease parents' economic burden.[11] Industrial employ- ment of juveniles offered financial relief in some instances but was not conducive to adoption of the middle-class norm of the child as an immature being in need of care and protection. The differences in parenting patterns between the middle class and the 'ragged class' inspired much disparagement of the behav- iour of parents and children from poor homes, but commentary of this kind has been disregarded.

Although Mayhew wrote in the 1840s, the evidence suggests that circumstances were similar in the 1820s and 1830s when most of the convicts were transported. Colquhoun reported much the same pattern for the last years of the eighteenth century, and Tobias confirms that there was only gradual change in criminal lifestyles and patterns of interaction. A more difficult matter is the typicality of London. There is no doubt that London was different: it was not an industrial city, employ- ment opportunities for casual labourers fluctuated sharply according to the seasons, and the metropolis because of its size and diversity was a beacon for new values and lifestyles. On the other hand, those who mixed seasonal work with part-time crime were highly mobile geographically; probably many had been born outside London, for Burnett has estimated that in 1851 nearly two-thirds of all inhabitants of English towns were first generation town-dwellers. Further, autobiographical material compiled by Burnett suggests that the life-experiences of many deprived working people who lived outside London were broadly similar to those of persons convicted in London. We accept that London's criminal community was exceptional, but not to a degree that invalidates the interpretation. The convict who had been socialized in London came to exercise a disproportionate influence on hulks and transports and the chain-gangs of New South Wales and Van Diemen's Land. Just as Australian language and accent has its generic links with the East End, many of the country's more distinctive values and norms can be traced to the rookeries of London.

Contemporary observers of the first half of the nineteenth century are agreed that juvenile delinquency and petty theft were frequently the first steps in a criminal career. The progression through juvenile vagrancy and street selling associated with petty pilfering, leading to pickpocketing and finally to more organized crime recurs repeatedly in experts' reportage and informants' autobiographical recollections. By mid century, defective parental care was held responsible for the proclivities of budding criminals. Early reformers thought that education would be a powerful tool in inhibiting criminal tendencies, but by 1850 some observers suspected that the Ragged Schools helped to spread juvenile crime. Certainly, the institutionalized violence which characterized many schools was unlikely to countermand feelings of mistrust and hostility towards society in general, and authority in particular.

Family life and childhood experiences of the street folk of London, the beggars, thieves, pickpockets, and prostitutes were seldom such as would foster consistent and constructive socialization and a positive self-image. A writer in Fraser's Magazine in 1832 stated in relation to juvenile offenders:

in the majority of cases, there has either been no parent, or those of such habits and temper as would have rendered orphanship a blessing; and that, in all probability, most of them under their care never had a kind or affectionate sentiment imparted to or drawn out of them, by any human being they could look to as a friend; and that they have in a manner been driven to take up arms against society, meeting from their earliest recollections, with nothing but an enemy in man.

The picture which emerges is characterized by parental neglect and indifference accompanied by lack of discipline. Mayhew pointed to the 'thousands of neglected children' who were to be seen 'loitering about the low neighbourhoods, and prowling about the streets, begging and stealing for their daily bread' and he deplored their lack of instruction and the 'bad example' set for them 'by their parents and others with whom they came in contact'. Not infrequently children were abandoned or rejected by parents or relatives and pushed into the streets to fend for themselves at an early age.[12] In other instances, accounts of parental harshness and tyranny feature repeatedly in the stories of youngsters who have run away and then lived precariously in the cities. Mayhew recounts:

The brute tyranny of parents, manifested in the wreaking of any annoyances of disappointments they may have endured in the passionate beating and cursing of their children, for trifling or for no causes, is among the worst symptoms of a depraved nature. This conduct may be the most common among the poor, for among them are fewer conventional restraints; but it exists among and debases other classes. Some parents only exercise their tyranny in their fits of drunkenness, and make that their plea of mitigation; but their dispositions are then only the more undisguisedly developed, and they would be equally unjust or tyrannical when sober, but for some selfish fear which checks them. A boy perhaps endures this course of tyranny some time, and then finding it increase he feels its further endurance intolerable, and runs away.

According to Tobias, orphans, runaways and deserted children all 'ran a high risk of ending up as members of the criminal class' in association with the children of criminals. Likewise, their mortality rate was above average. Images of the bullying father[13] who beats his 'wife' and children indiscriminately, especially when drunk, the absent or grudging mother, the resentful and punitive step-mother abound in contemporary reports[14] and in the personal accounts of street folk and recidivists interviewed by Mayhew. Even where one parent was described in positive terms, their effectiveness often had been over-ruled or subverted by the other partner, leaving the child resentful and confused.

Mayhew thought that a large proportion of felons in the metropolis were 'born in the houses of habitual thieves and other persons of bad character',[15] but such was not always the case as life-stories collected by him indicate. Nor was resort to a life of crime always a consequence of sheer economic necessity and the struggle for survival. In many instances the example of parents, siblings, peers, and other associates was instrumental in representing the inducements of easy money, an idle and self-indulgent lifestyle, and the spice of defiance of law and society in such a way that the values of a criminal sub-culture were endowed with personal immediacy. In the context of a criminal sub-culture, adoption of a criminal *modus vivendi* could take place with minimal moral scruple. Values and norms of this sub-culture established frameworks[16] for defining situations quite at odds with those of law-abiding citizens. Awareness of the consequences of concentrations of criminals and the poor in rookeries and dense slum areas stimulated moves in larger cities to clear and break up areas which provided havens and bases of social support for habitual criminals. In his 1840 study of 'Juvenile Delinquency in Manchester', W. B. Neale contended that a class of juvenile delinquents was to be found concentrated in certain quarters of Manchester which were a source of both moral and physical 'contagion and pestilence', such that children born and reared in them were 'predestined' to a life of crime.

Neglect and lack of guidance constituted prevalent patterns of child-rearing among the poorest city dwellers. Among street sellers, for example, young children were usually left alone all day to amuse themselves while their parents worked.[17] Mayhew recounts:

She is away at the stall, or hawking her goods from morning till night, while the children are left to play away the day in the court or alley, and pick up their morals out of the gutter. So long as the limbs gain strength the parent cares for nothing else. As the young ones grow up, their only notions of wrong are formed by what the policeman will permit them to do.

They were seldom sent to school, and when they were it was 'done more that the mother may be saved the trouble of tending them at home than from any desire that the children shall acquire useful knowledge'. For these youngsters, the streets offered richest opportunities for acquiring knowledge and finding entertainment. Much of the child's socialization took place unsupervised among its peers and siblings amid bullying, exploitation, and mistrustful competition. The children were alternately deprived, indulged, abused and exploited. Drinking habits of the parents tended to take precedence over all else so that children sometimes lacked bare essentials such as food and clothing, while on the other hand they were likely to be intro-duced early to the tap-room and made drunk for parental diversion.[18] Public houses provided important venues of social life, particularly as churches decreasingly fulfilled this function for the city poor, who regarded religion as something for well-to-do and respectable persons. Furthermore, they provided popular diversions in the form of melodrama, song, and favoured blood sports such as rat- and cock-fighting.

As soon as the children of street sellers could shout loud enough or carry a basket, usually around the age of seven, they were taken along to assist their parents or sent into the streets selling on their own—usually with cheap stock such as flowers, fruit, nuts, or matches. The money they earned was handed over to the parents. The fact that many were beaten if they failed to return home with sufficient money at the end of the day encouraged some youngsters to take up stealing. At some stage in adolescence, a youth would leave or be turned away from home after a quarrel with his father and would then start for himself, often in competition with and underselling his parents. Girls left home to 'keep company' with a youth of similar age to themselves, or were forced to leave home to make a living as best they could. Aversion to continuity and steady work was prominent among boys and girls of this class and most professed to 'like a roving life'.

Street selling was taken up not only by the children of coster-mongers, but also by neglected children, runaways, and orphans who had no other means of survival and by young thieves and prostitutes who used it as a cover for their main trade. Social interaction between thieves and street sellers was common, and they shared interests and attitudes, including hostility to the police and an inclination to rove the countryside. Lack of alternative employment was probably a factor which forced many young people to the streets and into crime as a way of making a living. During the Napoleonic Wars, crime is reported to have decreased not only because there was employment for many 'depraved characters' and 'mischievous members of the community', but also because youngsters who were given occupation had less incentive to crime. On the other hand, many youngsters who existed by begging, vagrancy, and various forms of larceny had a strong aversion to steady work. 'Sam', a young carpet-weaver turned vagrant explained:

I couldn't bring myself to work somehow. While I sat at the work, I thought I should like to be away in the country: work seemed a burden to me. I found it very difficult to stick to anything for a long time; so I made up my mind, when my time was out, that I'd be off roving, and see a little of life.

And as 24-year-old Ellen Reece explained shortly before her transportation after ten years of criminal activity and several convictions: 'When I left home I did not mean to work any more at all.'

The roving propensities and general restlessness of the London poor were attributed in the main to the harshness of either parents or masters, and a consequent failure to inculcate the habit of industry and a sense of purpose. The fact that a nomadic existence was often chosen at the cost of personal privation weakens the argument that this mode of life was chosen solely out of economic necessity. The summer when many young people left the metropolis was the time when most work was offering there. However, 'prospects of making a dishonest penny seem to have been better in the provinces', while London was better provided with refuges for the winter period.[19] Tramping around the countryside offered a change and the possibility of mischief and adventure, often in the company of other young persons of both sexes. Mayhew estimated that 80 per cent of vagrants were male. Seasonal excursions might include casual employment at harvesting, fruit or hop-picking. Then there were the country fairs and racecourse meetings where some might exploit opportunities for pilfering offered by the crowds. During these summer months, 'skippering' or sleeping under hedges and haystacks or in outhouses and barns was common, while some relied on getting a bed in the 'casual wards' of the unions.

For the essentially non-working tramps and beggars, their travels encompassed a well-known round of 'casual wards', 'good' halls and houses where handouts were available, goals and 'reliefs' in search of 'scran' or provisions and dodging work. Failure to receive anticipated relief could provoke angry retaliation and vandalism. A male informant described to Mayhew how at the Romsey Union:

a lot of young fellows broke all the windows they could get at because they were too late to be admitted. They broke them from the outside. We couldn't get at them from the inside.

And one young woman recounted how she and another girl took their revenge on a private citizen who failed to come up to expectations:

At last, when our clothes got bad, I and the other girl—she still kept with me—determined to break the parson's windows at Battle. We broke one because the house was good for a cant—that's some food—bread or meat, and they wouldn't give it us, so we got savage, and broke all the glass in the windows. For that we got three months.

This pattern of vagrancy was one of dependence. Vagrants and migrant workers travelled in the expectation of 'living off the country', so that farmers and smallholders became sensitive to raids on crops, gardens and livestock (usually poultry). When offenders were imprisoned for petty thieving or for vagrancy itself, the law at the time made scant allowance for the age of the culprit. Sometimes minor thefts were perpetrated with the express intention of securing food and shelter in prison, particularly as it was felt that thieves received better treatment in jail than vagrants. Sojourns in jail were accepted as a part of the life-cycle and in turn offered a chance to develop further criminal skills and contacts.

In a sense, these wayward juveniles became 'trained to prison life' and sought institutionalized food, shelter, and clothing as a matter of course, even while they rebelled against and evaded authority and restraints. On these grounds contemporary criticism was levelled against the penal system which was perceived as 'vomiting forth hordes of minor delinquents, who serve as recruits to the more desperate gangs, and remain in a course of turpitude until cut off by the commission of higher offences'. It was shown that criminal activity began early in life and reached a peak between the ages of sixteen and twenty-five, and that a majority of those sentenced were under the age of twenty-five. The general failure of the penal system to rehabilitate convicted persons and the fear which their return into society aroused were initially important factors in promoting transportation.

The blame that was attached to parents for this pattern of juvenile behaviour reflected widespread middle-class rejection of the realities of childhood and parenting among the poor. As noted, the lifestyles of street children defined middle-class conventions of protection and discipline, but condemnation of parental shortcomings failed to confront the basic human problems of adjustment to conflicting social standards and unfamiliar situations, which beset many adults in this period of rapid social transition. In addition to economic and environmental deprivation, many poor parents did not enjoy the emotional strength to impart basic trust in their parental roles. Erikson has framed with great clarity the relationship between the key role of motherhood and the social environment:

Biological motherhood needs at least three links with social experience: the mother's past experience of being mothered; a conception of motherhood shared with trustworthy contemporary surroundings; and an all-enveloping world-image tying past, present, and future into a convincing pattern of providence. Only thus can mothers provide.

These needs had not been met in most of the mothers (and fathers) of the street children: frequently their own experiences of being parented had been infused with an underlying hostility often manifest as indifference; contemporary surroundings were 'untrustworthy' which inhibited the emergence of valued norms of motherhood; there had been little constructive continuity in the life-experiences of most mothers and the prevailing world-image was one of antagonism. The consequences were children crippled emotionally by basic mistrust and imprisoned by excessive narcissism.

The profile of narcissism and under-socialization which emerges for the young street folk, thieves, beggars, and prostitutes of London is striking. Crude hedonism was expressed in precocious sexuality or greed for sweet confections and alcohol which suggests, when combined with lack of direction and tenacity, an almost infantile lack of restraint of libidinal impulses. Love of gambling was a further manifestation of the predisposition to rely on chance rather than personal effort. Many professed little notion of 'right' or 'wrong' in relation to their actions. Mayhew observed that: 'The only thoughts that trouble them are for their girls, their eating and their gambling—beyond the love of self they have no tie that binds them to existence.' This pattern of behaviour is consistent with an inability to form satisfying interpersonal relations in adult life, and may have its roots in infancy. An examination of attitudes to parents, of relations between men and women, and among peers will help to build a comprehensive personality profile.

Many of the thieves and vagrants whom Mayhew interviewed were highly ambivalent in their feelings towards their parents. In some instances, fierce resentment based on experience of rejections and cruelty dominated. More often, however, at least one parental image retained some positive attribute while the other was painted black. Treatment by fathers and step-mothers was most likely to be described as the reason for leaving home. In the story of one young thief and prostitute, for example, the dead mother was idealized while the girl and her sisters were ill-treated and deprived of essential food and clothing by the drunkard father 'who used to beat us and knock us about when he came home drunk', a situation which became doubly oppressive with the advent of a step-mother. Ultimately two girls escaped from home while the youngest, who remained, was allegedly 'almost dead between the pair of them'. In the recollections of a vagrant thief and house-breaker, the unloving harshness and coercion of his father was epitomized by his saying 'the bird that can sing and won't sing ought to be made to sing', but was offset by a kindly and indulgent mother who 'often kept me from my father's blows'. Yet, while this mother was portrayed as more affectionate and forgiving, there was an underlying suggestion that he felt betrayed by her and that her responses to his requests for money and assistance were perceived as grudging. Their basic ambivalence was illustrated, further, by the infrequency of expressions of concern for either mother or father. Remorse usually took the form of self-pity which contrasted their present penury and discomfort with 'what-might-have-been', but was seldom concerned with grief or hardship inflicted on their families by their own actions. The point needs to be underlined that in these life-stories we are dealing with an intrinsically subjective representation of events and persons as much as with historical actuality. For Ellen Reece, for example, youngest of three surviving children from a brood of eighteen, the mere fact of her survival was personal proof enough that her parents took, as she saw it, 'the greatest care as could be took of a child'.

The housing problems of the city poor prompted William Acton to describe the 'promiscuous herding of the sexes ... through want of sufficient house accommodation'[20] as an important cause of prostitution. Certainly, sexual relationships were entered casually and at an early age. Women were regarded as chattels and were exploited as cheap labour and frequently beaten and belittled to relieve their partners' feelings of frustration, inadequacy, and jealousy. Cruel and harsh treatment of the female partner was reported by many of Mayhew's informants. Males were especially susceptible to violent jealousy which usually provoked an attack on the female rather than risk a fight with the rival. The prevailing attitude was: 'The boy's opinion of the girl seems to be that she is made to help *him* or to supply gratification to his passions.' In casual relationships a girl was liable to be abandoned when she fell out with her partner, and while some clearly relished the freedom and changed partners to suit their convenience, others felt this to be unfair. If a girl became pregnant, 'the lads mostly sends them to the workhouse to lay in' explained one informant. Infant mortality was high and likewise infanticide. Temporary liaisons were especially common among those who led a roving life and formed part of the attraction of this way of life.

The transience of male-female relationships among youthful vagrants is indicated by these comments:

The female tramps mostly go down to Kent to pick up their 'young chaps', as they call them; and with them they travel through the country as long as they can agree, or until either party meets with some one they are better pleased with, and then they leave the other, or bury them, as they term it.

One 'quiet' 17-year-old who had worked in a cotton factory before running away, said of his fellow vagrants:

They often change their young women; but I never did travel with one, or keep company with any more than twelve hours or so. There used to be great numbers of girls in the casual wards in London. Any young man travelling the country could get a mate among them, and can get mates—partners they're often called—still.

Young boys among the street folk and vagrants quite often chose older women as their partners. In spite of these associations, most remained socially isolated. One young vagrant recalled:

I lost the young woman when I was put in prison in Manchester. She never came to see me in quod. She cared nothing for me. She only kept company with me to have some one on the road along with her; and I didn't care for her, not I.

Ultimately long-term relationships were formed by many street sellers and even prostitutes, although usually without benefit of clergy, and the children of these unions, although illegitimate, were at least acknowledged.

The image presented of the young female vagrants and habituées of the casual wards of London workhouses is not alluring. Many were thieves and prostitutes; some combined both professions and supported young men thereby. Mayhew describes them as follows:

The women were very rarely employed at any time, because there was no suitable place in the union for them to pick oakum, and the master was unwilling to allow them, on account of their bad and immoral characters, as well as their filthy habits, to communicate with the other inmates. The female vagrants generally consist of prostitutes of the lowest and most miserable kind. They are mostly young girls, who have sunk into a state of dirt, disease, and almost nudity. There are few of them above twenty years of age, and they appear to have commenced their career of vice frequently as early as ten or twelve years old. They mostly are found in the company of mere boys.

A young vagrant gives a more graphic portrayal which was corroborated by other informants:

Some of them are very pretty indeed; but among them are some horrid ugly—the most are ugly; bad expressions and coarse faces, and lame, and disgusting to the eye. It was disgusting, to hear them in their own company; that is, among such as themselves,—beggars, you know. Almost every word was an oath, and every blackguard word was said plain out. I think the pretty ones were the worst. Very few have children.

This passage gives a mild indication of the contempt in which such women were held by their male peers. This contempt was almost universal and efforts to maintain self-respect were likely to be met with mockery and overt hostility from members of their own and the opposite sex. Not surprisingly the women held an extremely low image of themselves and felt despised and rejected. Many resorted to drink as a refuge from their miseries.

The term 'mate' was used widely to refer to a partner or help-mate of the opposite sex, but it also applied to casual male or female acquaintances and companions of similar age and status. In neither instances does there appear to have been a basis of affection, closeness, or personal commitment in the relationships. Rather a mate satisfied a need for company, offered occasional support, and provided an appreciative audience for one's exploits and gratification of sexual impulses. An important element in these relationships seems to have been the feeling of equality: 'We were all in a mess; there was no better or no worse among us', as one youth phrased it. This was confirmed by the overt hostility shown to any whose behaviour implied superiority. To some extent these associations fulfilled a need for a sense of belonging and acceptance; they could provide appreciation of criminal exploits and cleverness which would support the feeling of personal worth of the individual criminal. Among vagrants it was common for boys or a boy and a girl to roam the countryside by day as mates 'vagabondizing' and at night to congregate in larger numbers in the small towns for gaming, singing 'blackguard' songs and story-telling.

Songs and stories of their own invention and those from popular broadsheets enlivened these gatherings. A fascination with crime, violence, sex, and the execution of convicted criminals predominated and was reflected also in broadsides and ballads sold by patterers and street vendors. Criminal characters such as Dick Turpin and Jack Shepherd were romanticized as popular heroes, and tales of their exploits were consumed eagerly. Stories of their own usually centred around a fellow named 'Jack' who defied authority and made fools of squires and parsons, ultimately gaining fame and riches (and occasionally respectability too). Mayhew records an interesting example of this genre, although it is too long to reproduce in full:

You see, mates, there was once upon a time, and a very good time it was, a young man, and he runned away, and got along with a gang of thieves, and he went to a gentleman's house, and got in, because one of his mates sweethearted the servant, and got her away, and she left the door open. . . . And the door being left open, the young man got in and robbed the house of a lot of money, 100*l*., and he took it to their gang at the cave. Next day there was a reward out to find the robber. Nobody found him. . . .

The narrative continues with Jack evading all traps set for him by the gentleman, enriching himself of a further £200 (in separate £100 amounts) and even assisting the gentleman to pay off an old score against the parson. Ultimately Jack is the only winner:

. . . and Jack got all the parson's money and the second 100*l*., and gave it all to the poor. And the parson brought an action against the gentleman for horsewhipping him, and they both were ruined. That's the end of it.

In this story, not only are 'respectable' authority figures outwitted, but Jack manages to win rueful admiration from the gentleman and to form a temporary alliance with him while the parson is being fooled into believing Jack is an 'angel' and obeying his behest. The fantasy of elevated status is extended further by the distribution of largesse among the 'poor'. The definition of authority figures as foolish, arbitrary, irrational and vindictive was an important element in their construction of reality.

Examples of mateship-type behaviour and sharing are reported among both males and females in Mayhew, but are not frequent. He felt that the 'hard struggle of their lives and the little sympathy they meet with' made the street children and their like selfish, so that while there might be companionship among them there was no friendship. Theft was seen as rife among this class and often led to quarrels, which might be provoked also by name-calling or derision among both men and women. However, fighting was relatively rare among themselves, 'even in the full swing and fury of their jealousy'. Among their own peer group, aggression was expressed through inter-gang skirmishes, larrikinism, and belittling of women.

Value was placed on 'helping-out', but this usually applied to behaviour expected of others (such as churchmen and relief agencies) and to themselves only where the personal cost was minimal. 'Taking in' persons in authority and the well-to-do with sob-stories, remorse, and crocodile tears was highly regarded, and advantage obtained in this way could be attributed to clever hoodwinking of gullible superiors which disguised the underlying dependence. The tone of one or two of Mayhew's respondents' stories suggests that he may have been the recipient of such performances on occasion. The prospect of outwitting the straight citizenry, and authority figures in particular, was attractive for its own sake, in addition to serving as a defence against feelings of inferiority and the horror of being patronized.[21]

Solidarity among street folk, especially costers, was most likely to be manifest when they banded together 'to thwart the police'. Common purpose in this instance was assisted by the fact that coster-mongers were subjected to continual harassment from police who interfered with selling pitches and seized barrows. In addition there was considerable overlap and informal association between costers and criminals such as thieves and receivers. Mention of the police, who were variously nicknamed 'peelers', 'bobbys' and 'crushers' was sufficient to excite hostility which was not lessened by the fact that 70 per cent of the metropolitan police who were comparatively well paid came from the provinces. Although in general the costers reportedly described themselves as 'Chartists', the principle element in their political outlook was hostility to authority as represented by the police who were perceived as arbitrary and despotic. Early childhood encounters in which police were the hated enforcers of prohibitions on street games and pranks, and agents of nemesis for those caught shoplifting or pilfering, compounded with basic mistrust and resentment of authority figures. This grew into lifelong habits of evading the eye and arm of the law. Among youths and vagrants, wilful defiance and outwitting of authority was considered laudable and they might band together to achieve this aim. 'We had pleasure in chaffing the policemen, and some of us got taken up. I always escaped', recalled one lad.

Another side of the relationship with authority was experienced by the Master of Wandsworth and Clapham Union, Mr Knapp:

They are very stubborn and self-willed. They have often broken every window in the oakum-room, rather than do the required work. They are a most difficult class to govern, and are especially restive under the least restraint; they can ill brook control, and they find great delight in thwarting the authorities of the workhouse.

This behaviour was contrasted with that of Irish beggars who were seen as more moral and orderly, less insubordinate and more inclined to seek employment than their English counterparts.

The Irish were prime targets for expressions of hostility towards outsiders. This arose out of mingled envy for the superior skills and assurance of the Irish and resentment of the threat they posed to selling and begging. The Irish were regarded as 'intruders and underminers' who had 'ruined' the best houses and unions and 'spoilt all the game'. As one female vagrant recounted:

We used often to say of a night that them Irish Greeks would ruin the business. They are much better beggars than we are, though they don't get as much as the English, because they go in such swarms up to the door.

It was quite common for vagrant lads to gang up against and rob Irish beggars suspected of having money on their persons:

At the time when juvenile vagrancy prevailed to an alarming extent the Irish hardly dared to show themselves in the casual wards, for the lads would beat them and plunder them of whatever they might have—either the produce of their begging, or the ragged kit they carried with them.

Juxtaposed with this envious attitude was their despisal of the dirty and diseased state of the Irish, and their propensity to 'eat anything' they could lay hand on. Contempt for the large Irish families which travelled together in part may have masked envy of the security in close personal relationships which these represented.

Tobias has postulated the existence of a 'criminal class' in nineteenth-century Britain which fulfilled an important supportive function for the large numbers of criminals who were otherwise isolated individuals.

Entry into the criminal class was a means of finding support; it was entry into an association, informal but nonetheless real, members of which could be found almost everywhere. In gaol or lodging-house or on the road, criminals could find companions in like situation, could exchange experiences and discover common acquaintanceships. To many of them the world had been an empty and friendless place;

many of them had never been able to find anyone to listen to them or sympathise with them, or speak to them save to command or criticise. Now all this changed. . . . *They were received on equal terms with others of their group, and were regarded as independent persons* [emphasis added].

One may query whether this shared ambit of experience consti-tuted the basis for existence of a 'class',[22] for while consciousness of being 'outside the law' might be common to all, discrepancies in status and lifestyles existed among criminals in differing lines of activity. However, a good case could be made to the existence of a sub-culture which might fulfil important functions for its adherents. Whereas criminals felt deviant and demeaned in association with a wider community, among other criminals their crime gave them standing and their worth as individuals was affirmed. The narcissism and low self-esteem which led them to shrink from relationships with 'straight' persons, where the threat of profound existential envy and self-dissatisfaction could arise, nevertheless permitted them to mix with others like themselves whose value system would affirm their identity.

Evidence on the extent of tangible personal support which might be expected from this source is inconclusive. Certainly, possession of a criminal record tended to isolate the individual concerned from most close relationships and employment opportunities among the 'respectable' community, and this could compel reliance on associates in the criminal sphere. Colquhoun lamented the fact that because those discharged from prison emerged 'without friends, without character, and without means of subsistence' they were forced to return to crime to survive. Contribution to raffles or whip-rounds for associates who had been jailed, or to celebrate their release, was one means by which a criminal could support his status in the group and demonstrate his capacity to pay. 'Flash houses' and the 'rookeries' provided meeting places where criminals might congregate and also facilities for disposal of stolen goods.[23] Training of green youngsters in the arts of picking pockets or theft was often undertaken in these venues. Sometimes this was done so that youngsters could be used as accomplices by a more experienced thief who could thereby reduce risk to himself (like Dickens's Fagin), but this motive may have been supplemented by the pleasure derived from instructing the novice and demonstrating one's superior skill. Casual associations within the criminal sphere could only be relied on up to a point. Betrayal and theft were prevalent. As one prisoner recounted, 'There is a sort of honour amongst us until we fall asleep or get drunk and then they will "barber" one another, "skewer them of all they have".' The 'honour among thieves' was based on mutual wariness and mistrust rather than on mutual warmth and loyalty.

Thus, although personal reassurance might be derived through association with others who shared a 'deviant' status similar to one's own, support from this source was unpredictable. Solidarity was most likely to be achieved in the face of external threat, but even then could not be relied upon fully.[24] Close interpersonal relationships were unlikely to develop because of the essentially enclosed self-centredness of these individuals and their lack of basic trust. Their anxieties about personal worth, and fears of commitment which could threaten ego-loss, precluded admission of a need for support and affection in close meaningful relationships so that their intense loneliness and anxieties remained unassuaged.

A profile of this 'type' of personality would comprise four basic characteristics. Although these are distinguished from one another for analysis, it will be appreciated that they interconnect and overlap.

The central characteristic is that of narcissism. Freud suggested that the narcissistic element which originated in the auto-erotism of the infant was present to some degree in all adults. However, a strong adult tendency to narcissism indicated, in Freud's terms, a reduced capacity for cathexes[25] with real external persons, and the ego-ideal which formed the basis for the super-ego. The libidinal energy which normally would be directed to real 'object' relationships in the external world would then be directed to the ego itself, 'thus giving rise to an attitude which we might call narcissism'. Inability to resolve satisfactorily the early dependency needs of the infant, combined with inability to form satisfactory object relationships in early childhood, principally with parents, left these individuals isolated, selfish and self-indulgent, trapped in the unsatisfying auto-erotism of the infant, and striving to repress frightening dependency needs. Erikson has seen this in terms of a failure to develop an attitude of basic trust towards both external reality and one's self. Where trust is lacking and a child has not internalized 'good' parental images, attempts at discipline may be rejected as self-interested and meaningless, and the parental model likewise rejected. Envy and resentment, withdrawal, depression, paranoia, and narcissistic isolation are some likely consequences of early deprivation and frustration of primary needs. Lack of self-confidence, negative self-image, weak super-ego resulting in poor control of impulses, and often delinquent behaviour round out the pattern resulting from parental neglect and emotional deprivation.

Closely related is intense anxiety about personal worth and competence and a consequent heightened fear of failure. This is indicated by reluctance to set goals which require directed purposive effort, and by nervousness of conflict situations which are not structured to contain or minimize threat to the ego. Chance or luck may be relied upon to bring success rather than personal effort, and readiness to find a scapegoat for all mishaps points to unwillingness to assume ultimate responsibility for oneself and one's actions. Fear or hostility manifested towards others who differ from oneself, such as members of the opposite sex, different racial groups, or those of superior social status, suggests another facet of this anxiety and provides an external release for aggressive impulses. Projection of aggressive feelings in definition of persons and inanimate matter as somehow 'bad' and malevolent justifies hostility, but in turn may evoke a need to contain or appease the external threat or may result in a tendency to withdraw as 'life' becomes intolerable.

A further characteristic is the lack of restraint on libidinal impulse and unwillingness to accept restraints imposed from outside. Internalization of controls through the super-ego is likely to be impaired when discipline and frustrations are seen to serve only the selfish purposes of authority figures (notably parents) but lack meaning and intelligibility for the child. Harsh, erratic disciplinary measures, untempered by parental affection and providence, lay a poor foundation for consistent social values and individual conscience. This will be closely related to the first and second characteristics, and is also linked with hostility to authority. In particular, an unloving and punitive father who fails to provide for and protect his family is likely to be seen as a selfish and aggressive tyrant. Paradoxically, in this case, while patriarchal-type authority is defined and rejected with its implied frustrations and threat to self-image, the erstwhile victim of oppression may in turn assume the role of oppressor when he is in a position of authority, particularly as father.

We suggest that the time has arrived for a deeper understanding of the social implications of the convict system. In this endeavour, recognition of the continuity of the individual human organism as a psycho-social and biological entity is central. For every individual transported, the episode formed part of a continuum of living, and its impact on personal identity and subjective construction of reality was linked with past and future situations and experiences. As Erikson has explained, 'Man is not organized like an archaeological mound, in layers; as he grows he makes the past part of all future, and every environment, as he once experienced it, part of the present environment.' The convicts may have been transported from Britain; they were not transported out of themselves. Their social perceptions were moulded by an English childhood which alternated hostility with indifference; eyes which perceived a harsh and inhospitable antipodean landscape, and lips which jeered and swore in defiance of decency, deity, and appointed authority, responded out of previous experiences of other persons. We will not proceed far in our examination of the psycho-social dimension of the convict heritage unless we appreciate the uncomfortable fact that key behavioural responses were evoked by the lack of basic trust towards others, and that this personality trait was unlikely to diminish swiftly on reaching Australian soil and without first making an important contribution to social life and institutions.

The distinctive patterns of behaviour so long associated with Australian convicts and later with their heirs, including the bushmen, appear to share features in common with the vagrants and street folk of London. Because of their numbers and relative homogeneity, their common experiences, shared values and language, the convicts socialized in 'London's Underworld' were highly influential culturally among their peers in the emerging colonial society. Their behavioural characteristics included restlessness and unwillingness to accept the personal investment and self-discipline implied by continuity of work and purposeful action; uncertain restraint of libidinal impulses illustrated by periodic bouts of excessive drinking; the evocation of fantasies of independence which masked an underlying reluctance to assume responsibility for oneself or one's actions, demonstrated by reliance on chance and addiction to gambling on the one hand and a tendency to rely on externally provided support on the other; the juxtaposition of this dependency need with a habitual quest for scapegoats to bear the blame for failures; hostility to outgroups and authority figures; release of aggression in acts of cruelty and savage humour, abuse, swearing, and vilification; wariness of personal intimacy, and an underlying mistrust between men and women which reflected an inability to relate to the opposite sex on a basis of mutuality; ambivalent and reticent relationships between 'mates'; and a marked preference for egalitarian modes of social behaviour which would minimize anxiety occasioned by manifestations of difference. These characteristics were expressions not so much of innovative social codes of behaviour in response to an alien and seemingly hostile environment. Rather, they represented a style of personal adaptation which was an integral part of personality structure, and served to confirm and defend a fragile identity. These defensive arrangements, which were consolidated during the life-cycle, stemmed from a profound feeling of inferiority and bore the imprint of formative personal experiences and their cultural setting.

7. Sydney and the Bush: An Urban Context for the Australian Legend

Graeme Davison

'It was I', recalled Henry Lawson in his years of fame, 'who insisted on the capital B for "Bush" '.[1] Lawson, as it happened, was not the first writer to adopt the convention and his pursuit of the bush idea was only one strand in a broader movement during the 1890s to make the rural interior a focus of Australian ideals. Though the bush, with and without a capital B, had figured in earlier writing, it remained for an expatriate Englishman, Francis Adams, in his book *The Australians* (1893), to identify the 'bushman' as a distinct national type. It is interesting, in view of the significance that the 'bush' was later to acquire, that Adams and Lawson should also have promoted the matching terms, 'city' and 'cityman'. 'Bush' and 'city' were plainly important literary touchstones to the writers of the 1890s and their symbolic counterpoint provides a vital clue to the sources of the 'Australian Legend'.

Historians of Australian cultural origins have generally sought the explanation of the 'bush' myth in the social context of the bush itself. Russel Ward, its most influential interpreter, has traced the 'Australian Legend' to a popular tradition of ballad and yarn that developed first among the convict settlers and itinerant workers of the pastoral frontier. Invoking the 'frontier hypothesis' of Frederick Jackson Turner, Ward argued that while America, a small man's frontier, had produced a national ethos of individualism and privatism, Australia, as a big man's frontier, created a tradition of egalitarianism and collectivism, of 'mateship'. Towards the end of the nineteenth century, through the powerful influence of the Sydney *Bulletin* and the 'new unionism' these traditions were imported from the pastoral frontier to the coastal cities where they formed the basis of a national, rather than merely sectional, culture.[2] As the 'bush' became the 'Bush', folk tradition was transmuted into literature.

It is a tribute to Ward's persuasiveness that, through a new generation of historical writing, *The Australian Legend* remains the standard account of Australia's cultural origins. Even as he was writing in the late 1950s, the foundations of his interpretation—the rural-export model of the Australian economy, his simple two-class model of pastoral society, the Turnerian concept of the frontier—were under attack. American historians were tracing their legend back from the far West to the popular song and story-writers of the great cities. In the early 1960s, Norman Harper, reviewing the history of the American and Australian frontiers, urged Australian historians to shift their vantage point 'from back of Bourke to the coast' and Michael Roe reminded them that 'whereas the appeal of the bush has been the great myth of Australian history the appeal of the city has been the great fact'.[3] Yet 'fact' and 'myth' have remained strangely unrelated, not least because the few casual attempts at an urban interpretation of the 'Australian Legend' have lacked a definite intellectual and social context.

A fundamental weakness of folk history—a genre of which Ward's book is a superior example—derives from its assumption that popular values may be abstracted from creative literature without direct reference to the ideas and special situation of those who created it. We are required to look beyond the mediating author to divine the *conscience collective*. The hazards of this method are obvious even with an unselfconscious, traditional culture, but they are greatly multiplied when we apply it to a post-industrial, culturally derivative society like nineteenth-century Australia. In such a culture, I suggest, we do better to begin, as we would any other exercise in the history of ideas, with the collective experience and ideas of the poets and story-writers themselves.

This experience, it must be emphasized, was of an emerging urban intelligentsia rather than a dying rural folk culture. All but a few of the *Bulletin*'s staple contributors and most of its occasional 'correspondents' lived in the coastal cities, especially Sydney and Melbourne. But only a handful had apparently grown up as city dwellers. The most outstanding group—Henry Lawson, Bernard O'Dowd, Edward Dyson, A. G. Stephens, the Lindsays—came as fortune-seekers from the declining gold-fields, their intellectual interests already often kindled by small-town self-improvement societies. 'Banjo' Paterson was the one important figure with even fair 'bush' credentials. Moreover, while it may be true, as Geoffrey Serle has claimed, that 'there is hardly one major creative artist, after Marcus Clarke and Buvelot, who is not a native Australian',[4] a striking number of the *Bulletin*'s second rank—James Edmond, G. H. Gibson, Ernest Favenc, 'Price Warung' (William Astley), Victor Daley, D. H. Souter, Will Ogilvie, Will Lawson, F. J. Broomfield and Albert Dorrington—had arrived in Australia from Britain as adolescents or young adults. Rather than bush—or Australian city—origins, the recurrent feature in the biographies of the *Bulletin* writers was their arrival in Sydney or Melbourne as lone, impressionable, ambitious young men.

In some, literary ambition had been fired by the frustrations of more conventional pursuits. Drop-outs from law or com-merce, like Roderic Quinn; failed matriculation candidates like Lawson; disillusioned schoolteachers like Mary Cameron: all clamoured for a place in the one calling, open to talent and con-sistent with literary aspirations, which a colonial city provided. 'Journalism', G. B. Barton noted in 1890, 'is at present the only field in which literary talent can find profitable occupation'.[5] The 1880s were a prosperous time for the press. Expanding colonial trade and a growing urban reading public produced a rapid growth of newspapers and trade journals and, in turn, an encouraging stimulus to literary effort. The number of 'authors, editors, writers, and reporters' counted by the census-taker in Melbourne more than quadrupled from 89 in 1881 to 359 in 1891. But even in these best of times a journalist's apprenticeship was hard and the long hours, low pay, and drudgery of police rounds weeded out all but the most determined. His work, by its very nature, put the young reporter constantly on call and this 'enforced irregular life' and 'weakening of domestic influences' were reckoned to confirm the 'bohemian tastes' and lifestyle of the average journalist.[6]

Many would-be writers had already cut adrift from 'domestic influences' when they came to the city and, like other young urban immigrants, lived alone in lodgings. In 1890 Sydney, with its large floating population of dock labourers, seamen, and seasonal workers, had over 300 listed boardings-houses, most of them crowded into a narrow 'transitional zone' between the terminal areas around the waterfront and railway station and the central business district. (See Map 1.) The city's boarding-house district extended from the high-class boarding-houses on Dawes Point south into a notorious skid-row of seamen's lodgings in lower George and Clarence Streets near the older Chinese quarter and the Quay; there were further clusters of cheap rooming houses adjacent to the main 'red light' district around the Town Hall and amid the pubs, music halls, and paddy's market near Belmore Park and the Haymarket; then, a little further out, a crescent of respectable white collar and artisans boarding-houses stretched from Redfern Station through Surry Hills towards King's Cross.[7] Sydney's boarding-houses were more than twice as numerous as Melbourne's and, since they lay athwart the main transport arteries, they were also more conspicuous. By the late 1880s, rising unemployment and the city's chronic housing shortage had swollen their population to crisis point. High population densities and residential mobility, a preponderance of unattached men and the volatile mixing of the poor, the vicious, and the exotic gave the region a distinctive ethos.[8] These were the tidelands of the city: a staging point for immigrants; a haven for the drifter, the outcast, the man or woman with a past; a twilight zone of rootlessness and anomie.

This was the sleazy urban frontier which provided the social context for the *Bulletin* writers' confrontation with the city and

MAP 1: SYDNEY BOARDING HOUSES, 1890

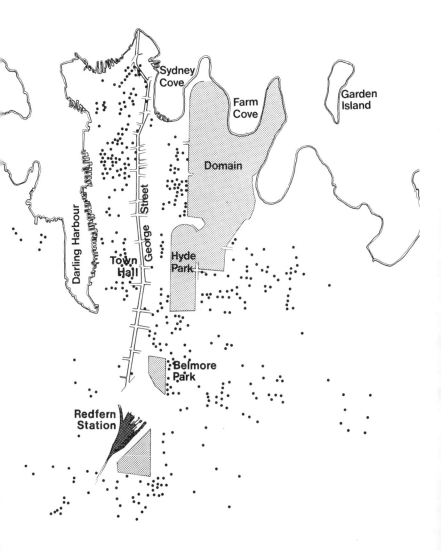

Source: *Sands' Sydney Directory*, 1890

MAP 2: RADICAL SYDNEY IN THE 1890s

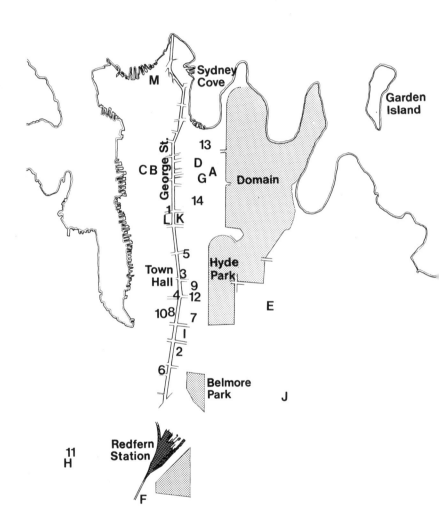

Sources: *Sands' Sydney Directory*, Sydney Electoral Rolls 1889, 1894 (Dixson Library), biographies, letters and memoirs

from which, as we shall see, they fashioned reactively their conception of the 'bush'. Map 2 shows the residences, during the late 1880s and early 1890s, of some of its leading members and their associates. It remains necessarily incomplete: perhaps because of their 'irregular' lives, several important figures have left no trace of their movements in directories, electoral rolls, memoirs, letters or other sources. But the evidence is sufficient to suggest the close connection between the residential habits of the writers and the life of the 'transitional zone'.

Throughout their early stories and verses there are vivid glimpses of boarding-house life. We meet the landlady, blowzy and familiar, and drawn—as we might expect with young men away from home—affectionately and rather larger than life. James Edmond describes one such 'wild' bohemian establishment':

There were ten of us there . . . including Bem, the humorous Polish tailor, who was vaguely understood to have thrown bombs at all the royal families of Europe, and then gone into exile. We paid seventeen shillings a week each, not including washing; and we lived riotously on boiled mutton. There were more empty beer bottles in the bedrooms, and more laughter, and more grease slopped on the floor, and the candle-ends got in the soup oftener in that boarding house than in any other I ever heard of. Also the neighbours got less sleep than anybody ever did in the vicinity of any other boarding-house. The dining room had not been papered since the beginning of history, and the landlady had only one eye; also her daughter had recently eloped with a non-union printer. She, the landlady, was aged about 40, and wore a green dress, and in the evening she used to sing songs to us with her hair down.[9]

But beyond the rough good fellowship of the boarding-house, the city melted into the fleeting images of the twilight zone: Chinese opium dens and sixpenny restaurants, drunken youths swaying under gas lamps, painted women waiting on street corners and the ceaseless tidal flow of faces in the street. Henry Lawson, who traversed the region daily on his way from Phillip Street to Redfern Station, gave us the essential vision:

> They lie, the men who tell us for reasons of their own
> That want is here a stranger, and that misery's unknown;
> For *where the nearest suburb and the city proper meet*,
> My window sill is level with the faces of the street—
> Drifting past, drifting past
> To the beat of weary feet
> While I sorrow for the owners of those faces in the street.[10]

None of Lawson's early poems establishes so precisely his marginal urban situation or attests so poignantly to his legacy of loneliness. The dilemma—'Sydney or the Bush?'—had been inherent, from the very beginning, in the emotional conflict between Lawson's parents, the brooding bushman Peter Larsen and his ambitious, city-struck wife, Louisa. Louisa had married Larsen, she later confessed, to escape the claustrophobic atmosphere of her parents' home but, as a selector's wife, she soon repented her blunder. (Misalliance was to become the emotional core of her feminism and a central theme in her later fiction.) Torn between this ill-matched pair, young Lawson grew up dreamy, solitary and deprived. When he was five, he visited Sydney for the first time, an experience he still recalled, with the pain of outraged innocence, thirty years later. He wandered into a brothel, ate cakes with the ladies of the town, and was scolded by his mother. With some playmates he stole some wood shavings from a neighbouring coach factory but was detected by the boss who chased the young delinquents down Castlereagh Street, shouting, 'Cut off their heads.' Young Harry hardly stopped running until he got back to Gulgong, marked for life with a distrust of city ways and city people.[11]

When he was sixteen the Lawsons' dismal marriage broke up and Louisa brought her four children to Sydney. They squatted with relatives at Marrickville for a few weeks then, in 1884, rented four rooms in Phillip Street, amid a cluster of lodging houses near the Quay. On their first night the children, unaccustomed to the noises of the city, lay awake listening to the clatter of feet on pavements, the mewing of tom-cats and the rattle of trams around Hunter Street corner. For Louisa the city was at first a lonely and difficult place and a few years later, in a thinly disguised autobiographical story, she described the difficulties of a separated country wife making her way by doing odd jobs and taking in boarders. The problem of simply surviving as one of that 'greatly ill-used, landlord-cursed class, the boarding-house keeper' was compounded by the 'undeserved loss of caste' in being a married woman apart from her husband. She was, in her own eyes, 'a social outcast'. 'I was unknown and uncared for', she wrote, 'lost in a great city'.[12]

The helplessness of the rural emigré, their exclusion from respectable society, and Louisa's highly developed religious sensibility all combined to bring the Lawsons into the orbit of Sydney's radical intelligentsia. Within three or four years Louisa, with Henry at her apron-strings, had extended her manic energies to the full spectrum of 'progressive' causes, ranging from secularism and spiritualism to republicanism and feminism. A letter to George Black in 1888 reports on a typical week's activities:

Mr Bell has gone to the northern districts and in consequence we expected no [Republican] meeting in the Domain Sunday but Mr K[eep] reports a good one. The speakers were Mr Manley and others. ... Good crowd, fine day etc. Mr K. attended Mr Collins lecture title Resurrection Myths last evening fair house. Mr K. says it was a splendid discourse. I went down to Lyceum where Mr Hubbard the medium was giving clairvoyance tests with fair success. ... I went down to the Town Hall on Sat Eve to hear what the Australian Natives Association had to say for themselves they were well received ... I also attended the Anti-Chinese meeting in the same buildings.[13]

The close interconnections between radical organizations suggested by Louisa's routine are further substantiated by their geographical concentration in the inner city. The overlapping circles of secularists, republicans, land-reformers, feminists and socialists, which together comprised Sydney's infant 'counterculture', focussed their activities on a small triangle of the 'transitional zone' between the Town Hall, Hyde Park, and Redfern Station. (See Map 2.)

Its nucleus was the Hall of Freedom in George Street where, under Thomas Walker and W. W. Collins, Sydney's freethinkers continued to preach the doctrines of Thomas Paine, just as their great contemporaries Charles Bradlaugh and F. W. Foote did in London. Many of the Association's stalwarts were themselves apparently refugees from London's declining trades: hard-working hatters, drapers, upholsterers, and compositors whose secularism, crude and iconoclastic, had reflected the disappointments of their lot. But economic aspirations denied by Clerkenwell and Finsbury found more encouragement in Sydney and by the late 1880s many older secularists had left the mean environs of George Street for Woollahra and Paddington. With their dispersion something of the old militancy was lost, and in 1889, at the opening of a new Freethought Hall, these 'sons of Albion' were ardent in praise of their 'Southern Home'. Indeed, it was not resentment of England or a peculiar sense of being Australian so much as fidelity to the Paineite tradition that made some of Sydney's leading freethinkers, like Thomas Walker and William Keep, theoretical republicans. For them, kings and princes, like bishops and priests, were part of an outworn fabric of medieval superstition and oppression. It was only among a smaller cadre of native-born secularists— including, notably, the Lawsons, mother and son—that republicanism became the basis of a more distinctive nationalism. Other *Bulletin* writers who may be numbered, formally or informally, as republicans in the late 1880s include George Black, E. J. Brady, J. le Gay Brereton, John Farrell, Roderic Quinn and, away from Sydney, Bernard O'Dowd and A. G. Stephens.

From the attack on priest-and-princecraft, it was only a step further to an attack on inheritance. Since the days of the Land and Labour League in the 1860s, the causes of republicanism and land nationalization had been closely associated in London radical circles and during the 1870s Charles Bradlaugh had made land reform a main plank of his electoral platform. In

Sydney, secularists and republicans appeared, with the *Bulletin*'s W. H. Traill, among the leaders of the New South Wales Land Nationalization League. The radicals of the inner city had good reason to crave 'the abolition of that poverty which manifests itself in all large cities of the world' and the *Bulletin* urged them on with slashing exposes of rack-renting in lower George Street. The scapegoats for the city's housing problem were the hated Chinese. The pressures created by redevelopment around Circular Quay had forced them to abandon their old haunts in lower George Street and move south to the new market area near Belmore Park, an area which, with its boarding-houses and bookshops, the radical intellectuals regarded as their own. Their champion, George Black M.L.A., led the anti-Chinese campaigns of the late 1880s and early 1890s while the *Bulletin*'s illustrators led by Phil May depicted the squalid interiors of Chinese gambling houses, brothels, and opium dens.

The outlook of Sydney's radical intellectuals was, therefore, a product of two mutually reinforcing influences: the transplanted artisan culture of late nineteenth century London and the pressures of day-to-day life in Sydney's transitional zone. One cannot but remark how closely their ideological preoccupations—secularism, republicanism, land reform, and anti-Chinese feeling—match the 'anti-clericalism', 'nationalism', bush sentiment and 'race prejudice' which Ward has identified as the defining features of the 'Australian' ethos. Indeed in this chapter I argue that the projection of these values, born of urban experience, onto the 'bush' must be understood in terms of a concurrent movement to establish the 'city' as a symbol of their negation.

The city depicted in the writings of the *Bulletin* school is one that a dispassionate historian would find hard to recognize in contemporary photographs of Sydney's dishevelled townscape. But their lurid imagery, we must remember, was more symbolic than photographic, and owed less to observation of the Sydney scene than to the rich stock of urban imagery which the *Bulletin*'s 'hard-reading crowd', along with other colonial city-dwellers, imported from London. The primacy of London and their stereoscopic vision of the nearer urban scene is nicely suggested in a line of Lawson's, written 'to speed enthusiasm in favour of the London poor'.[14] 'I looked o'er London's miles of slums', he wrote, 'I saw the horrors here/And swore to die a soldier in the Army of the Rear'.[15] (His first and only journey to London still lay fifteen years in the future.)

For J. F. Archibald, founding editor of the *Bulletin*, the experience of London merely crystallized and reinforced an already dismal view of the colonial city. He had first come to Melbourne in the 1870s as an apprentice journalist from the Western district and for eighteen months scraped along as a part-time stone-hand, living alone and depressed in a South Melbourne boarding-house. A few years later, after becoming well established in journalism, Archibald arrived in Sydney. He was 'ill and tired' at first but gradually established himself and in 1880, with his partner John Haynes, founded the *Bulletin*. But the metropolis continued to exert its fatal attraction and in 1884 he arrived in London. Sick and burdened with financial worries, he lived for almost two years on the margins of Fleet Street, shut out from regular employment but supplying the *Bulletin* with leaders and 'pars' that reflected his acquaintance with contemporary radical journalism and the mounting sense of crisis in 'Outcast London'.[16] The experience reinforced his distaste for the 'selfish', 'hysterical', and 'callous' ways of the city but, paradoxically, increased his reverence for London standards. Under his influence the *Bulletin* in the later 1880s continued to project its view of local affairs onto a rolling backdrop of metropolitan events: the West End riots, the rise of the Social Democratic Federation, the fortunes of Charles Bradlaugh, and the Dock Strike.

Among the paper's contributors over the following decade, it is possible to distinguish three main styles of urban writing, each firmly rooted in the London context. As bookish schoolboys in the 1860s and 1870s the *Bulletin*'s writers naturally fell under the pervasive influence of Charles Dickens's rich, but essentially segmental and antipathetic, view of London. Henry Lawson, for example, claimed that 'every line that Dickens wrote/I've read and read again' while his friend Jack Brereton recalled how 'Lawson and I used to wander into all sorts of queer corners and neglected backwaters of Sydney, and he pointed out to me the localities which he fancifully associated with the one novelist with whose work he was fairly familiar, Charles Dickens'. Unhappily it was the weaker side of Dickens—the pathos of young Oliver and Little Nell—rather than his powerful vision of urban landscape which Lawson emulated in his 'Arvie Aspinall and Elderman's Lane stories.[17] But then the value of the London influence lay not in the quality of these imitations so much as the later, less obviously derivative, work for which they provided a scaffolding.

Archibald's stay in London had also coincided with the success of the journalist and light versifier, George Robert Sims. As a protege of Douglas Jerrold and G. A. Sala and a patron of the National Sunday League and the Hall of Science, Sims united the sympathetic, but otherwise separate, worlds of literary bohemia and militant secularism. Today he is remembered mainly for the impact of his book, *How the Poor Live and Horrible London* (1883), on the housing debate of the 1880s, but he was equally celebrated in his day as the author of *Dagonet Ballads*, a book of light verse dramatizing the condition of the London poor. (It included 'It is Christmas Day in the Workhouse' and 'The Lights of London Town'.) The *Bulletin* regarded Sims as 'undoubtedly the most read light litterateur in the world' and reprinted his verse on several occasions.[18] With his use of colloquial speech and the ballad convention, and his theme of rural innocence and 'urban degeneration', Sims may have exerted a powerful influence on the style and anti-urban bias of Australian popular verse.

The third, and most seminal, influence on the *Bulletin* writers was the tradition of rhetorical, quasi-religious verse which descended from the late eighteenth century through Blake and Shelley, persisted in Chartism, and returned to fashion in the radical movements of the 1870s and 1880s. For Dickens, the city was mainly a *theatre* of human character; with Sims, it was a *cause* of human degeneration; but among the radical poets it became a gigantic *symbol* of corruption and exploitation invested with the apocalyptic shades of Sodom and Gomorrah. The most formative English exponent of the style was the 'poet laureate of freethought', James Thomson, whose 'City of Dreadful Night' first published in 1874 enjoyed a vogue during the 1880s. In Australia he was followed by the 'Arnoldian Socialist' Francis Adams whose collected verse, published in Sydney in 1887, was, according to E. J. Brady, 'a notable incident in the pre-socialist period'. Adams's gloomy view of London, 'the City of Wealth and Woe', reflected his deep hostility to the land and class of his birth but became, through its resonance with the marginal urban situation of the *Bulletin* poets, a pivotal image in the verse of J. A. Andrews, George Black, E. J. Brady, Edward Dyson, Henry Lawson, and Bernard O'Dowd, who all served for a time as poetic footsloggers in Adams's 'Army of the Night'.[19]

These three styles of urban image-making corresponded roughly with different kinds of social and political consciousness and the gradual predominance of the third over the first and second is one index of the deepening sense of urban alienation among *Bulletin* writers around 1890. Only careful attention to the chronology of their writings discloses the connection between their increasingly dismal view of the city and the rise of the bush ideal. Until about 1890, for example, Henry Lawson's writing had consisted mainly of republican 'songs for the people', verses on urban themes ('Watch on the Kerb') and semi-autobiographical sketches on gold-fields and selection life. But in that year we find his interests moving further inland. In a series of newspaper articles he discussed the idea of decentralization and land reform, arguing that 'if some of the surplus suburbs of Sydney were shifted up country a few hundred miles, New South Wales would greatly benefit by the change'. Almost simultaneously his verse leaps 'Over the Ranges and into the West':

> We'll ride and we'll ride from the city afar
> To the plains where the cattle and sheep stations are.[20]

In the late 1880s 'Banjo' Paterson may have stood closer to the rest of the *Bulletin* crowd than he did in later life. It is true that he joined few of their campaigns and lived in semi rural seclusion across the Harbour at Gladesville, but his solicitor's office was within a block of the city's most sordid flophouses and in one of his first published pieces, a tract on land reform *Australia for the Australians* (1888), he invited his readers to

take a night walk round the poorer quarters of any of our large colonial cities [where] they will see such things as they will never forget. They will see vice and sin in full development. They will see poor people herding in wretched little shanties, the tiny rooms fairly reeking like ovens with the heat of our tropical summer. I, the writer of this book, at one time proposed, in search of novelty, to go and live for a space in one of the lower class lodging houses in Sydney, to see what life was like under that aspect. I had 'roughed it' in the bush a good deal. . . . But after one night's experience of that lodging I dared not try a second . . . I fled.[21]

In his flight from the horrors of the city, Paterson retreated inland; his solution to urban ills was to open up 'the rolling fertile plains' to closer settlement. The city and the country were established as separate moral universes: the poet worked in a 'dingy little office' in a 'dusty dirty city' but his better self, on permanent vacation, rode with the 'western drovers', sharing the 'pleasures that the townsfolk never know'.[22]

With E. J. Brady, the flight from the city took a new direction. Brady had grown up in Carcoar, a mining town on the eastern slopes, but spent some of his school years in the United States where, he later claimed, he was converted to republicanism. Back in Sydney, Brady and Roderic Quinn, a schoolmate at the Marist Brothers High School, actually designed an emblem for their future 'Republic of Australia'. After matriculation and a brief trial as an engineer's apprentice, Brady followed his father into Dalgety and Co., becoming a timekeeper in their bondstore on Circular Quay. The Harbour, in his eyes, was to become a 'golden portal' between the mean environs of the Quay and 'the wide mysterious domains of Glory and Romance, spreading out and away across the world'.[23] He wrote a first slumming article on the Chinese gambling dens of lower George Street and learned a lot about 'ships and sailormen and stevedores' which he stowed away as material for the sea-shanties and ballads which expressed his nautical variation on the 'bush' themes of mateship and manly toil. His intellectual horizons were broadening too. From Chateaubriand and the *Lives of the Saints* he moved on to Kant, Mill, Darwin, and Marx—teachers who took him far from the faith of his childhood and created a rift with his parents who became 'so opposed to my secular opinions that I could not discuss my religion or politics within the home circle without disagreeable conflict'. These tensions emerge clearly in Brady's unpublished verse of the late 1880s: two of his poems—'Ruth' and 'Ishmael'—express feelings of 'mental isolation' and territorial estrangement, while others—'Eden: The Dream of the Disinherited' and 'The Land of the West'—project his vague utopian longings beyond Sydney Harbour into a mythical land far from 'the shore/Of Time, whose restless changing sea/The fleeting prow/Of mortal *How*/Sails to some far-off *To Be*'.[24]

The dream-like 'Land of the West' which emerged in the late 1880s as an anti-type of the city began to acquire a more definite character during the urban conflicts of the early 1890s. With the Maritime Strike of 1890, the Sydney waterfront, already ridden with unemployment, overcrowding, and racial tension, became a frontier of class conflict. There was rioting on Circular Quay and unionists held almost daily meetings in the Haymarket. Battle lines were strictly drawn and the radical intellectuals, occupying the narrow divide between the eastern (middle-class) and western (working-class) sectors of the city, were bound to take sides. E. J. Brady refused his employer's instructions to enrol as a special constable and was dismissed without credentials. He was now a 'marked man', shut out from regular employment and disowned by friends and relations. 'I very shortly learned what it feels like to go without regular meals, and what it feels like when the soles of your boots preserve but a nodding acquaintance with your uppers and your only coat is out at elbows and turning a faded green.'[25] He tried to organize a clerks' union but his brother clerks, loyal to the white collar, held aloof. In 1891 he was appointed secretary of the Australian Socialist League whose members, for a brief moment of radical solidarity, spanned the range of anarchists, social democrats, Georgists, and labourites and extended from the intellectuals of the transitional zone to the working-class respectables of the western suburbs. Roderic Quinn wrote euphorically of a new unity of 'Labour and Thought' and many of the *Bulletin* crowd—including Lawson, George Black, Mary Cameron, Con. Lindsay, and 'Price Warung'—were active in socialist circles at the time. The engagement of their sympathies laid an ideological basis for the 'egalitarian' and 'collectivist' elements of the bush ethos and began the transformation of socialism into 'being mates'.

The headquarters of socialist activity was the boarding-house and bookshop run by W. H. McNamara next door to the League's rooms in Castlereagh Street. Henry Lawson was a frequent lodger and it was here that he met his wife-to-be, McNamara's step-daughter, Bertha Bredt.[26] Later, in 1893, William Lane, on his long odyssey from non-conformist Bristol to 'New Australia', kept a similar establishment further west on the borders of Chippendale. It cannot have been Lane's first visit to Sydney for his novel, *The Workingman's Paradise* (1892), contains an acutely observed sketch of the 'moral geography' of George Street:

There were no street-walkers in Paddy's Market, Ned could see. He had caught his foot clumsily on the dress of one above the town-hall, a dashing demi-mondaine with rouged cheeks and unnaturally bright eyes and a huge velvet-covered hat of the Gainsborough shape. . . . Then he had noticed that the sad sisterhood were out in force where the bright gas-jets of the better class shops illuminated the pavement, swaggering it mostly where the kerbs were lined with young fellows. . . . Nearing the poorer end of George Street they seemed to disappear, both sisterhood and kerb loungers, until near the Haymarket itself they found the larrikin element gathered strongly under the flaring lights of hotel bars and music hall entrances. But in Paddy's Market itself there were not even larrikins. Ned did not even notice anybody drunk.[27]

As a mind-scarred refugee from the English class system, Lane was prone to interpret Australian conditions in terms of London stereotypes but his working-class characters, like Mrs Phillips with her doomed aspirations for a Sunday 'room', nicely catch the predicament of inner Sydney families squeezed by rising rents and irregular employment while the salon conversation of his radical intellectuals exposes, even as Lane himself attempts to repair, their fragile alliance with the working classes. For as long as it persisted, the intellectual-working class partnership strengthened the influence of the socialist muse upon the *Bulletin* poets and intensified their apocalyptic vision of the city:

> In the bye ways foul and filthy—in the dark abodes of crime—
> Revengeful fate is counting out the gathered sands of time,
> In the hovels of the helots—in the narrow city slums
> An army lay in waiting for the beating of the drums.[28]

E. J. Brady's 'dirty, smoky city', peopled by drunks, harlots, and legions of the oppressed was, as we have seen, conventional among English radicals, but it also mirrored life as he saw it from his room in an umbrella shop in Regent Street, Redfern. ('I have rented me a room/In the close oppressive gloom/Of a narrow street where I/Watch the people passing by . . .)[29]

Writers, as a group, had experienced a sharp reversal of fortune. As a boom occupation, journalism was hard-hit by the depression. Full-time respectable reporters set up an Institute of Journalists to defend themselves, but the part-timers and free-lancers of the colonial Grubstreet had little collective strength left to exert. For a few months in 1891 Brady had been editor, at £3 a week, of the *Australian Workman*, but he fell out with the freetraders who controlled the paper and was elbowed aside by

George Black. 'With nothing else for it', he went over to John Norton's *Truth* where, for the next few years, he eked out a 'sordid' livelihood at 10s. 6d. a column. It was galling to be a mere 'wage-writer':

> You may hold your own opinions and you hold them dearly too,
> But the journal that you live on has a 'policy' and you?
> Why, you barter those opinions for the things you wear and eat,
> And sell your very virtue, like the woman of the street.[30]

In Melbourne, Edward Dyson's one-man imitation of the *Bulletin*, the *Bull Ant*, struggled bravely against the flood of cheap English magazines but foundered in 1892. Lawson wrote a lament for 'southern journalism' in 'The Cambaroora Star' (1891). During the depression the *Bulletin* became one of the chief sources of outdoor relief for unemployed journalists and it is no accident that older family men—'Price Warung', Edward Dyson, and Ernest Favenc—were its most prolific contributors during these years. The depression also took a heavy toll on writers' wives and saw the break-down of several marriages, including those of Brady, O'Dowd, Black and Becke.

For Melburnians especially the 1890s were a period of terrible disillusionment. Even with their ideological defences up, the city's radical intellectuals could not help sharing the optimism of the land boom era and the fall of 'Marvellous Smell-boom', as the *Bulletin* cruelly dubbed the scandal-ridden metropolis, destroyed the illusion of urban progress and brought them a step closer to the dark city of the revolutionary poets. During the good years Edward Dyson had migrated to 'a very exclusive suburb, out at the far end of a methodical and cautious railway' but by the mid 1890s he had been forced back 'In Town'.[31] Bernard O'Dowd, who fled with his in-laws when their Carlton bootshop failed, looked down from its windswept northern perimeter on a city cursed—as he was himself—with disease and poverty.

> The City crowds our motley broods
> And plants its citadel
> Upon the delta where the floods
> Of evil plunge to hell.
>
> Through fogs retributive, that steam
> From ooze of stagnant wrongs
> The towers satanically gleam
> Defiance at our throngs.
>
> It nucleates the land's Deceit;
> Its slums our Lost decoy;
> It is the bawdy-house where meet
> Lewd wealth and venal Joy.[32]

O'Dowd's was possibly the most protracted and overwrought response to the depression crisis and it was more than a decade before his celebrative poem 'The Bush' (1912) provided a symbolic counterweight to the despair of 'The City'.

Under the impact of the depression, Sydney's boarding-house zone had deteriorated almost to the level of 'Outcast London'. As well as the familiar 'boozers', 'loafers', and 'spielers', hundreds of respectable working men were wandering aimlessly through Hyde Park, eating frugally in the 'Full and Plenty Dining Rooms' and sleeping under newspapers near the old Fruit Market. Henry Lawson, who spent much of 1892 in doss-houses round Dawes Point, left a grim picture of boarding-house existence during the depression in his story 'Board and Residence' (1894). He describes his hypocritical Welsh landlady, her uninviting board of warm grey tea and thin white bread, and the dumb resentment of her guests. 'This', he reflects, 'is the sort of life that gives a man a God-Almighty longing to break away and take to the Bush.'[33]

At last, at the end of 1892, Lawson broke away from Sydney and made his famous journey out to Hungerford on the Queensland border—the brief, unhappy episode that was to be, as A. G. Stephens noted, 'his sole experience of the outback'.[34] He had gone prepared to be disillusioned for already, after a less arduous trip 'up-country' the *Bulletin* had published the verses which sparked off his famous duel-in-doggerel with 'Banjo' Paterson:

I am back from up the country—very sorry that I went—
Seeking for the Southern poets' land whereon to pitch my tent;
I have lost a lot of idols, which were broken on the track,
Burnt a lot of fancy verses, and I'm glad that I am back.
Further out may be the pleasant scenes of which our poets boast
But I think the country's rather more inviting round the coast.
Anyway, I'll stay at present at a boarding house in town
Drinking beer and lemon squashes, taking baths and cooling down.[35]

Hungerford confirmed his worst apprehensions about the county 'further out' and, in a letter to his 'Aunt Emma', Lawson resolved 'never to face the bush again'. Even so, he was the exception among the *Bulletin* writers in testing experience against the bush ideal and, though others came to his defence in the controversy with Paterson, few in practice adopted as sardonic a view of outback life.[36] After Hungerford, even Lawson remained in two minds on the question, for the savage realism of his best stories depended for its effect on the continued cultivation of a bush ideal, a process which Lawson the poet himself assisted by his adoption, in the mid 1890s, of the 'capital B for Bush'.

The 1890s have been rightly interpreted, by Russel Ward, Vance Palmer, and others, as a watershed in the creation of an 'Australian Legend'. But that 'apotheosis', as Ward calls it, was not the transmission to the city of values nurtured on the bush frontier, so much as the projection onto the outback of values revered by an alienated urban intelligentsia. How far itinerant bush workers absorbed these values, or shared them already, remains very much an open question. The most, perhaps, one could say is that urban experiences, intensified by the economic crash, might almost suffice in themselves to explain the value-structure, if not the mythological setting, of the bush legend. With anti-urban sentiment flowing strongly in the wider community, the depression years fixed the rural ideal, and by the end of the decade the original negative image of the city had slid silently away, leaving the bush to acquire a new reality of its own.

As the depression lifted, the *Bulletin* writers made their belated escape from the inner city. Most moved back into regular journalism and under A. G. Stephens, fresh back from London, were drilled into a self-conscious literary school. Stephens was convinced that 'it was in the cities, not the bush, that the national fibre [was] being . . . slackened and destroyed' and the collected editions of *Bulletin* material he published around the turn of the century omit most of the writers' earlier city-influenced verse and prose.[37] By now most had dropped their old radical associations. The scandal of George Black's 'domestic infelicity', blazoned forth in John Norton's *Truth* in 1891, sowed the first seeds of suspicion between the 'intellectuals' and the 'horny-handed sons of toil'.[38] Con. Lindsay was expelled by the socialists and Brady by the Redfern Electoral League, while Lawson passed from socialism to anarchism and on to alcohol. Most of the *Bulletin*'s young radicals had forsaken their old haunts in the twilight zone for the pleasanter pastures of Darlinghurst and Paddington. 'Banjo' Paterson married and moved to a big house in Roslyn Gardens; Rod. Quinn, Victor Daley, F. J. Broomfield, 'Price Warung' all lived in the vicinity of Glenmore Road, Paddington; while several of Stephens's newer discoveries, Alex Montgomery and D. H. Souter, moved further out along the Bondi Road.[39] Their association was more convivial and artistic than ideological, their one common cause the defence of 'art for art's sake'. They gathered, now, only in the boozy fellowship of the Dawn and Dusk Club, affecting the strenuous bohemianism that was their last defence against the encroachment of suburbia.

8. Mateship in Country Towns[1]

Kenneth Dempsey

Many of the values and beliefs traditionally associated with the idea of mateship are held by the menfolk of country towns. Country men value physical courage, resourcefulness, toughness and independence, group solidarity in the face of adversity, and loyalty to one's mates. They believe that Jack is as good as his master, or even better; that mates must never bludge on one another; that a man's word is his bond; that women are inferior to men; and that the company of mates is preferable to the company of women. However, the opportunities for expressing such values and beliefs are severely limited. Insofar as they do find expression it is in the private, rather than the public sphere, and in leisure, rather than work-type activities.

An examination of men's behaviour with their mates, and of the impact of this behaviour on themselves, their women, and their relationships with their women provides most of the content of this chapter. I will argue that there are no signs of these patterns and processes weakening in country towns; on the contrary, current cultural, economic, and demographic trends should ensure their continuance for the indefinite future.

The country towns I am talking about are small, possessing populations between 500 and 4000 people. There are several hundred such towns in Australia functioning as service centres for nearby rural hinterlands. The material I present here is based on research I have carried out in country towns and on

131

many conversations with friends and acquaintances who have lived in them.

Before proceeding to a discussion of this material, however, a word of warning should be sounded. I am not claiming that the types of mateship behaviour reported in the following sections are peculiar either to Australian country males or to Australian males generally; nor am I suggesting they are peculiar to the working class. The occurrence of similar patterns of behaviour—at least among disadvantaged groups in other societies—is well documented. I have witnessed such behaviour on many occasions in Australian provincial and capital cities, as well as in country towns, and among the middle and upper middle classes, as well as among the working class. Nevertheless, I suspect that the milieu prevailing in country towns is more conducive to mateship activities than that prevailing in the cities. In a country town everyone is known and visible, there is a relatively short supply of potential male mates, and few alternative leisure activities to those described below. Together, these characteristics serve as powerful inducements for men to participate in mateship behaviour. These characteristics also make it likely that country men at the extremes of the social hierarchy will get together for mateship activities. I must stress, however, that these are conjectural statements and that until more evidence is available—particularly on urban men's behaviour—they must remain so.

The Development and Expression of Mateship Values

The values associated with mateship are instilled in boys from their earliest years. They are taught to compete, especially in body contact sports, to be self-reliant, and at all costs, to abhor the 'sissy' behaviour of girls. Whatever class he belongs to, a country boy absorbs the implications of this training: girls and women are inferior, and it is only in the company of boys and men that he will find fulfilment. By his teens he has formed friendships with boys which are different from, and, he believes, superior to any friendships he will ever have with girls. Here is what one 17-year-old said, and it is typical of the comments made by teenage youths.

Girls can be friends but never mates. Friendships die, especially friendships with girls. You stick to your mates for life. If you fight with your girl it may be all over; but a fight with your mate never ends things. After all, he's your mate!

Although men may value mateship highly, opportunities for expressing mateship values are quite limited. They are probably more limited than 100 years ago and certainly more limited than in the situations described by the great nationalist writers of the 1890s. Nature no longer provides a common adversary: the bush is tamed, and the development of modern machinery has reduced both the number of workers and their need for each other's assistance in wresting a living from the land. Furthermore, because there are many small employers rather than one or two big ones, workers who remain in the town are separated from each other in their daily employment. Group solidarity does not develop and trade unionism is usually ineffectual.

At the same time, the economies of country towns are stagnating, and the jobs that are available provide few opportunities for individual advancement or satisfaction. Before they are out of their teens most workers have reached the high-watermark of their 'careers', and the sons of businessmen and farmers are aware of the relatively poor returns on their family's capital investment and the unlikelihood of any significant change in the future. The workers, in particular, usually find themselves in routine, tedious, and frequently lonely work that offers little opportunity 'for a man to prove himself' by demonstrating physical prowess, or exercising power over other men, or making a great deal of money. Nevertheless, the further up the local class ladder one goes, the more likely it is that working conditions improve. Local businessmen, professionals, and farmers enjoy some job autonomy and, on occasions, they make profits as opposed to 'just getting wages for all their slog'. They can increase their personal satisfaction and enhance their public reputation by providing good service, or producing fine crops and first-class live stock. Yet, for most, the rewards offering in work and public spheres are not enough. While home and family are possible alternative sources of satisfaction, the responsibilities of both home and work frequently clash with, rather than facilitate, the expression of manliness and the pursuit of mateship activities. Neither the garden nor the unploughed paddock is an appropriate venue for the display of male courage and resourcefulness. Furthermore, for middle-class and working man alike, such commitments reduce the amount of time and money available for what he sees as more rewarding activities: talking, drinking, watching sport, and occasionally playing it. These are all primarily leisure activities of a fairly passive and undemanding kind.

Talking and Drinking

At the end of a working day, men of all classes—labourers, tradesmen, school teachers, a solicitor or two—habitually visit the hotel, the Workers' Club, or the R.S.L. Club. Many of them return again following their evening meal to spend time drinking and yarning with whoever might be around. This includes farmers and graziers, who have come to town following their day's work.

On these occasions the talk is escapist and self-glorifying. It is ritualistic, facilitated and coloured by drinking, often to excess. The same conversations are repeated day in and day out, week in and week out, year in and year out: what the weather is like, the state of the crops, the chance of the football team winning next Saturday's match, the chances of 'making it with the new sheila' in town, the relative merits of Holdens and Fords, and so on.

Self-glorifying talk takes a number of forms. Stories of past successes are recounted in a ritualistic manner: 'the day I kicked six goals in the grand final'. Then there is talk about current achievements risking life and limb 'doing a ton in the ute down the highway'; and 'blasting the brains out of fifty or so bloody bunnies the night before'.

Men inflate their self-importance by reaffirming together the inferiority of women as a class, stereotyping them as silly, sentimental, and prone to gossip. Women are portrayed as men's jail keepers: '. . . so you've got another leave pass tonight, Jack, you must be in good with the missus'. An absent mate will be gossiped about for being weak in the face of his wife's protests about spending so much time with his mates. During a drinking session, men will ridicule one of their mates for preferring the company of his new girlfriend to their company.

Much of men's talk is a form of fantasizing, especially about making money. They will spend hours discussing in great detail what they will do if they win Tattslotto: the trips they will take, the type of car they will buy, or 'the bird they'll leave the wife for'.

Boasting about drinking, and the effects of drinking, has a major place in the conversation of mates, particularly because excessive drinking is one of the few realistic ways open to most country men to make a mark in life. They will boast about 'drinking themselves silly under the table'; recount the number of times they were sick, and measure the success of a night out with the boys by how sick they became. They regularly engage in drinking games where the most acclamation is given to the man who can stay longest on his feet. Although drinking to the point of inducing physical illness is probably more common among younger men than among middle-aged or older men, men generally are considered weak if they *don't* drink, and it takes a lot of moral strength to resist the pressure of mates to engage in heavy drinking. A man is likely to be accused of being tight-fisted, or tied to his wife's apron strings, if he resists.

Generally speaking, there is little serious talk when country mates get together. Repeatedly men have said to me: 'I can't remember the last time we (that is a group of mates) talked about a serious subject'. This is something of an over-statement because I have frequently heard farmers complain about government policies, or the ineptitude of the Shire Council, and workers discuss the threatened closure of the mill. What this kind of statement is referring to is that such matters are usually not discussed heatedly, or at length; that there is an absence of talk about religion or party politics—particularly if the group is composed of men of different religious and social class affiliations—and that talk among mates serves as a means of escape from daily problems, rather than as a context for airing them.

Men may or may not unburden themselves when alone with a male friend. The information I have on this point is inconclusive. But in my experience in the company of a *group* of mates, they keep their problems to themselves. Fears about the future, problems at work, sexual, family, or money worries are not discussed except in terms that shift the responsibility onto others: their boss, their wives, their girlfriends, or 'the system'.

Sport and Mateship

Discussing sport avoids most of these problems, and sport is a perennial topic among mates. Sport is very important in country towns. On a Saturday, it is not uncommon for all members of a family to go their separate ways to engage in one of a variety of sporting activities such as netball, tennis, cricket, bowls, golf, and football. Members of a family take a keen interest in one another's sporting activities, but especially in the sporting activities of the men, for men play the important sports: football and cricket. Even when they play the same sports as women— tennis, golf, and bowls—it is tacitly understood that men's sporting achievements in these areas are more important and therefore of greater interest than those of women or girls.

Far more public interest surrounds football than any other sporting activity in a country town. In football men can display their physical courage and resourcefulness, and share the euphoria of battling with a common adversary, the thrill of victory, or the pain of defeat. Football, of course, is a young man's game. Most men in country towns are beyond the age for playing football, yet they talk incessantly about it with their mates. Over a weekend mates will travel hundreds of kilometres to watch the home team play. They will meet at the pub with friends before the game to discuss its outcome, and meet again after the game to celebrate its success, or mourn and analyse its failure. Saturday is followed by more postmortems and prog- nostications on Sunday morning around an eighteen gallon keg at the club rooms; often while wives and children attend church.

More than anywhere else in the life of a country town, we see in the fetish of football the vicarious and egalitarian qualities of modern mateship.

Mateship and Egalitarianism

Joe Smith is one of the top farmers in this district. He must be worth at least a million, and yet he'll always call out and say hello even if he's on one side of the main street and I'm on the other. He calls me 'Bill' and I call him 'Joe' and I'm only a grease monkey. If we happen to be in the pub at the same time we'll have a drink together. Now that proves, doesn't it, that there's no classes in this town. Of course, there are a few snobs who think they're better than anybody else, but you're just as likely to find them among the workers as among the farmers or the business men.

Bill Williams
Service Station Attendant

The strong belief in egalitarianism in a country town fosters the mingling of men of different classes and status groups. Some workers—but by no means all—will point to such practices as that of wealthy graziers drinking and playing sport with labourers as evidence of the essential equality of men's relationships in the town.

Although it is true that egalitarian beliefs play a significant part in producing cross-class mixing, it is also facilitated by structural factors such as the geographical isolation of these towns, their small populations, and their limited financial resources. There is not enough money, for example, to provide one bowling club for the district 'silver tails' and another for the rest. Consequently, men who want to pursue such special interests must be prepared to mix informally—even to become 'mates'—with men of other classes who share their interests.

Nevertheless, there are limits to inter-class mixing. Many towns that are too small to offer separate sporting facilities for men of difference classes are big enough to support several hotels. In these towns there is some interaction between classes in the public bars, but the practice develops of farmers congregating at one pub, blue-collar workers at another, white-collar workers at a third, and so on. Yet even in towns with one hotel, limits to class mixing always exist. So while graziers may regularly drink with workers at 'the pub', the graziers will belong to a circle of landowners, and perhaps professionals and businessmen, from which the worker 'mates' are excluded. The members of this wider group will exchange dinner engagements, attend picnic races, and in some instances form ties of marriage.

Mateship and Women

The segregation of the sexes associated with mateship behaviour is manifested in many aspects of life in a country town. Bowling is one such context. Men prefer to bowl with one another and, only grudgingly—at least overtly—play mixed bowls. Women bowl at the club on the off-days (that is, when men do not want to play) and they bring their own refreshments. When men play, the women provide morning and afternoon teas and, on special occasions, lunches and dinners. Women appear to enjoy doing this and compliment one another on the quality of the food.

Usually, women are kept well away from the activities of the Rotary Club and the Masonic Lodge but they are permitted to enter this 'charmed circle' on Ladies' Nights; not as equals, but as guests, whose subordinate status is clear to all. Sex segregation also occurs on less formal occasions. After church on Sunday morning, for example, men and women form their separate informal discussion groups; when suppertime comes at dances, men congregate at one end of the hall and women at the other; and at parties, the men will stand outside, or drink in the kitchen, while the women talk together in the lounge-room.

Football is not only a major mateship activity, it also exposes clearly the effect of mateship upon women. While women may be just as enthusiastic about football as men, they are, neverthe-less, excluded from the male rituals; it is men who engage in physical combat on the football field; who 'understand' football; who tramp to the locker-room at half-time to urge the team on; and who congregate together while the women sit together in the cars and mind the younger children.

Only courting couples or newly weds are seen in one another's company at a football match. If other men choose the company of their wives, they provoke derogatory comments and are stereotyped as 'sissies' or 'sheilas' for doing so.

During a football match, the male supporters will call out to a player who is faltering: 'A sheila could do better than you, yer got a yella streak down yer back. Get in there and fight like a man, yer mug', or words of that kind.

The segregating and ridiculing of women, and the stereo-typing of them as an inferior group builds the bonds of mateship and strengthens the masculine identity of men. Men, however, pay a heavy price for these gains. In particular, it seems to render them incapable of entering into equal and mutually rewarding relationships with women. There is an ironical aspect to all of this for while men are dependent on their women for many things, their women—forced to take major responsibility for house and children—learn to do without them. It is women who provide them with their base; who feed them, wash their clothes, and so on, and enable them to return to the world of work and find relaxation with their mates. Yet, as the women point out, the men always return home to pour out their worries for fear of being ridiculed if they discuss them with their mates.

Mateship often increases the bonds between women, for the absence of the men forces them to find emotional satisfaction in one another's company. It also develops in many of them a resentment which frequently turns to bitterness when they realize the impossibility of escaping from their situation. They are trapped not only by the strong traditional norms surrounding marriage, but also by economic dependence, for country towns are communities where opportunities for paid employment for married women are extremely scarce.

Younger women are more likely to be angered or embittered than older women for often their consciousness has been raised by the feminist movement to the point where they believe they have a right to happiness achieved through pursuing their own interests, rather than as a derivative of their roles as wives and mothers. Most older wives, however, tenaciously hold to the idea that life for them is a calling to service and that personal satisfaction is to be found, particularly, through service in the home. They compensate by engaging in activity outside the home that enables them to enhance their status as homemakers by displaying their domestic skills at fêtes, street stalls and in the craft classes of the Country Women's Association. Such women will resign themselves—albeit grudgingly—to a situation in which the husband prefers the company of menfolk to their company.

As this last comment implies, many women do not find the situation I have been describing here as entirely negative, and there are others on whose lives it has a minimum impact. All men put in some time at home, take holidays with their families, exchange gossip, and discuss the children with their wives. Many women report they welcome their husband's regular and predictable absence, preferring their major emotional involvment to be with their children, woman friends, and relatives. Maintaining a balance between time spent in leisure activities with mates and time spent in leisure activity with wives occurs in all classes. But is is probably more common among middle-class men, as is the practice of bringing together the world of men and women by forming couple friendships. Such couples exchange dinner dates and sometimes take holidays together.

Finally, some women are married to men (drawn from all classes) who shun mateship behaviour altogether, preferring the company of their families or the pursuit of their hobbies. The wives of such men report that they have better marriages than most of the women of the town and that they are spared the 'indignities' and neglect that are part and parcel of mateship activity. Yet even these women acknowledge that because of the strength of tradition and the ways in which social behaviour is structured in country towns they and their husbands are, from time to time, caught up in sex segregated activities that cast women in an inferior role.

The Future

As the impact of the feminist movement penetrates country towns, it is likely that some wives will manage to gain a greater share of their husband's leisure time. Some may also gain a greater degree of independence from husband and family to pursue personal interests. Developments of this kind are more likely to occur among transient middle-class women than among locals, for the transients bring with them experience of greater autonomy and, even if they are not working, they usually possess greater financial resources than most local women. Furthermore, because of their transient character, they are in a better position to withstand the trenchant criticism of the town's older women. These women make a habit of attacking young wives and mothers who pursue their own interests, reputedly at the cost of their husbands and children.

For most younger townswomen, however, the likelihood of their dependence and subordination continuing is being increased by the growing proportion of older women and by the chronic short supply of paid employment. Unless women have professional qualifications, the work that is available is usually menial, laborious, part-time, and poorly paid. There are no signs of this situation changing. Consequently, the only alternative for women dissatisfied with it is for them to leave for the city in the hope of achieving economic independence and a more satisfactory life.

What about the situation of men? The tradition of mateship has such a firm hold in country communities that its present momentum will probably carry it forward indefinitely. It is difficult to see any alternative. For we have seen, these men, like their women folk, are trapped in economically stagnating communities that provide few opportunities for tangible success or satisfaction in the world of work.

It is predictable and understandable, therefore, that many men will go on seeking what personal satisfaction and social recognition leisure activity in the company of their mates offers them. Moreover, the pub will continue to be the focal point of this activity for in the words of a recent country and western hit song these men

> . . . love to have a beer with Duncan,
> Love to have a beer with Dunc.
> We drink in moderation and we never, ever, ever
> Get rolling drunk.
>
> We drink at the Town and Country
> Where the atmosphere is great.
> I love to have a beer with Duncan
> 'Cos Duncan's me mate!

9. Mateship and Egalitarianism: The Failure of Upper Middle-Class Nerve[1]

John Carroll

There have been three main influences on Australian culture: upper middle-class Victorian values and institutions, working-class (significantly Irish) egalitarianism, and twentieth-century consumerism.

Australia was colonized by the British and virtually all its institutions—governmental, administrative, judicial, financial, educational, religious, cultural, and trade union—came out of the British mould with, at the most, minor adaptations.[2]

In the cities, moreover, the middle class settled itself in British-style suburbs, built British houses, planted British trees, sent its children to British-style private schools and whenever possible on to Oxbridge, and its successful males relaxed in London-style clubs. It traded, travelled, dressed, and patronized charities and the arts in a British manner. It valued civility, prosperity, and civic pride. At the same time many Victorian bourgeois attitudes were reinforced by the strong influence of Presbyterian Scots, notably in education.[3]

Working-class attitudes have permeated the more general Australian culture since the middle of the nineteenth century with an egalitarian ethos. The pressure for social equality has carried with it an intolerance of respectability and manners, a hostility to authority, a talent for improvisation, and an idealization of male comradeship. Such attitudes were strengthened by a disproportionately strong Irish influence in the early working class, transporting into Australia a distaste for British middle-class authority. There have been many attempts by the literati to give the egalitarian-mateship theme a greater dignity and mythical weight by locating its origins among the early convicts, and finding it amplified in the lives of the bushmen who took on the harsh conditions of the great outback, in the exploits of the bushrangers, and in particular Ned Kelly, in the experience of the gold rushes, and finally in the Anzacs.

The third influence on Australian culture is consumerism, and as in all Western societies its importance has been growing right through the twentieth century. It constitutes an attitude to life cultivated by the economic needs of advanced industrial societies, their technology, their high levels of production, their material affluence, and their welfare states. These needs are pervasively articulated by the modern mass media. Consumer-ism is indicative of a process of social change in which progress-ively higher degrees of uniformity are imposed, both within and between different Western societies.

Consumerism poses a peculiar problem for a relatively new society like modern Australia. Its pressure towards international modes of taste and behaviour, applied across the total spectrum of social life from clothes, houses, and motor cars to political styles, music, and hero images, threatens the local culture with killing off any of its unique elements before they have had a chance to establish themselves. The first and most important question for any study of national culture is what is singular to it. In the Australian case it may be a task of looking for an animal that was always rare, but now shows signs of extinction.

So what is unique to Terra Australis? First and foremost there is the landscape, the light, the flora and fauna, which are all powerfully distinct and represent a force of nature that will always dwarf and humble the humans who inhabit the conti-nent. But culture is the various works of man, and it is those works with which we are concerned here.

In answer to the question 'What is typically Australian?' there has been a remarkable unanimity among the commentators, whether they were visitors or locals: the egalitarian-mateship

ethic and its practice. I do not wish to argue against the prominence of the ethic and its practice. However, this prominence is
often exaggerated, to the degree of calling Australia the most
egalitarian society in the Western world. The commentators
have usually either explicitly or implicitly taken Britain as the
basis for comparison (most of the visitors came from Britain,
and Britain was the society that Australians knew best). It is true
that compared to British society there is less social distance in
Australia and Australian manners are sometimes more gregari-
ous and easy-going. But British class differences endure in
Australia. It is, for example, the norm in a country town for the
lower class to gather socially in the pubs while the higher class
meets in its own clubs. Accents vary substantially. Generally the
attitudes, prejudices, interests, and manners of working-class
Australia are notably different from those of educated, upper
middle-class Australia.

Switzerland is a more genuinely egalitarian society than
Australia. It has often been described as a wholly middle-class
society. It has its proportion of blue-collar workers, but they are
not distinctive culturally. The Protestant ethic remains strong
and softens class difference: while a man works, whatever his
vocation, and does not live ostentatiously, he is respected. It is in
no way obvious, moreover, that Australian society is more egalitarian than that of the United States.

The egalitarian-mateship ethic has also been prominent in
Australian literature. The poems and stories published in the
Bulletin in its early years, the work of Lawson, Furphy, Paterson,
and Steele Rudd were all aggressive in their assertion of these
values. The ethic also recurs, although in a more problematic
sense, in more recent literature, for example Kenneth Cook's
Wake in Fright, Alan Seymour's *The One Day of the Year*, and Jack
Hibberd's *A Stretch of the Imagination*. Carrying with it its own
range of attitudes to work and to intimacy, it remains central to
many Australians' perceptions of themselves.

This version, however, is not very plausible set up as the
foundation stone of Australian identity. Neither its origins nor
its essential nature belong to Australia. The most systematic and

influential modern attempt to examine the egalitarian-mateship ethic, its origins, its history, and its influence—and to argue the case for it defining the Australian identity—has been that of Russel Ward. Ward tries to defend himself against the charge that the actual events were different from what the legend maintains by claiming that he was writing the history of the legend itself. However, his account is full of inferences that Australia was like its legend, and indeed that the legend tells the most important story about Australia—describing what is singular and typical. It is crucial to Ward's thesis that the legend is unique to Australia. But this is quite simply false. The egalitarian-mateship ethos, the core of the legend, has little to do with the peculiarly Australian experience of convicts, bushmen, gold-diggers, and so on.

In the first place, there are grave doubts about whether the procession of truly Australian groups, as Ward lines them up, from convicts to Anzacs, can legitimately be characterized as obeying a mateship code. As the Schedvins argued in Chapter 6, the evidence suggests that the convicts were if anything egoistical, delinquent types, out for themselves, and showing little inclination or capacity for companionship, or indeed constancy of any form. It would be understandable for them to have disliked authority, but this is hardly any qualification for the egalitarian-mateship ethic. The character types that were common among the nineteenth-century urban poor, the social stratum from which most of the convicts came, were a most unlikely source for mateship. I imagine that the bushrangers, too, can be lumped in the same bracket, and I remain sceptical that the gold-diggings would have provided an environment much more conducive to feelings of solidarity than a Birmingham slum. Which leaves the bushmen themselves, a thin peg on which to hang a nation's leading legend.

The Anzacs are a special case. I see no evidence to doubt that the romancing historians, including Bill Gammage, have built their legend on real foundations. Comradeship was deep and pervasive among Australians at war. Interviews with returned soldiers conducted by some of my own students confirm that the mateship ethic was first and foremost, and the finest memory of war years. However, one of the students, Ruth Krake was told by a dozen returned soldiers that this mateship was not peculiar to Australians. It was something that war generated among men, and was equally noticeable in the British and the German armies. Here are the social and psychological roots of the band of blood brothers, and an extension of the fact that warrior societies tend to have been egalitarian (the Nuer and the Homeric Greeks provide two examples). When Ruth Krake asked whether there was anything special about Australians at war, the soldiers replied that the only thing they would stress was less separation of officers from men, and that officers were judged more as individuals than by rank, and were more likely to fraternize with the men than in other armies. We have at last found one special egalitarian trait.

The Anzac case exemplifies one of the two main reasons for rejecting the Ward thesis. The mateship ethic is not essentially Australian: it can be seen in many other societies, probably in all societies at one level or another. Thus not only did Ward imagine mateship where it did not exist—among the convicts and bushrangers—but that very mateship which he tried to derive from conditions peculiar to Australia is common to many and varying social conditions. One reason for the prominence of the Anzacs in the Australian imagination has depended on the same false hope, to consolidate an evanescent legend with the vitality and virtue of uniquely Australian traits—ones that turn out not to be unique.

The second main reason for rejecting Ward is that the ethic's origins are not Australian. The history of its development in Australia is quite different from that constructed in *The Australian Legend*. The same egalitarian-mateship attitudes are deeply rooted in the British working class—especially the preference for male company, gathered in pubs or watching sport. Moreover, Australia has always, and especially since the late nineteenth century, been a heavily urbanized society, and it is implausible to look to rural life for the sources of its leading values. Indeed there is no need to search further for an explanation of the Australian mateship ethic: it was imported from Britain and Ireland, and reinforced by an experience of working-class life similar to that in the countries of origin. It is by and large a class product, deriving from a shared experience of economic subordination.

In the Australian case these attitudes developed in the latter half of the nineteenth century, not before, and were taken up in the 1890s by urban intellectuals and glamorized into a legend, that of the bushman. Graeme Davison has shown in Chapter 7 how the bushman legend was dreamed up by poor inner-city intellectuals suffering from the chronic economic depression of the time, and compensating with an Australian version of the clichéd Romantic fantasy of going back to nature, of finding redemption in union with the simple and the primitive, in the arms of mother nature. These Antipodean Rousseaus set up their bushmen heroes as antidotes to the poisons of city life: they were the noble savages flourishing in the bush, great improvisors living off and in harmony with nature, real artists in the bush yarns they told.

I am not doubting that such bushmen existed: they very likely did, and still do. Nor am I denying that they may have been some of the most interesting Australians, and in some sense the most genuine native products. What I am doing is criticizing the legend that has grown up, its amplifications, the attempts to give it a greater historical plausibility, and the almost complete misreading of how egalitarian-mateship attitudes really developed in Australia.

To summarize the argument so far, the only thing that is typically or singularly Australian about the egalitarian-mateship phenomenon is that it is more widespread than in other Western societies. Let us now ask why it has become more widespread. The argument might be put that this ethic has been prominent in Australia because of the peculiar nature and strength of the working-class experience. The argument could run two ways. First, it might be suggested that the working class in nineteenth-century Australia was confronted by conditions of peculiar hardship. As a result it was bonded together in the face of common adversity. This argument fails for the simple reason that apart from one or two brief periods the working man was much better off than his British counterpart. Two difficult periods were the late 1850s and early 1860s in Victoria, when large numbers of unsuccessful gold-diggers retired to the towns where opportunities were severely limited; and the 1890s, during the depression that hit Australia with particular extremity. From early in the twentieth century, however, tariff protection was introduced to ensure comparatively high basic-wage levels. Anthony Trollope concluded his lengthy study, *Australia and New Zealand* (1873), by advising English men and women who were willing to work to emigrate to Australia, for there they would find a paradise: their whole condition of life would be changed in a society that respected labour rather than regarding it as servile.

The second argument for the peculiarity of the Australian working-class experience is one of unrealized expectations. We can assume that the material aspirations of those who migrate are higher than those who stay at home. In the Australian case from the middle of the nineteenth century a majority of immigrants saw themselves as coming to a new land full of promise, offering a prosperous and independent way of life. This was particularly the case for the uncharacteristic population that was attracted to Victoria in the 1850s—a high proportion of educated middle-class people and skilled tradesmen. Many of this group of immigrants found themselves in reduced circumstances in the new country, at least in the short term, making them leading candidates for the role of ideological radicalism—becoming hostile to a social order that had not allowed them to satisfy their own high ambitions. However, before long most newcomers to Victoria improved their living standards, and in the words of one historian of the period, Geoffrey Serle, 'For a large minority ... the rise in living standards was sufficient to meet all reasonable hopes.'[4] We may assume that the unreasonable were in the minority, and indeed that large sections of the immigrant population in the latter half of the nineteenth century did not suffer from frustrated aspira-

tions to a degree acute enough for them to constitute a significant moral or political factor in the formation of the Australian
identity.

A large majority of Australians when asked to name the
national hero answer Ned Kelly. This does not mean that they
know very much about him, or feel strongly about the issue.
What is significant for our purposes here is the confirmation
that Australia lacks the pantheon of national heroes normal in
other countries. The Cromwells, Nelsons, Napoleons, and
Lincolns who save their nation in a moment of great trial or
who lead their people on to great deeds do not have a place in
Australian mythology. This is not for the lack of potential candidates: Deakin and Monash immediately suggest themselves.
Moreover, there is nothing exceptional about having a Kelly-
style hero, the man of humble origins, abused by corrupt
authority, who fights ably and courageously against that authority—the Schedvins mention similar heroes among the vagrant
poor of urban Britain. Robin Hood is partly equivalent, although
it is significant that he was fighting for the good king who was
away—there is no counter-balancing image of benign authority
in the Kelly legend. Even more importantly, Ned Kelly is not
complemented by heroic figures who unite and integrate the
society, who confirm it in its higher purposes. The middle class
has failed to incarnate its own values in exemplary figures from
the past.

The examination of hero and villain models provides one of
the roads into the heart of a culture. In the Australian case it
immediately supplies the key clue to the prominence of the
egalitarian-mateship ethic: that the upper middle class, or the
bourgeoisie, has not been able, from lack of confidence rather
than from lack of strength, to enshrine its own values. While it
has differed little from its British and American counterparts in
terms of occupation, income, styles of living and consuming,
and patterns of leisure, it has failed to imprint its own ethos on
the nation as a whole. Its manners, for example, have remained
the preserve of a small section of its own kind. As a result the
values of that part of the working class that has seen itself as

under siege, in conflict with the more economically privileged social strata, have had little competition. Their influence has seeped right through the society largely because they met with little resistance. The strength of working-class egalitarianism has been less to do with its own peculiar vitality than the absence or weakness of possible alternative philosophies of life. It has succeeded *faute de mieux*.

Thus the key question about the genealogy of Australian culture has nothing to do with a distinctive egalitarianism, or a particularly assertive working class; it is a question of why it was that the upper middle class failed to consolidate its own culture. My own tentative answer is that the formation of Australian society coincided with a general development in the West whereby the upper middle class came progressively under the influence of an egalitarian bad conscience. Its British, and to a lesser extent American, counterparts had an established tradition to offer them some protection against the growing self-disgust that they harboured. At this point Tocqueville's work is illuminating: his predictions about the future path of democracy, and in particular its pathologies, fit Australia much more acutely than the United States.[5]

Tocqueville argued in his more pessimistic second volume of *Democracy in America* that, in spite of their many advantages, democracies tended to suppress excellence and individuality; they stimulated an impatience with constraint and a disdain for hierarchy; and they made it inevitable that central government would steadily grow in size and power. Above all their egalitarian spirit legitimated the envy of difference, and in particular of those who were better or had more. It is one of the characteristics of the workings of envy that those who fear that they might be envied set up disarming strategies: they disguise or underplay whatever is likely to be coveted. Such a fear of envy has been one of the factors contributing to the modern middle class's bad conscience about its own privileges, forcing attempts to conceal some of the public signs or manners of its lifestyle.

There are other sources of this guilt. Middle-class civility imposes its own strains, sometimes to an intolerable degree, forcing rebellious identification with the underprivileged. Again, the goal that most members of this class have today attained, that of comfortable consumer affluence, does not satisfy them; it leaves their more important spiritual needs undernourished and makes them feel in some sense that they have been cheated.

The main reason, however, for the low confidence of the upper class in promulgating its own values is that it hardly believes in them itself any more, and as a result has lost its rationale. It has lost faith in the good Puritan virtues that gave its forbears a strong sense of purpose, the virtues of hard and disciplined work, pious and frugal living, the sanctity of conjugal love, and responsibility for the community. The authority that backed these values collapsed with the decline of Protestant Christianity. For a few generations these values survived, passed on by parents still strongly attached by disposition to Puritan ways, but doubts increased all the time as the religious supports rotted away. This process was the more rapid in Australia, as I have suggested, because the upper middle class had less of a tradition behind it to support its flagging morale.

The egalitarian bad conscience was one of the consequences of this development. As I have argued at length elsewhere,[6] the collapse of the authority of the old culture led to people turning against what that culture had stood for, and identifying with its victims (or rather, imagined victims)—the lower classes, the deviant, the criminal, the insane. From the 1950s we have seen identification with working-class habits and the proclamation of egalitarian ideals. This has happened in all affluent Western countries. In Australia it took one step further the history of a culturally bashful middle class, now turning against itself and identifying with its traditional enemies. This whole process is deeply rooted in high levels of guilt, no longer harnessed by a culture that explained it and told anxious men what to do in order to be saved.

The psychology of the upper middle-class bad conscience is not new to post-World War II Australia. The myth-makers of the 1890s were urban middle class. They, too, had little or no faith in the dominant values of their own class, and out of their own moral vacuum turned to the bush. Indeed the mythic strains invigorating the egalitarian-mateship ethic are the product of middle-class guilt, seeking to idealize some dynamic element in other parts of the society, above all an element opposed to the middle-class city, its traditions and its values. Thus the culturally feeble seek an emblem of vitality with which to identify, and through which to punish themselves.

Where does all this leave the Australian quest for identity? Nowhere, as far as the egalitarian-mateship ideal is concerned. Just as the origins and the nature of this ideal are not related to any peculiar local conditions or events, so too the enabling factor that I have focussed on—the failure of upper middle-class nerve—is not exclusive to Australia. It is a phenomenon common to all Western countries, one that at the most may have developed a little more rapidly in Australia. I believe that there is a much better candidate than egalitarian-mateship to represent something peculiarly and formidably Australian. I will discuss it in my concluding chapter.

Part III
Modern Visions of Australia

Most of Australia's thinking about itself has taken place in the twentieth century, and in by and large a post-bushman and post-Anzac society. We might expect that a new understanding of national identity, new myths—or at least revised myths—must have appeared. In this part of the book we look at the four areas of artistic vision in which Australians this century have probed with most promise new images of themselves. Peter Fitzpatrick looks at drama, and in particular the nationalist drama that emerged in the late 1960s, outlining the images of society that were portrayed. Jack Clancy surveys the renaissance in Australian film in the 1970s and shows that its handling of national myths has been pretty much at odds with the classical legends. Mary Eagle looks at painting, and especially the nationalist figures of the 1940s: Boyd, Nolan, and Tucker. She rather turns our enquiry on its head, arguing that the obsession with national identity, both among the painters and their public, has had an inhibiting effect on the quality of Australian art. Finally there is a chapter on literature. Patrick White is the one great writer the nation has produced, and his work towers over our fiction. He has put at the centre of his novels the task of giving imaginative form to what Australians have made of settling their vast continent. Veronica Brady examines what is at the heart of White's vision of Australia, and suggests some lessons we might learn from it.

10. Australian Drama: Images of a Society

Peter Fitzpatrick

Australian plays seem always to have been much preoccupied with seeking to define the distinctiveness of the culture. Perhaps this is to be expected of any fledgeling national drama—it is hard to find suitable comparisons, given that so much of the culture and so many of its people have been so recently trans-planted. It is true that in the late seventies several playwrights emerged who have very successfully, and sometimes quite dogmatically, provided exceptions to that general rule.[1] But the concern to create images by which we might recognize who we are has remained a remarkably consistent one, and the plays and playwrights taken up by the theatrical establishment have very largely been those purporting to show us ourselves, or our friends, or, most often, the people we think we know but would never ask to dinner.

The durability of this concern with cultural self-definition is itself suggestive of the peculiar difficulties of the quest, and the number of dead ends to which it has led. The efforts of writers like Louis Esson to create a theatre defiant of the conventions of English drawing-room drama were limited by the models by which they tried to establish what was different about this country. The figure of the bushman, as defined by Russel Ward and other writers, is fairly thoroughly non-theatrical. His conflicts were mostly elemental ones, in which his stereotypical virtues were pitted against floods, fires and famines, which were

157

resistant to the received mechanics of naturalistic staging and plotting; his taciturnity gave him little capacity to talk about them. And his way of living was alien to the experience of most audiences. That figure, and the values of physical endurance and mateship for which he stood, had to wait until Ray Lawler's *Summer of the Seventeenth Doll* (1955) for a satisfying presentation on the stage; and although Lawler is clearly sympathetic to those values, the presentation is a critical, and, more importantly perhaps, consciously retrospective one. By bringing his cane-cutters Roo and Barney south to suburban Carlton, Lawler is able to throw the traditional qualities and verbal awkwardness into relief in a way that does justice to the complexity of the opposition. It represents also, in a number of ways, a closing of the subject.

The difficulties faced by Esson were more widely based than the depiction of significant human action and the discovery of an appropriate stage language, recurrent and enduring though those difficulties were. They also seem to stem from the lack of any highly developed cultural myths, in the theatre or in litera-ture generally, to define or express recognizably Australian qualities or aspirations. The comparison with American writing reinforces the sense that the task facing the Australian play-wright who sought material in the distinctive life of his own culture was not one of holding up mirrors to nature, or even of drawing on existing orders of cultural symbolism, so much as the making of myths. While the myth of the American dream has roots, like the Australian bushman ethos, in men's confront-ation with the new frontier, it is a unifying myth, expressing the values and aspirations of the Puritans and a wide range of other distinct immigrant groups. It is a myth which transfers readily from rural to urban society, and has proved strong enough to provoke and to focus strong reactions in plays like Miller's *Death of a Salesman* and Albee's *The American Dream*. And its power of generalization is sufficiently grounded in strong traditional systems of belief to make it a source of powerful stage meta-phors which are frankly and unembarrassedly mythic in their scope, like the house in O'Neill's *Desire Under the Elms*, or the baby in Sam Shephard's *Buried Child*.

Australia lacked not only a unifying myth of this kind, but also the sort of diverse regional life that enriches the drama of the United States and, more especially, of Britain; and in that respect the attempts to define a representative national 'type' were a response to something genuinely distinctive about this society, its relative lack of strongly developed regional cultures. For all the vastness of its distances, Australia is a country in which discriminations based on representative attitudes or styles of language have much more to do with social and educational differences than with geography.

The most significant breakthrough in this connection was the appearance of the Ocker, who rode in rudely on the 'new wave' of Australian writing in the late 1960s and early 1970s to focus much of that concern with cultural definition, and to liberate the local drama from some of the constraints of action and language which had previously hampered it. It is not easy to remember whether there really were ockers before the loud-mouthed young men of David Williamson's and Jack Hibberd's early plays; but it is certain that there have been a great many more since the theatre created the model.

The image is not simply to do with big paunches, big drinking, and big talk about sex at the male end of the barbecue, although these are among its outward signs. The ocker is defined neatly in *The Australian Pocket Oxford Dictionary* as 'a boorish person; person who is aggressively Australian in speech and behaviour, often for humorous effect'. It is the consciousness of effect that distinguishes the figure, on the stage at least. Even the relatively poorly educated ockers, like Kenny Carter, the victim in Williamson's *The Removalists* (1971), are not quite as crude or as simple as they appear; Kenny describes himself, affectionately, as 'a beer-swilling slob', but that is a role he chooses, and at several points he speaks in ways which underline that he is perfectly capable of assuming other, less offensive, roles when he wants to. The highly educated young men of Williamson's *The Coming of Stork* (1970), and their older counterparts, the sentimentally disillusioned professional men of *Don's Party* (1971), have a similar versatility, except that in their case the effort is to shed surface refinements for a 'how-yer-going-yerold-bastard' cameraderie that looks, at first glance, more 'real'.

The ocker is almost always funny, and there is a sardonic 'no bullshit' habit about his talk which is easy to mistake for candour. The predominantly comic mode of most recent Australian drama is epitomized in him, and while in his early appearances, in plays like Hibberd's *White with Wire Wheels* (1967), he was at least partly the object of satire, he became increasingly its agent; not of any very discriminating satirical view, but of something more like a reflex cynicism about life. In this way his development conformed to a tendency in the new theatre of the late 1960s, which established a rough-house satirical style in the service of a strong political vision that became, as the ideologies were lost or left behind, a very skilful but sometimes fairly aimless form of debunking. That process was understandably most evident in the coming to respectability of new writing in the early 1970s, when writers like David Williamson and Alex Buzo became desirable properties in establishment theatre.

The ocker made theatrical capital out of two of the factors which had created problems in earlier attempts to present Australians convincingly and interestingly on the stage. The first was the absence of strongly based regional variations in language. Talk is such a useful index in this culture of the social class to which the speaker belongs or aspires that one might have expected that sort of discrimination to come fairly easily to playwrights with a more or less sociological interest; but in practice in earlier plays that recognition led to fairly wooden oppositions of working-class vernacular and neutral 'good conversation' which ignored the tendency of many Australians to slide quite smoothly between those poles, usually in unconscious adjustment to present company.[2] The habit was essential to the ocker, and his freedom to range among the available idioms was extended by the remarkable censorship breakthroughs of the late 1960s.

The second of the problems turned to advantage in the ocker figure was the very cultural vacuum which writers like Esson had sought strenuously to fill. A number of writers have recorded their sense of Australia as a country without a soul; it is the kind of intuition which gathers some measure of self-substantiation because it is impossible to refute. The ocker comedies implicitly conceded the pointlessness of the search. Their concern was with social roles and strategies of evasion, and just occasionally with the emptiness that can lie behind them. But the nature of the ocker is to reveal very little of that 'withheld self' which D. H. Lawrence in *Kangaroo* thought he detected under the 'great geniality' of male intercourse.

Louis Nowra, in rejecting the Australian vernacular as a means to the revelation of any significant human feeling, has said of it:

It's a language which allows little or no feeling to emerge from below the surface. It shows itself to be male oriented, with the anti-female impulse and immature attitude to sex, yet perversely, it is one of the most colourful, funny languages in the world. As a means of communication between people it has always struck me as a thorough camouflage for sensitivity, compassion and understanding.[3]

That overstates the case somewhat, and attributes to language itself an entire social style which finds discomfort in seriousness. But it does neatly define the theatrical strengths and limitations of ocker conversation; for all its colour, the ocker's volubility takes us no closer to a centre of self, if there is one, than the taciturnity of the heroes of the outback dramas.

The notion of the lack, or elusiveness, of a centre has some implications for the structure of the ocker plays, as well. The outback plays were characteristically linear, with plots built around a clear progression of incident; the social realist plays of working-class life which sought to emulate the style and scope of *The Doll* typically resolved their conflicts in an eruption of arbitrary violence, followed by a reaffirmation of domestic sentiment—Richard Beynon's *The Shifting Heart* (1957) is a superior instance. But the ocker is a man of surfaces whose conflicts are resistant both to climax and resolution. A figure like Bentley, the born loser in Buzo's *Rooted* (1969), is 'rooted' (in the sense of 'stuffed'), but really he has no roots; the portable assets (car, wife, and stereo) by which he defines his identity are all vulnerable, and the people of his play change possessions, lifestyles, friends and lovers with the greatest of ease and fatuity. Increasingly that aimlessness produces in the plays images of circular or recapitulated action. The notion of absurdity is explicit in perhaps the first of the ocker plays, Hibberd's *White with Wire Wheels*, when the boys' impulse to drive nowhere, but very fast, produces a Beckettian close:

MAL: Let's go!
ROD: Which way?
MAL: The same way we went last time, naturally.
SIMON: No short cuts?
MAL: No short cuts.
ROD: The same route for everbody. It's easier that way.
MAL: Let's go!
(They stand still. Darkness.)

The glimpses of personal panic and emptiness, and the wider cultural tendencies they represent, ensure that the ocker in these plays rarely remains simply a figure of fun.

The ocker is no longer much in vogue. He has been succeeded in the theatre of cultural definition by a rather less socially representative, but rather more cultivated, figure, with a similar capacity for being entertainingly insecure. We meet him in plays like Williamson's *A Handful of Friends* (1976) and *What If You Died Tomorrow* (1974), Buzo's *Martello Towers* (1976) and *Makassor Reef* (1978), and Barry Oakley's *Bedfellows* (1975) and *Marsupials* (1979). He is more self-conscious than his predecessor, and far more at ease with the style of self-analysis which will demonstrate his complexity and pre-empt analyses by other people; his articulateness has a much more literary bent than the ocker's, and he is rarely very crude. He is a jester, with considerable skill in sending up all pretensions, including his own, although his readiness to be funny at his own expense allows a good deal of self-sentimentalizing as well. The principal forms of his insecurity, and consequently the subjects of most of his jokes, are aesthetic (the preoccupation with the iconography of social class) and sexual (the pursuit of passionate love as a reassurrance of genuineness, the interest in adultery as a token rebellion and a means of proof and, above all, the fear of impotence.)[4]

The jester is presumably much closer than the ocker to the kinds of people who write and see plays, and although in the ocker plays there often seems some uneasiness about the form and direction of the satire, and the degree to which it seeks to expose or indulge him, the question is still more problematic in these more recent works. There is some danger in each of the plays mentioned above that their ingratiating central characters are to be taken at their own sentimental self-assessments, articulating as they do so many of the familiar crises of the educated middle-class male. That seems especially true of the Oakley plays, which lack the cool detachment of Williamson's treatment of power games, or the idiosyncratic wit and moral energy of the best of Buzo. A play like *Marsupials* dramatizes, and at the same time seems itself to demonstrate, a kind of parodic impulse out of control. The difficulty of the playwright, who depends on the charm and cleverness of the talk for much of the energy of the play, is to find any uneroded standpoint from which to direct his satire—he risks sharing, as well as exposing, the predicament of his central character.

The ocker, for all his limitations of boorishness and philistinism, did effectively free Australian stage language from the constraints of inarticulateness and prissiness. The sophisticated parodists who have succeeded him have offered no comparable expansion of possibilities, and Nowra's strictures retain their measure of truth. The art of the send-up is so much second nature to such a talker that richness of metaphor, or even genuinely exploratory talk, becomes difficult to sustain. It is hard to restore the value of a vocabulary of the feelings when it has been so cleverly discredited.

Perhaps for that reason the recent plays of this type characteristically return to the familiar resource of the bushman plays for the suggestion of a particular emotional intensity—the power of understatement. It is a device which sometimes seems to point to a failure of responsibility on the playwright's part, by leaving the audience to supply the force of an undefined emotion, but it has proved a powerful weapon. Roo's silent fury as he smashes Olive's souvenirs at the close of *The Doll*, and the final image of his stumbling exit with the support of his mate Barney, represent the culmination of the earlier tradition. In the plays of the 1970s, it recurs as an intimation of the fearful vacancy when the wisecracks run out, and perhaps a tacit admission by the playwright of the insufficiency of the words available to him. That feeling is there in the self-enclosure of Andrew with his building blocks in *What If You Died Tomorrow*, and there are signs of it as the lights fade slowly on Russell and his sister Jill in their separate acting areas in *A Handful of Friends*; it is there in the final image of *Martello Towers*, when Vivien is left alone holding her heavily symbolic torn panty-hose, and we feel it strongly in *Makassar Reef* in Weeks Brown's look of despair as he clings to the bars of the cage-bed to which Beth has brought him; it is there in Carol's 'bleak and direct' gaze across the bed at Paul in *Bedfellows*, and in the silence that follows the clasping of hands in *Marsupials*.

Thus, while the common view that Australian drama has been standing still in the wake of the 'wave' is, from this point of view and others, a misconception, some of the limitations of earlier attempts to dramatize distinctively Australian experience remain. The preoccupation with notions of representativeness and social externals has kept the theatre responsive in its reflections of cultural changes, but it has left some aspects of the quest unfulfilled. It remains, too, very skewed in the kinds of experience that are dramatized. Like the plays about bushmen and ockers, the plays about the current crop of jokers are concerned almost exclusively with male attitudes; there was no female equivalent of the figures of the bushman and the ocker, and the only female counterpart to the new parodist is the exuberantly bitchy central character in Buzo's *Coralie Lansdowne Says No* (1974). The male stereotypes tend also to be of a particular age, and come from solid Old Australian (or British) stock. It is a very selective form of representativeness.

It seems odd that recent Australian plays have been relatively unconcerned with retrospection, especially since the cinema in the same period has devoted a good deal of attention to the way we were. The alternative theatre of the late 1960s, at La Mama and the Pram Factory in Melbourne and Jane Street and the Nimrod in Sydney, presented a number of plays with a historical basis; but the style of satirical revue, and the concern to draw contemporary political parallels, limited the extent to which an understanding of the past might inform a sense of cultural distinctiveness. And although *The Doll* exerted a very strong influence on many of the plays that followed it, none tried to reproduce the sense of the intersection of old and new cultural images and values which is part of Lawler's achievement in that play. Indeed, it was twenty-five years before another play emerged that similarly focused an awareness of things passing in a thoroughly credible present; and that play was also able to ground its universality of theme in a carefully particular set of social understandings.

David Williamson's *Travelling North* (1979) has more in common with *The Doll* than just the feel of a major play. Although its setting is contemporary, the presentation of its central character Frank has, like Lawler's treatment of his cane-cutters, an element of valediction. Frank is a thirties socialist, and epitomizes a type which has all but disappeared; an intelligent man, inclined to passion or crankiness in argument, surprisingly erudite about some things and with a fierce concern for his own independence and honour. He is a proud, prickly, and immensely likeable man. The type has not been tried much in our literature, but in *Travelling North* it focuses a number of the qualities which Australians have liked to think of as national characteristics, and does so authentically. Partly the context in which they appear is the social laboratory familiar from the other Williamson plays, in which familiar conflicts are played out among familiar types; here the problem is the slightly uneasy one of the marryings of old people, and the still more awkward subject of septuagenarian sex, and the attitudes for analysis are particularly those of three recognizable types of modern young women, Frances's daughters Helen and Sophie and Frank's daughter Joan. But beyond this the play, like *The Doll*, is concerned with larger issues which are explored the more convincingly for their very solid grounding in times and places. Through the play Frank is dying, and the play is sufficiently successful in establishing the seriousness of its approach to that subject, and the dignity of the man dying, to get away with a bizarre comic moment at its close. Frank's corpse suddenly jolts upright in what might be a resurrection, or a last twitch before rigor mortis, but turns out to be a quirk of his reclining chair. It cuts through the sentimentality of the little wake as the man himself might have done, but does not trivialize the death. It seems an aspect of a great generosity of treatment, and its effect is bracing.

Travelling North and *The Doll* work with the same metaphors of place, and although they both set up a basic opposition between the exotic and exciting North and the South where it is mostly winter in the suburbs, in neither case is the antithesis a simple one. North for Frank and Frances might offer an escape from illness and baby-sitting and a feeling of redundancy; but despite its warmth and the burgeoning vegetation, the people we meet are all in fairly graceful withdrawal from life, and the 'regular little paradise' is the scene of Frank's invalidism and death. Melbourne, for all its bleakness, is the home of all the younger generation, and teeming with its babies. The ambivalence of the symbolism of place is focused in Frances's curtain line when asked if she plans to 'go back down' to her family: 'No, I think somehow I'll go travelling further north;' the North is both a legitimate focus for aspiration towards a richer kind of life and a mirage fostered by a rather feckless discontent with things in general. The complexity of treatment in both *The Doll* and *Travelling North* is partly a product as well of the generosity with which the contending attitudes are presented. Seeming caricatures like the prudish Pearl in Lawler's play, and Helen and Freddie in Williamson's, are allowed surprising degrees of sensitivity and vulnerability as we get to know them better.

Travelling North has a breadth of thematic and metaphysical reference which is rare in the plays which have made some form of cultural discrimination their business. It avoids a number of the problems which face the writer who focuses on articulate and quite interesting youngish men rather like himself. It also achieves a balance through its quality of retrospection which makes one wonder whether that is a necessary ingredient of the business of myth-making. A number of the plays mentioned in this chapter seem weakened—both as social observation and as theatre—by an uncertainty of distance from their central people, and it may be that the events and social forms are also too close. There is a good deal of value in that enterprise, and it has produced plenty of entertainment in the last fifteen years. But catching the surfaces as they pass has tended to produce satirical stereotypes rather than the archetypes of a sustaining myth. The urgency of the quest is understandable; writers in Australia at present are caught between empires, and the sense that the distinctiveness of the culture is rapidly being eroded may be behind a number of the recent plays which seem to take the absence of a dominant myth as their premise and even their subject. Perhaps it will take a keener sense of our recent history to discover stage images that will define the way we live now, and what we have lost.

11. Film: The Renaissance of the Seventies

Jack Clancy

It is probable that a majority of the Australian population has seen an Australian film at some time in the last decade. I have no way of establishing whether that is the case or not, but I am tempted to assert the same kind of proposition in a different form: that it is probable that more people have seen an Australian film during the last decade than have read a serious work of Australian literature, or examined an Australian painting or experienced an Australian play. And I do this only as a way of pointing out the particular nature of cinema—that it is popular, and accessible at a popular level. It is at the same time, in a certain sense, serious; fewer people would have seen an Australian film in the last decade than would have seen examples of Australian television drama, but there is, about a good number of feature films, a tone that suggests that they are intending to deal with important matters at a level of seriousness which exceeds the ambitions of a television series.

Film has often, and in different countries, been analysed for the light it has shed on a society and its culture. The resurgence of Australian film in the decade of the seventies provides just such a temptation. The period is both neatly defined and interesting in itself—a period of social change and economic and political turmoil. The films, on the evidence of a certain, albeit fluctuating, level of popular local acceptance and considerable overseas response, hold the promise of some kind of perspective

168

on the interests, attitudes, and values of the film makers themselves, as well as of the audiences to whom they were directed,
or at least the film makers' perceptions of those audiences.

The great majority of the films of this period, and especially of
those with larger budgets and ambitions for general release
(that is, the ones most deliberately designed to be popular) were
made with, and could not have been made without, substantial
assistance from public funds. Public sector support for film
making, late in coming though it was, was seen to be desirable
for a number of reasons, not the least of which was some
vaguely articulated notion of national identity. At the beginning
of the seventies, amid all the excitement, there was a not unreasonable expectation that, of all the contemporary art forms,
films might be able to reveal something of Australian life, to
present, as cinema must, the appearance and something of the
reality behind the appearance.

How then has Australian cinema, a body of about 150 narrative feature films in a decade, represented the classical legends
dealt with in this book? A survey of the films provides a varied
set of answers. The surprising response of the film industry to
the bushranger legend, and particularly the Ned Kelly story, has
been largely to ignore it. The ground was pre-empted by the
Tony Richardson version, a foreign production made in 1970.
One of the last films of the co-production era, it suffered from
the casting of Mick Jagger in the title role, and from a script and
a directorial style that appeared more concerned with atmos-
pherics and superficial dramatics than with any attempt to
probe the reasons for Kelly's importance in the Australian
consciousness.

Although it might have been expected, despite this, that the
bushranger figure would provide an attractive source of material for Australian film makers, only one film in the decade has
dealt with a bushranging story—Phillipe Mora's *Mad Dog
Morgan*. In social terms, the strongest comment is made by the
way the Anglo–Saxon, establishment authorities deal ghoulishly
with the dead bushranger, their determination to exhibit,
dissect and anatomize his corpse suggesting the depths of the
superstitious fear he inspired.

Other 'Australian Westerns' have neglected the outlaw hero. The mixed genre essay of *The Inn of the Damned* (1975), the exploration of fantasy in *The True Story of Eskimo Nell* (1975) and the frolicking of *Raw Deal* (1977) did nothing towards any development of the bushranger legend. Only one other film has presented an outlaw hero, but Fred Schepisi's *The Chant of Jimmie Blacksmith* (1978) is rather an assault on white conscience than any celebration of the Aboriginal rebel.

The bushranger can be taken as the extreme embodiment of the rebel–outlaw hero. Despite his being on the wrong side of the law, perhaps because of the very acts and impulse which put him there, he is attractive because he represents a stance of defiance, a challenge to established society, a threat to the complacent acceptance of things as they are. If it is significant that this legendary type has been little dealt with in over 150 Australian films, it is equally significant that Australian film narrative has also eschewed structures that involve a purposeful journey. In moving pictures, the idea of an actual (physical) or implied (emotional, psychological) journey is the most familiar plot structuring device, suggesting as it does a sense of purpose or goal, of something to be achieved.

Australian films in the seventies have been remarkably static, caught in episodic anecdotal structures in which any sense of purpose or goal is difficult to find. Despite rare exceptions like the unfortunately neglected *In Search of Anna* (1979), or even John Ruane's *Queensland*, where the journey north that is the central issue of the film is never taken, set locations and situations which are concerned with a state of being, and often with the impossibility of changing that state, are the norm. Taken with the neglect of the rebel theme, and the stoic defeats which are the lot of Australian film heroes, they represent overwhelmingly a resigned submission to a land of spiritual status quo. Only in the considerable achievements of *Caddie*, *The Getting of Wisdom* and *My Brilliant Career* is there any sense of the protagonist's triumph. That the protagonists are all women is of significance as obvious as the fact that traditional Australian legends except, and almost incidentally, the pioneer legend, have little to say about women.

If, in the practical and very commercial world of film production, the Richardson/Jagger *Ned Kelly* is the reason for the dearth of other outlaw films, there is an equally practical reason for Australian cinema's failure to treat the Anzac legend. Budgets, so far, have been limited, and battle scenes are expensive to stage. The David Williamson/Peter Weir version of *Gallipoli*, in post-production at the time of writing, has by far the biggest budget, at almost 3 million dollars, of any wholly Australian film so far. The only other film to refer specifically to the Anzac legend was *Break of Day* (1976), notable first for the fact that the battle sequence referred to in flashback betrayed very clearly the production's budget limitations, and second for the way the narrative used the Anzac background only as a way of revealing it as, in this case at least, a sham. The central character has become a town hero by returning wounded from Gallipoli, but is revealed to have wounded himself to get out.

More significant, however, are two films which centre directly on the experiences of Australian soldiers in foreign wars. Although the wars are at different ends of the century so far, surprising similarities can be observed. *Breaker Morant* (1980) is set in the Boer War, *The Odd Angry Shot* (1979) in Vietnam. Both wars were unpopular (or at least controversial), both were 'dirty' wars, demanding the kinds of tactics against guerrilla fighting that were unlikely to lead to military glory. Yet both films, while avoiding a simplistic celebration of jingoism and chauvinism, manage to endorse qualities which tend to be connected in the national consciousness with the best of the Anzac tradition.

In each film there are carefully placed elements which undercut the traditional simplicities. Lieutenant Handcock, Morant's mate, has joined up for reasons that have nothing to do with patriotism, Empire or even adventure, but a great deal to do with the need to support a wife and child in times of high unemployment; Morant has admitted to the need for a brandy before getting on a wild horse. *The Odd Angry Shot*, avoiding any mention of volunteers or balloted conscripts, pays token deference to the demythologizing of militarism by having one character point out that wars are fought by working-class boys and that people back home don't know or care.

Yet in both films what is re-inforced is the male camaraderie, the mateship, which must have often made possible and was more often used to justify Australia's participation in foreign adventures, and which to this day ensures the survival of the Anzac rituals. Notwithstanding the ironies of *Breaker Morant* (colonial Australians joining imperialist British to fight colonial Boers, and getting shot by the British for doing so, Morant's status as legendary figure and the first hero in a decade of Australian film coming from his death rather than his sordid life, and Morant being, anyway, an Englishman) and the ending of *The Odd Angry Shot* (where, asked by a barman if they are just back from Vietnam, one of the two veterans simply says 'No') there is no real questioning in either film of the basis of the Anzac legend, and the strongest elements in both are those which have supported it. Neither film has much of substance to say about the motives Australians have for taking part in these wars, and although *Breaker Morant* does acknowledge the existence of the complexities of moral responsibilities, *The Odd Angry Shot* goes its way in total disregard of such matters.

Australian films in the seventies have effectively caught and presented the element of egalitarian-mateship in Australian life. Although, regrettably, they have not gone beyond that, they can claim to have carried out this first obligation of the unspecified brief which lies behind public funding. Another part of that unspecified brief, which might be defined roughly as 'doing those things which cinema does best but doing them in Australian terms' might have involved not only Australian cultural phenomena like mateship, or Australian legends like Anzac, but Australian landscape. This was a challenge to which Australian directors and cameramen responded with eagerness, and what resulted was some extraordinarily creative versions of Australian light, horizons, and atmosphere. It was probably inevitable that in seeking landscape, film makers would seek the bush, and the outback, and that in doing that they would also seek the past. Thus time and place should have combined to produce the chance for some reference to the bush legends. And indeed there was a period in the late seventies when the most common charge levelled at Australian films was that they were involved in some conspiracy of escapist nostalgia, in that films dealt with the past or the bush, or both, rather than the urban present. The charge is not sustained by the facts. In just over one hundred films produced between 1975 and 1980, I can find only sixteen which are set in the rural past, with most of these concentrated in the three years 1975–77. Among those sixteen, however, are some films which demand examination in terms of both the bushman and the pioneer ideals.

The most obvious is *Sunday Too Far Away* (1975). What is most striking about it is that, if one returns to Ward's account of the bush nomad type, one has almost a point by point description of Jack Thompson's Foley. A shearer, Foley is occupationally within Ward's nomadic group, and if he does not emerge in the film as being 'content with a task done in a way that is near enough', it is because the element of pride in his own physical prowess, and in sparking competitiveness is paramount. His attitude to authority is best expressed in his comment on the grazier fretting about his stud rams: 'If he carries on running up and down like a headless chook, the place'll be ankle deep in pedigree balls.' As for scabs, he shouts, rather ineffectually, to the incoming strike breakers, 'You're scabs. You're the lowest form of life.'

The film takes a detached and yet affectionate look at the shearers' way of life, and yet, set back in 1956, it has a tone of elegy about it, as though the attitudes and values these men represent belong to the past. *Sunday Too Far Away* excited Australian audiences. In several viewings with urban audiences, I sensed the excited recognition of something familiar. That this response was achieved despite the awkwardness of the narrative (the result, it would seem, of production difficulties, disagreements, and compromises)[1] leads me to the difficult business of speculating on the reasons for that audience response. While few of the people in those urban audiences would have direct experience of the kind of life being depicted in the film, the response to the film's laconic humour, and to the qualities embodied in Foley, suggests that the kind of ideal which Ward's nomadic bushman represents can strike responsive chords in urban Australians, even if this is finally a matter of cultural conditioning.

The other film demanding notice here is *The Irishman* (1977) directed by Donal Crombie from Elizabeth O'Connor's novel. Here the setting is North Queensland in the twenties and the Irishman of the title, Paddy Doolan, is a teamster in charge of a superb team of twenty Clydesdales. Doolan is not as fully the nomad character as Foley, since he does have a home and family, and the narrative is awkwardly divided between his failure to see that his way of life is being overtaken by the motor vehicle, and his inability to come to terms with his oldest son, who can see this very clearly. What had become, by 1977, the familiar narrative difficulties of Australian films were almost outweighed here by the splendid photographic style, which gives the film a kind of patina. This is no mere indulgence in nostalgia, but a recognition that something has passed, and that its passing carries a sense of loss, all the greater since the view-point in the film is largely that of the younger brother, whose allegiance is transferred from his father, to a substitute father, more firmly established in the real world and aware of its changes.

Foley and Doolan are, like most of the male protagonists in Australian films, defeated. Foley survives, his crown as gun shearer taken from him, his money gambled away in one reckless night, but the qualities that make him representative remain intact. Paddy Doolan dies, but even before his casual, accidental, inevitable end, he has been by-passed, and his death only confirms what the film has already made us recognize.

If there are few approaches to the archetypal 'nomadic bush-man', any reference to, let alone treatment of, the pioneer legend is even more difficult to find. The 'old world people', with 'hearts to dare' who 'wrought with a will unceasing', make no appearance. The opposition between selectors and squatters has never received the dramatic treatment it might have seemed to invite, although American cinema has dealt extensively with a parallel conflict between large and in different ways privileged, land-holders and small settlers; any student of the Western will be familiar with the free-range cattlemen who fight to keep out the small farmers, the despised sod busters, who want to fence the land. Perhaps only in *My Brilliant Career*, and then peripherally, is the contrast drawn between the elegant life of the squattocracy and the grime, dirt, and physical toil of the small farmer.

Seventies' Australian cinema, having shown its attraction towards rural Australia but little inclination to take up the classical legends with any literalness, nevertheless begins to reveal an interesting pattern. (There are many patterns, it should be noted, to be found in the decade's output. I have traced elsewhere the film portrayal of Australian sexuality,[2] and there are other patterns, ones for instance to do with the treatment of the family, the ocker figure, migrants and comic themes.) The rural myths which develop and reflect a nation's dreams are inevitably, especially in Australia, the myths of urban man. Paterson's 'Clancy of the Overflow', with its vision splendid, its bush with kindly faces, opposed to the dusty dirty city with its hurrying, haunted, stunted people, is the broadest expression of that rural romanticism which is a product of urban escapism. And in a 1970s Australia, more urbanized and troubled than ever before, one might have expected the film makers' eagerness to take up the challenge of Australian light and landscape to have produced a further instalment of the idealization of the bush. If not that, then perhaps a return to the 'hayseeds' strain of thirties' films, which allowed city folk to laugh at their unsophisticated country cousins, while still allowing noble rural virtues like simplicity, openness, and honesty to emerge triumphant.

But, as American cinema discovered, the seventies are a long way on from the thirties, and simple idealizations of earlier decades were no longer adequate in that serious and troubled period. In the seventies, films like *Easy Rider, Deliverance, Jackson, Country Jail, Prime Cut* and *The Texas Chain Saw Massacre* have presented rural America as no longer the great good place, but as filled with hostility and menace, which proceeds from man, from nature, and sometimes from both. In this inversion of the theme of a pastoral utopia, a loss of the sense of the goodness of nature is combined with a sharp sense of the threat provided by the red-necked ignorance and inbred primitiveness of rural populations.[3] Urban romanticism has given way to rural gothic. It is significant, too, that American cinema saw the decline of the Western from the anti-Western, the 'dirty' Western, the post-Western to the virtual demise of the genre.

There is no lack of rural gothic in Australian films of the seventies, and in a surprising number of them Clancy's vision splendid of the sunlit plains extended has suffered a very nasty transformation. Occasionally it is the people, more often it is the place, which suggests the hostility of the rural location, but in one key film, both are involved. The film is *Wake in Fright* (known overseas as *Outback*), and although in thematic terms it is a key film, it is also a preliminary film: it was first shown in 1971, and thus largely precedes the main part of the seventies revival; and it was not an Australian film in the strict sense but a foreign film made in Australia.

Adapted from Kenneth Cook's novel and directed by Canadian Ted Kotcheff, *Wake in Fright* begins in the small country town where the sole teacher, John Grant, is leaving for his summer holidays. There is nothing attractive about the town from which Grant is so obviously escaping—a school, a pub, a railway station, and endless arid plains—but he never reaches the city. His stop at a provincial town involves him in a nightmare of drunkenness, brawling, gambling, attempted seduction by a female, a homosexual assault, a kangaroo hunt that turns into an orgy of drunken slaughter, and attempted suicide. The intermittently inter-cut image of a bikini-clad girl in the sparkling surf of a Sydney beach stands as a civilized contrast to the bush nightmare.

The nightmare is seen to proceed from the people of the town, in particular the Chips Rafferty policeman, helpful and efficient but making no attempt to disguise his complacent authoritarianism, and Donald Pleasance's alcoholic doctor, a grotesque portrait of a figure whose only saving grace is his total lack of any illusions about himself or the world. And yet these two, and the others like the kangaroo shooters, are seen by the film as the products of the rural environment. Grant, the teacher, yearning for civilization, is a total foreigner among them.

The directly realist style of the film, and what seemed to them its scathing social criticism, did not win favour with local audiences, and few Australian films since then have mounted such a direct frontal assault. But in all sorts of oblique forms, the views of rural Australia which have emerged have been largely negative ones.

The rural gothic elements in wholly Australian films probably started with Peter Weir's *The Cars That Ate Paris*, where the ironically named Paris is a country town where the local population deliberately engineers car crashes, so that they can profit from the wrecks, vehicular and human, which result. The old plot device of the assault on the lonely traveller in an out-of-the-way place enables Weir to make some sharp comments on motor-car madness, the road toll, and the human suffering and heartless profiteering which result.

Weir's next film *Picnic at Hanging Rock* (1975) was one of the great successes of the first half of the decade. Here it is the bush itself which threatens. The rock where the girls disappear looms ageless, mysterious and indefinably threatening, and the bush itself seems determined to resist the encroachment of an alien culture. This sense of resistance to intrusion is heightened by Victorian-era trappings: the clothes, manners, civilized inhibitions, and repressed longings of the girls seem absurdly out of place in the landscape that resists them. There is one scene— where the camera pans across a neatly manicured lawn past a string quartet playing Mozart, and then comes to the end of the lawn beyond which is wilderness—which sharply points up the tiny impression made by this alien culture on the vast body of the ancient continent.

There is something of a parallel here with Tom Cowan's *The Office Picnic* (1972); both involve a group of people on a jaunt to the bush, which results in the disappearance, never explained, of some members of the party. Each film plays on a disturbing sense that the bush is somehow hostile, not only capable of swallowing up urban dwellers, but in each case choosing as victims those who are young, beautiful, and most intensely sexual.

Bush settings have been used to hide a dark past or a sinister secret in *Summerfield*, *Weekend of Shadows* and *Break of Day*, and only *Dimboola* (1978) has attempted a comic celebration of country life with, it must be added, indifferent results. But the two films which are most central to the city—country division make remarkably strong statements on the theme. Colin Eggleston's *The Long Weekend* (1978) has a young, very urban, very 'with it' couple escaping from their city home, and attempting to escape from their marital tensions, by going camping in a coastal bush setting. The central action and the central meta-phor of the film has the bush and its creatures unaccountably threatening, and finally destroying them. Though not complete-ly successful in its working out, *The Long Weekend* is remarkably direct in its presentation of the estrangement of the urban Australian from the bush. Ill at ease, and dissatisfied to the point of neurosis with the normality of familiar Australian suburban life, the two seek meaning, even redemption, in nature, only to find that, as the publicity for the film puts it, they are 'trespassers' unable to understand or finally to withstand the hostility of the environment they sought.

Peter Weir's *The Last Wave* (1977), a daring exploration of those areas of the mysterious and irrational opened up in *Picnic at Hanging Rock*, adds to the pressures bearing on civilized urban man—in this case a Sydney solicitor—the forces of nature and the mysteries of Aboriginal culture. The sense of nature going awry, if not actually threatening civilization, is combined with the opposition of Aboriginal law and custom—organic and alive—to the sterile formalism of white law.

In the 1970s Australian cinema, the bush, the source of so much of the strength of the legends, has turned against man. Even those films like *The Picture Show Man* (1977), *The Mango Tree*

(1977), and *The Irishman* (where, as the producers said, there was an attempt to capture 'that wonderful Tom Roberts look') are either weakened by sentimentalism or infected by defeat.

Defeated heroes, a hostile bush and a lack of any sense of goals to be achieved or triumphs to be won; all this sounds like a catalogue of pessimism, especially if we add to those defeated males the images of the mentally retarded Tim, the wheelchair bound hero of *End Play* (1975), the comatose *Patrick* (1978), the repressed or dying males of *The Night the Prowler* (1978), and the silenced Trenbow of *Between Wars* (1974). Despite the hard-won victories of women in *Dawn* (1979) and *Journey Among Women* (1977), as well as those mentioned earlier, and the brave attempts to confront contemporary urban life in *F.J. Holden* (1977), *Mouth to Mouth* (1978), *Kostas* (1979), *Cathy's Child* (1979), and the admirable *Stir* (1980), the decade of Australian cinema suggests as much about Australia by what is not there as by what is.

12. Painting an Australian Identity

Mary Eagle

Australians like to find heroes among their painters and to keep them prominently on view. According to our folk history, there have been two isolated peaks in our art, the Heidelberg School and the angry Expressionists of the 1940s. No matter that the ground on either side of them had to be dug away to make them eminent, the result is 'heroic'. Each group of painters has been made to stand forth as the beginning of a vital new era, the story being that Australian painting began with Roberts and company, and began all over again with Boyd and Nolan. Head shakings and occasional rude demonstrations from art historians have not knocked the heroes from their pedestals.

This folk history makes too much and too little of our painters. The picture it gives needs evening out. Even the 'heroes' among Australian painters when they have sought inspiration in art abroad have rarely, if ever, chosen what was avant-garde. On the other hand, there has never been a question of generations of painters turning their backs on the world and refusing outside influences. Quite the reverse. Painters throughout the nineteenth and twentieth centuries have consistently looked to art centres abroad for inspiration and, with few exceptions, have prided themselves on doing so.

Avant-garde artists since the Romantics have typically perceived themselves as battling against established taste. It was therefore to be expected that Tom Roberts and his friends, the Expressionists sixty years later, and a string of artists in between, would insist upon their newness and use the claim to sting the establishment. But instead of tamely accepting the painters' Romantic perception of their role, we should ask whether they were in fact revolutionary. The answer—not nearly as much as they claimed to be. Sidney Nolan's exciting 'new' approach to painting, for example, had precursors in earlier paintings by Sam Atyeo, Danila Vasilieff, Peter Purves Smith, and Russell Drysdale. We could multiply instances showing that even the most innovative artists have fed upon ideas around them . . . but the folk heroes would continue to stand!

Folk history, the most powerful we have, is allied with the Australian legend—more than allied, it is married to national identity, despite embracing what appear to be contradictions. Although it would seem logical to disqualify a painter who intro-duces outside stylistic ideas from being representative of national expression, the reverse applies. Paintings by Tom Roberts, Arthur Streeton, and Charles Conder which have been generously interpreted as the first Australian intimations of French Impressionism have also been received as the first truly Australian expression in art. Likewise, the valiant torch-bearers of modern European styles in the 1940s were announced as a second renaissance of genuinely Australian art. We see that the two periods of supposedly greatest stylistic advance in *inter-national* terms are also the recognized peaks of our *national* vision. I am sure this is not coincidental. One springs from the other, as they simultaneously declare the two sides of our cul-tural endeavour.

The second anomaly is the unspoken condition that to become 'great' the artist must make a contribution to national identity. Our pantheon of painters shows how true this general-ization is. Streeton, Roberts, Conder, Heysen, Drysdale, Boyd, Nolan, Williams, and Whiteley—their appeal has been as painters of an Australian vision. Others who produced work of equal or superior quality, such as Grace Cossington Smith, Roger Kemp, Ralph Balson, Ian Fairweather, Hugh Ramsay,

Clarice Beckett, and Joy Hester, were enclosed either within the 'feminine' worlds of their time, or the narrow environs of a lonely personality or specialized milieu, and *they have not entered the pantheon*. I am suggesting that only those artists have been elevated in popular regard who are recognized as contributing to our national image, as distinct from a personal or universal expression. Putting this more firmly, nationalism is the *only* large challenge Australia has offered artists.

The more I consider this habit of selective heroicizing, the more false, pompous, and powerfully persistent it appears. At bottom it has to do with internationalism. We persuade ourselves, as we persuade the world, that what is special in the work of our heroes is the flavour of Australia.

Sidney Nolan, Fred Williams, and others have been categorized 'Australian' even more energetically outside this country than within. Introducing Williams's paintings to those Americans who visited his exhibition in New York's Museum of Modern Art in 1977, William Lieberman spent more words describing 'the world's oldest continent', its 'immensity' and 'undeveloped' interior, than Williams's style which, he stressed, was strictly narrative and factual rather than abstract. 'Fred Williams is a painter of the Australian landscape. . . . His images may at first seem abstract, but they in fact describe actual times and places. . . . Fred Williams' colors are those of the continent itself . . . [his] vision is authentic. . . .'[1] Australian commentators have never placed Williams's art at the service of national identity quite as nakedly as Lieberman does here.

London reviewers over more than a hundred years have looked first for signs of national identity. A 1953 London showing of work by twelve Australians was reviewed in *The Spectator* (31 July 1953) in predictably national terms. 'As the country reaches its era of self-discovery and nationalist aspirations, its painters become intensely and emotionally aware of whatever is peculiar to the local scene, to the expanding horizons of a land freshly opened up. . . .' Like Lieberman, the English reviewer commented that among the twelve Australians, 'None of the abstractionists will cause much excitement here'.

Very briefly, we might consider just how peculiar to Australia was the art of those 1953 exhibitors, Nolan, Boyd, Drysdale, and so on. I am sure most Australians who have visited art galleries in Italy, England, and the United States have discovered striking stylistic likenesses between the work of our artists and their contemporaries in other countries. For instance, Nolan's Kelly paintings (1946–47) compare closely with Robert Motherwell's 'Little Spanish Prison' (1941), his 'Pancho Villa Dead and Alive' (1943) or 'The Poet' (1947). (The two painters were also linked by their interest in French poetry, and Mexican art.) We could go on making stylistic comparisons of this sort, for earlier and later artists besides Nolan. If we want to be historically rigorous, we won't find what is *unique* to Australian art where people have looked for it, in the broad outlines of style and subject. If ever this uniqueness is to be located it will be by patiently analysing the stylistic and ideological habits shared by artists of the same milieu. Inevitably, the search would first uncover particular locational identities (Sydney, Melbourne) and national identity would emerge only later. Compared with the positive pronouncements we are accustomed to hearing, it would be a vastly diminished identity, revealed rather as the odds and sods of artistic habit, traditions, types of imagery, and stylistic manners that persist and have had a part in shaping Australian art over long periods. Hardly the sort of heroic identity the world looks for!

As a generalization, it is fair to say that people worry about identity if they are afraid of losing it. Our painters are caught in something akin to the dilemma of the first-generation migrant. They have had to learn another culture's language (English, French, American), had to translate it into terms appropriate to their local culture—and the preferred cultural symbol is our landscape. The landscape looms in Australian art like the externalization of our struggle to make ourselves and not give in to the dominant reality outside.

Not surprisingly, the landscape has been evoked more compulsively by those artists who have felt the pressure of an overseas reality most keenly than artists who have stayed at home.

Patrick White and Sidney Nolan have drawn on the idea of the interior, stretching vast and virtually untouched, behind a thin outer ring of coastal cities, interpreting it complexly, both as psychic self-exploration and a mirage-filled mirror of nineteenth-century venturings. Speaking of racial identity, the American writer James Baldwin has suggested, 'History must, in one way, be a metaphor for the techniques of survival people have used.' Australian art history discloses a persistent strategy of exteriorization. National identity (surely a *social* matter) has been externalized as landscape. True, the pictures of two centuries often include one figure or more which might lead us to suppose that national expression was the figure in landscape. However, the many declarations made about national identity as it is to be seen in our painting have almost unanimously pointed to landscape and its attributes of light, gum trees, space, and so on. Introducing 'The Exhibition of Australian Art in London, 1923', Lionel Lindsay explained the historical roots of the national tradition:

Lawson, Paterson and Edward Dyson were making the characteristics of Australian life into literature in the same hour that Arthur Streeton and Tom Roberts approached them with the brush; and it is with these two painters that the true Australian movement in our landscape art begins. Although Roberts painted incident, and later George W. Lambert, pictures like 'The Breakaway' and 'Weighing the Fleece' have been unfortunately the exceptions in Australian painting. It is to landscape, therefore . . . that we expect the English people to look for whatever is fresh and original in Australian art.

Landscape bore the brunt of national expression at least until the 1950s, and still continues as the major theme. If we accept that identity is revealed by what people go out of their way to *avoid*, as well as by what they choose, then it is notable that our painters and writers have preferred to hide behind a screen of heroes, myths, old stories, and above all, the landscape. They have avoided coming to close terms with their own selves or the people around them. When personalities creep in (as in Dobell's portraits, and Hal Porter's and Patrick White's prose) they are caricatured, treated in a mannered way, and thereby defused slightly. The public is evidently uneasy before works of art which cut close to the bone, such as Joy Hester's vulnerable people, Mike Brown's 'Mary Lou', John Brack's 'Collins Street, 5 p.m.', or Albert Tucker's 'Images of Modern Evil'. The personal or social truth of these paintings is undeniable, yet they haven't the currency of Nolan's fey Ned Kelly series, or Boyd's pleasant Wimmera landscapes, which are reproduced in magazines and calendars and hung on the walls of dentists' waiting rooms. Nolan, Boyd, and White explore their inner selves but do so behind a barrier of national types, national figures and nineteenth-century history. They have been encouraged to do so.

I wish now to distinguish the finders from the keepers of art. Artists are not the creators of the cultural strategies their society involves them in but, being involved, they make the most of them. Thus Fred Williams, returning to Australia in 1956 after spending six post-student years in England, switched from the predominantly figurative subjects of his English period to mainly landscape themes. Excluded from the Antipodean group, who were all painters 'of a similar generation, all known to him personally and apparently sharing the same kinds of concerns in their art',[2] he re-thought the premises of his art, with the result that through the 1960s he increasingly identified with abstract, international tendencies then emerging in Melbourne painting. Although the manner of this stylistic drift was not confrontational, the trend was in direct opposition to the nationalism and image-bound expression of the Antipodeans.

Williams has been loudly hailed in recent years as the foremost painter of his day, the stylistic exception whose innovative discoveries (in line with international styles) became the rule for local followers. He has also been credited with forging a new vision of the Australian landscape, by this double achievement qualifying for entry into our pantheon of great painters. Yet he made each of these decisions not by a shrewd analysis of how to win success locally, but in the course of grappling with the artistic terms of the Melbourne art world. Who is to say what his success would have been if he had remained fifteen more years in England?

To see the artist in the act of making his primary choices we need to move in closer upon his creative milieu. As we do not yet know enough about what Williams said, did, and thought about art and life in the fifties and sixties, we must turn to other painters ... to Nolan and Albert Tucker at the outset of their careers.

Later Nolan and Tucker were recognized abroad as proponents of Australian identity, and I wouldn't blame anyone for feeling that by the mid sixties they had capitalized on this. I, for one, grew up prejudiced against the small group of expatriates who, having made overseas reputations as Australia's exotic export, periodically descended upon the local market with cooing blandishments and high prices.

In George Johnston's novel, *Clean Straw for Nothing* (1969), one of the expatriates describes how he kissed the soil on arriving back in Australia. 'I got the best press I've had since I left the bloody place. You see, out there you've got to do this sort of thing or they'll kick you to pieces ... we've got to go back repentant, and singing there's no place like home.'[3]

The expatriates had ambivalent feelings about their homeland (who hasn't!) but to doubt, therefore, the veracity of their artistic expression is unwarranted. Tucker's and Nolan's beginnings show how they became involved in expressing national identity; they show also how the imaginative framework of their mature work was predicated in the early paintings.

Hoping for identity, as many Australian poets and painters did in the forties and fifties, may seem to us in the eighties as futile as trying to catch a glimpse of one's 'true' self in the mirror. As anyone knows who has tried, reflected appearances are legion, and the most one can expect from the mirrored image is recognition. Nonetheless an understanding of what was meant by 'identity' is essential if we wish to look back at the painters of the forties. Compared with their search for identity, recognition is a much lower aim. The identity-seeker wished to penetrate beyond appearances to another, definitive 'reality'. Recognition is passive compared with the spirited communion between artist, subject, and image, which justifies the word 'identity'.

The difference between Albert Tucker, writing about 'Art, Myth and Society' in 1943, and a disbeliever of the 1980s is firstly that, unlike most modern thinkers, Tucker believed in a basic, unchanging reality, intimated to mankind as 'archetypal forms'. Secondly, he pinned his faith on *myth*, 'a symbolic reflection in the minds of men of the forces of nature and society, a picture of reality, compressed and imaginatively completed in accordance with men's desires; its realization becoming *the object of his behaviour*' [my italics]. He believed, as most of us cannot, that history progresses towards a gradual unveiling of fundamental reality: meanwhile myth fills the gap between what is known and what is sensed. He wrote, 'The function of myth is to imaginatively complete that which the intellect does not know. . . . [It is] the means by which people express and systematize their fundamental notions of life and nature'. Finally, myth for Tucker is truly myth only when it comes out of 'the deepest levels of the collective unconscious' and is an active force in society.

A similar desire to 'express and systematize fundamental notions of life and nature' was the central rationale and push behind Nolan's myth-making and elliptic type of poetic imagery, and Boyd's even more personal imagery. Identity, they realized, may only be found, and certainly only expressed, within the larger context of a view of life, society, and human nature. For these painters, personal identity thus became a matter of history and geography, their psychic explorations an expression of national identity.

Tucker's style of painting, as of writing, was forceful and analytical. Nolan's way has been that of the palimpsest, each statement paralleling and partly erasing previous formulations. With a very different creative habit from Tucker, he nevertheless demonstrates a like notion of creativity. Nolan wrote in *Angry Penguins* (1944):

... to discover the constants of experience, the only material by means of which an artist can be articulate—as history is articulate—to treat these circumstances with the same objective poise with which we observe a work of art, is surely the peak of imaginative courage and the necessary condition of penetrating the turbulence of life.[4]

In view of his own future use of myth, and need—as he later admitted—of a hero, what he wrote of Max Harris's 'The Vegetative Eye' is enlightening: '... the legendary figures that Max uses are made peculiarly true of his own experience and interpreted in the only way that art can be interpreted, by means of more art'. This was to be his own method. Returning to the same legends again and again at various stages of his life he experienced each time anew the life and poetry of the Australian landscape and its stories.

As a young man he already saw the landscape in story terms. Writing from the Wimmera, where the Army had stationed him in 1942, he was overcome by images of *history*:

Sometimes the silos look so powerful here, that seen from a distance standing up from the trees you could imagine them as made by the Aztecs for no other reason than to worship the sun, which would not be out of order either, with the sun the dominant factor in this country.[5]

As demonstrated by his choice of myths he accepts the history of all places as his—and Australia's—by right of knowledge. The silos reminded him of the Aztecs, the landscape was 'as old as Genesis'.[6] Nevertheless he felt a special need to read and to hear the stories of his own country, writing:

... a desire to paint the landscape involves a wish to hear more of the stories that take place within the landscape. Stories which may not only be heard in country towns and read in the journals of explorers, but which also persist in the memory.[7]

Nolan did research in Melbourne's Public Library for the first Ned Kelly series, painted in 1916–47. His instinct to create has been more than usually bound up with the poetry and stories he has been thinking about: art creating art through the medium of his experience. Responsive to art, his senses have recognized in nature the sorts of concrete images which could be colonized for art. So that, although Nolan's ostensible subjects have been descriptive of landscape and legend, the theme throughout has been his own internal history.

Nolan's use of imagery compares with Baudelaire's 'correspondances'—the attempt to make art which captures what is indefinable (magic, symbolic) in objects. The original stimulus becomes also the measure by which to judge the success of the work of art; its seedbed is memory, its moment the shock of recognition; thus image, artist, and participant commune together through a vital and *familiar* experience. Nolan encountered the idea in French literature, in Baudelaire, Valery, Proust.

In the mid sixties Nolan defined his aim as 'a reconciliation between experience and ideals'—an attitude he described as very Australian.[8] He sympathized with Bertrand Russell's hope that before dying he would say something definitive about life—not any specific aspect, but the stuff of life, its totality. Nolan's English interviewer contrasted 'this need for a solution, the optimistic belief that man can understand and master the confusion of life' with the more typical '20th century despair of finding a cohesive pattern'. The optimism, he and Nolan agreed, may be peculiarly Australian. Said Nolan, 'There is a certain innocence about being an Australian. It is being part of a dream which hasn't been shattered or burnt out'. Whatever we may feel about its 'Australianness' this need to say something about Life distinguishes Nolan, Tucker, and other painters of their generation and the next. Tucker's 'Art, Myth and Society', and Nolan's statements over many years document the peculiarity of Melbourne's 'identity' painters, who operated between positions of nineteenth-century optimism (the sheer ambition of their need to bridge the gap between experience and archetypal truth) and a twentieth-century awareness of the complexities of the psyche.

The evidence of Nolan being chiefly preoccupied with his own internal identity contrasts sharply with the vulgar way his art has been transposed to be part of the Ned Kellyisms of national identity.

In conclusion I wish to criticize the keepers of our culture who are governed by the traditions, types, and often-repeated subjects of art and discussion, as if the national culture resided in its classifiable parts rather than in genuinely creative achievements. Quality has nothing to do with national habits, yet the art market, popular opinion, and art history indicate that Australians value the national typology more than they value quality. Great art is original and cannot be identical with typical art. An expression that is alive, newly truthful, perceptive of what lies at the heart of experience is almost always lonely, unusual—if it is also 'great', it manages to be universal in its expression and long-lasting in its power to move us. Shakespeare's plays are not great because they embody the human contingencies of his time (which they do brilliantly) but because they effortlessly transcend the foreign language and exotic social context of Elizabethan England.

As a *focus* of art, national identity has a deadening effect. Art's true inspiration is life, not tradition. No more than Macbeth represents the identity of Shakespeare's society does Ned Kelly represent our culture. Australians don't believe their identity is represented by Kelly, Gallipoli or Eureka. *God* still has power to move some people to prayer or protest, but the national figures neither live nor cause society to act. Their place is at second remove, within traditions of art and history where, as in the case of Nolan, they occasionally come to partial life as a touchstone of sensibility. We ought to look to Nolan not to Kelly, to the paintings and not the myth, to contemporary society rather than its legend, when we ask what are the characteristics of Australian society just after World War II.

Our perceptions of our society and country are always changing. Far from being locked up in legend, 'Australianism' is a flavour no sooner recognized than dispersed. The unknown interior, painted since the war by Nolan and Drysdale, and written about by Randolph Stow and Patrick White, had by then already passed from the camel trains of the explorers to the laden transports of modern commerce.

13. Patrick White's Australia

Veronica Brady

With a little perspective, good novels come almost to resemble natural phenomena. We forget they have authors and accept them as we accept stones or trees because they are there, because they exist.[1] So with Patrick White's novels. By now they have become one of the facts of life in Australia, but a fact of a difficult kind for sociology to grapple with since White writes within the Modernist tradition, that is, with an 'adversary intention'. The world he describes is not so much there to be seen as a possibility within the self to be rehearsed by means of images borrowed from the external world of commonsense. Far from resting on this commonsense, however, White contests it. Radically anti-cultural in this sense, his bias is towards everything in human experience that militates against custom, abstract order, and reason itself, towards the solitary and usually suffering self instead of towards existence in society. Elevating unconscious feeling over self-conscious perception, and intuition over intellection, he points up the limits of social events and institutions, centring his work on the 'flickering, barely experienced, obsessive moments with which the mind deals more fully after they had been stored up'.[2] To complicate matters still further, to a greater or lesser extent his works arise out of personal necessity, out of a need like Eddie Twyborn's 'looking at his reflection in [a] glass . . . [and trying] to convince himself of an existence which most others seemed to take for granted'.[3]

Evidently a writer of this kind who calls in question not merely the common perceptions and feelings of his society but the definition of reality and of value by which its inhabitants live offers a picture of Australia which is all his own. Although he has a sharp eye for detail and a remarkably accurate ear, he exaggerates and distorts what he sees and hears in the interests of his own obsessive vision so that his characters are often closer to caricature and his stories to rituals, constrained to follow predetermined patterns. Yet this is precisely what makes his work so interesting. By definition, the primary question posed by new societies like Australia is not, as in more traditional societies, 'what role must I assume?' but rather, 'what world am I to possess?'[4] Yet by and large, Australians are not metaphysically inclined and thus do not really face up to this question preferring to live in a 'sceptical and utilitarian spirit that values the present hour and refuses to sacrifice the present for any visionary future lacking a rational guarantee'.[5] White is interesting therefore because on the one hand he indicts this failure to take up the primary ontological question and on the other hand attempts himself to explore it, thus opening up further possibilities of existence in a society which he sees as pathetically complacent and ignorant. As a result, his 'adversary position' has social implications, implications of which he is very well aware. He has said, for instance, on his return to Australia in 1948 he wanted to contribute to the task of 'helping to make the people of a half-savage country a race possessed of understanding'.[6]

His work, then, is valuable for the study of Australia on three counts; first, for the criticism it makes, second for the possibilities it opens up, and third for the insight it offers into the situation of one particularly gifted and articulate Australian. If, as Raymond Williams has argued, a theory of culture involves the study of relationships between various elements in a whole way of life to which the key lies in the discovery of patterns of a characteristic kind, White's work as a whole gives us access at least to one of these patterns of feeling which represents a living response to the general organization of Australian society working upon someone who sets himself as a kind of shaman-figure, a lightning-conductor of the general experiences, anxieties, and aspirations of his tribe.

Broadly speaking White describes two Australias, the actual and the possible. To begin with the actual, the negative aspects of his vision, the burden of his indictment is that, accepting that it is as the historian G. E. W. Bean put it, 'a country still to make', Australia today in his view represents a gigantic failure of imaginative nerve. *Voss* concerns itself most explicitly with this failure, although it is also very important in *The Tree of Man*, which concerns itself with the faithlessness of society and of his fellows to Stan Parker, the man of good faith who is prepared, like Voss and Laura, to make the journey to the interior. Newly arrived in this country, Voss responds immediately to the challenge it offers, compelled by its difficulty and longing to test the greatness of his spirit by it. In contrast, the majority of Australians represented by the wealthy merchant, Mr Bonner and his circle shrinks from this challenge, preferring to huddle in Sydney, on the fringes of the continent and of themselves. As White sees it, the land itself is the primary fact of Australia so that the first task facing our culture was—and still is in his view—to come to terms with it, to establish the 'true relationship with [the] contiguous universe' which is for him as for Lawrence, the basis of any enduring culture. In his first published novel, *Happy Valley*, he turned his back on Australia as 'Egypt, the land of plagues, only not so mythical', because this relationship had not been attempted. There was no continuity between the people of Happy Valley and the world around them. The town was merely 'a peculiarly tenacious scab on the skin of the brown earth'[7] while they themselves were only half-living, 'the trousers hanging on but only just'[8] for lack of this vital relationship. Similarly, Mr Bonner and his circle refuse to follow Voss on his journey into the interior, a journey which is more a matter of psychic than of physical exploration. In contrast, Mr Bonner's niece even in Sydney is able to accompany Voss in spirit, to discover with him that to be human is to be finite, vulnerable, and subject to physical necessity and thus to achieve the 'true knowledge [which] only comes of death by torture in the country of the mind'.⁹ For Mr Bonner, however, the only realities are material: 'I do not understand what all this talk is about' he declares, when Laura suggests that Voss' expedition is important for all of them because 'we are not yet possessed of understanding' of the country but still afraid of it as something 'foreign and uncomprehensible' and goes on angrily:

'We are not children. We have only to consider the progress we have made. Look at our homes and public edifices. Look at the devotion of our administrators, and the solid achievements of those men who are settling the land. Why, in this very room, look at the remains of the good dinner we have just eaten. I do not see what there is to be afraid of.'¹⁰

Where this harsh environment manifestly calls, as Lawrence saw, for 'some sort of new show', Mr Bonner is content with 'money-having and money-spending'. In this he is representative of what White calls 'the great Australian Emptiness', the product of existential cowardice of this kind.

This kind of critique is common enough—indeed, it has become something of a literary cliché and suspect to many social scientists for that reason. White's position, however, is empirically based. *The Tree of Man* and *Voss* both originated in his own attempt to come to terms with the culture he found himself in on his return after being away for twenty-five years. The story of Voss offers to explain the existence of people like Mr Bonner who represent something he found threatening:

Although the money he had made was enough to have bought him absolution of his origins, Mr. Bonner had never thought to aspire to gentle birth. That was a luxury he left to his wife. . . . [but] he did love the fortune that rendered him safe, so he considered, from attack by life, for, in the course of living Mr Bonner had forgotten that the shell-less oyster is not more vulnerable than man. Safe in life, safe in death,

the merchant liked to feel. In consequence, he had often tried to calculate for how much, and from whom, salvation might be bought and,
to ensure that this last entrance would be made through the right
cedar door, had begun in secret to subscribe liberal sums to all
denominations, including those of which he approved.[11]

This disavowal of nature as irrelevant to human purposes has
become an article of faith for a culture committed to the closed
world of the Enlightenment which rests on the proposition that
the human mind is the measure of all that is. Man's relation to
the natural world is thus one of conquests. Developers shave the
natural vegetation of Sarsaparilla 'down to a bald, red,
rudimentary hill . . . to erect the fibro homes. Two or three days,
or so it seemed, and there were the combs of homes clinging to
the earth. The rotary clothes-lines had risen, together with the
Iceland poppies, and after them the glads'.[12]

Even on the fashionable North Shore there is no relaxation.
The Cheesemans, for example, live 'in an impeccably main-
tained, shamelessly illuminated, fairly recent colonial mansion,
surrounded by European trees and Japanese shrubs at a stage in
their development which suggested they must have increased
their rate of growth to keep up with their owners'.[13]

These people contrast with people like Stan Parker, Theodora
Goodman, Voss and Laura, and Ellen Roxburgh with their
attention to the land, prepared to 'let go and let be', prepared to
respond to what it has to teach them. In effect theirs is a different world view. For them body and spirit, nature and psyche are
not separate, still less antagonistic, but the two poles of the same
expressivity. In the austerity and silence of the land, therefore,
they explore their own possibilities, immersing themselves in a
state of humility and acceptance which is the direct opposite to
the violence and restlessness of the citizens of Sarsaparilla. This
is the state Stan Parker achieves at the end of *The Tree of Man* as
an old man in his overgrown garden when, in the midst of
physical decay, he becomes aware of himself at the centre of a
'large and triumphal scheme' radiating out 'with grace movements of life' to embrace 'all that was visible and material'[14] and

is therefore able to see God even in a gob of spittle, 'glittering intensely and personally on the ground'.[15]

In this contrast between two different kinds of people, White puts the traditional antithesis between the city and the bush in a larger context. As he sees it the crucial distinction is between those who are able to see themselves as part of this 'large triumphal scheme' and those who cling instead to the 'neat, self-contained shape it is desirable that souls'[16] should harden into in Sarsaparilla. 'City' and 'bush' thus represent a psychic rather than a geographical division. Even he lives in Sarsaparilla. Arthur Brown in *The Solid Mandala* is an inhabitant of the interior, the 'country of the bones'. Similarly, Laura accompanies Voss in spirit into the desert while remaining in Sydney.

This interpretation of the traditional vision has large consequences for the understanding of Australia, implying as it does that most Australians do not really inhabit their country but live in bad faith, evading the reality it represents, with no psychic means of support. What he calls 'the Great Australian Emptiness' is a kind of vice, the hell to which Dante condemned Pope Celestine V who made 'the great refusal', renounced the Papacy 'out of cowardice', the hell inhabited by 'the forlorn spirits . . . of those who spent life without infancy and without praise'. In this sense his attack on contemporary Australian culture and preference for a more 'primitive' consciousness is not an attack on civilization as such but on the false consciousness which is the basis of contemporary Western society, the product of the Cartesian separation of mind and matter. For White, 'the intellect has failed us'[17] because it imprisons people in their own minds, drifting across the surface of a universe without feeling or comprehension for it, although, ultimately, their lives are governed by its imperious necessities, above all the necessity of death.[18] So it is no accident that the house Mrs Flack lives in is called 'Karma'. On a visit, Stan and Amy Parker feel themselves threatened by 'anonymous waves of people' bound on the wheel of illusion.

The city was never stationary for long, nor they [its inhabitants], it was like dreams, only less personal. The glass caves into which the old people [Stan and Amy] looked, and especially in the purple night, were opening for others. It was the dream of someone else's dream that they were dreaming. When shall we be put down again? their faces asked. Their own dreams in monochrome, although at times suffocating by hate or strangling with love, did exact less.

So much for the failure to deal with the problem of place. White also accuses Australian culture of failing to deal with time. But here, instead of drawing on stereotypes, he overturns them. Where others make it their boast that Australia is the 'recordless land' outside history, White sees this boast as another evasion, just as disastrous in its way as the evasion of physical reality. By definition, of course, any colonial culture relates to the metropolitan culture and by implication to the mainstream of history with a certain ambiguity. But where Americans have been Promethean, attempting to master history and reshape it to their own ends, White's Australians generally have preferred to withdraw, affirming rather than contesting their state of disinheritance. Arrived in the new country, they set themselves to forget a past in which, like Mrs Brown in *The Solid Mandala*, they have been humiliated, in her case by the snobbery of her family or, like the Rosetrees in *Riders In the Chariot*, they have faced the horrors of Hitler's 'final solution'. So, the Rosetrees change not merely their names—from Rosenbaum—but their gods, becoming Roman Catholics, although the real god they worship is Mammon.

They are still persecuted from time to time by recollections of the richer culture from which they came, but their children, ideal citizens of the 'kingdom of nothingness', have no such memories.

They had learned to speak worse Australian than any Australian kids, they had learned to crave for ice-cream, and potato-chips and could shoot tomato sauce out of the bottle even when the old black sauce was blocking the hole.[20]

From time to time, it is true, history intrudes. Wars break out and carry men away to the other side of the world into regions of chaos and violence, 'men . . . fighting, killing, to live to fuck to live'.[21] But generally Australians are helpless outsiders, watching the procession of history passing them by, uneasily conscious that somehow it concerns them in a way they neither understand nor wish for. Thus Mrs Poulter knows that the appalling events which befall the Browns in Sarsaparilla are somehow bound up with the images on her television screen:

The flat faces of all those Chinese guerrillas or Indonesians, it was the same thing, dragged out across the dreadful screen. All those Jews in ovens, that was long ago, but still burning, lying in heaps. Lone women bashed up in Mosman, Maroubra, Randwick, places you went only in your sleep. Little girls held to the ground. The bleeding wombs of almost all women.[22]

By definition therefore this is a society of guilt, that is, of penalty divorced from responsibility.[23] Most people live by images, that is by the annulment of the real in an imaginary unreal. Mrs. Jolley is typical:

Mrs.Jolley did not know where to begin, and would stand kneading her bare arms, as if they might not have got her final shape. . . .
    Mrs. Jolley was a lady, as she never tired of pointing out. She would repeat the articles of her faith for anybody her instinct caught doubting. She would not touch an onion, she insisted; not for love. But was partial to a fluffy sponge, or butter-sandwich, with non-parallels. A lady could never go wrong with pastel shades. Or Iceland poppies. Or chenille. She like a good yarn, though, with another lady, at the bus stop, or over the fence. She liked a drive in the family car, to nowhere in particular, but looking out, in a nice hat, at faces on a lower level. Then the mechanism with which her superior station had fitted her would cause her head to move ever so slightly, to convey her disbelief.[24]

Cut off from traditional values, she moves to resume them, but this resumption is false; the symbolism of sin and defilement has no basis in the one-dimensional culture. She remains instead at the primitive stage in which good is a matter of conformity and evil is associated with misfortune or difference. As a result she lives in a state of bondage feeling herself somehow responsible for and captive to a world that is too much for her. In men this sense of captivity leads to resentment and to the 'paranoic pseudo-community' which is sometimes called 'mateship'. Unsure of themselves, their beliefs or their place in the world, people like Blue, Mrs Flack's 'nephew'—actually her illegitimate son—suspect a Jew like Himmelfarb, sustained by an inner life which accuses their brash emptiness. Catching sight of the Jew crossing the factory yard and dimly recalling that it is Easter time Blue is troubled and confused:

He was trying to remember—always a difficult matter where moral problems were concerned. His ear was aching with the effort as it pressed against the telephone of memory. But did at last distinguish the faintest . . . 'suffer every Easter to know the Jews have crucified Our Lord'. All the sadness pressing, pressing on a certain nerve. 'It was then, Blue'. All the injustices to which he had ever been subjected grew appreciably sadder. But for all the injustices he had committed, somebody had committed worse. Not to say the worst, so he had been told, the very worst, and must not go unpunished.[25]

The violence he then turns on the old man—he and his friends string Himmelfarb up in a mock crucifixion—is a projection of his confusion and anger against himself on its account. Lacking a centre of authority and by implication of intelligibility and value, such people live by resentment, unable to find any one individual responsible but feeling that guilt is entwined and mingled with everything, the property of everyone. So personal feeling is dangerous. Instead, their lives are ruled by compulsion, responding only when ordered or compelled to do so. Marriage is an arrangement of convenience, at best as with Stan and Amy Parker, a sharing of loneliness. So too with relations between parents and children. Ray and Thelma, the Parkers' children, begin moving away from their parents, drawn into their own orbits, Ray to a life of petty crime and Thelma to the social aspiration which is rewarded by her marriage to a solicitor. Both of them surrender themselves to the crowd and live by the feelings of others, to a life in which, as Ray says, 'nothing is for always'.[26]

Far from being the place of the new beginning, for such people Australia thus represents an end of the world, the place of A. D. Hope's 'ultimate men/ whose boast is not, we live; but we survive'.

What, then, of White's positive vision of Australia?

In a sense, this positive vision is implicit in the kind of attack he makes on what he dislikes. His tactic of disgust reminds one of Kierkegaard's determination to provoke his audience to use violence against him and so be forced to confront the evil within them. Also like Kierkegaard, he sees the source of evil in complacency, the readiness to be 'so deceived by the joys of life or by its sorrows that [they] never [become] eternally and decisively conscious of [themselves] as spirit'.[27] His positive vision therefore involves a change of consciousness, something like the Nietzschean 'transvaluation of value'. The true Australia is thus a 'land of vision', of the silence, simplicity, and humility which he sees as the only proper state, and the true Australians are those drawn into communion with this vision and, as in *Riders In the Chariot*, with one another through it. Granted that the majority, the inhabitants of the 'Great Australian Emptiness', live fixated on the unreal, the alternative he offers is a radical one, outside the terms by which they live—mere negation would still lie within these terms—and involves a redefinition of reality and value. Far from being incidental, his style thus becomes central. Undermining conventional habits of grammatical syntax and thus of the wider syntax by which words and things relate to one another, it moves towards this redefinition of reality towards a less mental, more intuitive and sensuous mode. The disruption and uneasiness occasioned by his style thus represent the desert through which it is necessary to pass on the way to the 'true knowledge [which] only comes of death by torture' there.[28]

Similarly the Australian landscape becomes important less as a metaphor than as the seat and homeland of all experience, the place where the truth of the human situation is most clearly manifest. Its vast austere spaces, more or less without image or positive character, serve as a kind of silent transparency reveal- ing the structure of physical necessity which rules the world and holds our bodies in subjection to it, despite the aspirations of our minds. White's proper Australians accept this subjection even as they continue to pursue a dream of 'a reality more intense than the life [they have] so far experienced',[29] which is to be found at the heart of this 'country of the bones'.

They are thus tragic people, and White thus takes up and enlarges the Australian preoccupation with the 'loser'. To a greater or lesser extent, all of his main characters are defeated by circumstances yet remain undeterred in their self-possession. They are also mostly outsiders, alienated from the easy-going hedonism of most of their compatriots by their hunger for reality. Even as a child Hurtle Duffield's mother, for instance, tells him that 'You're what Pa and me knows we aren't'.[30] At first sight such characters seem anything but typical. Yet, eccentric as they seem, they truly respond to the state of disinheritance and displacement described earlier. Where the inhabitants of Sarsaparilla are content to live without memory or authority, characters like Eddie/Eadith Twyborn, Theodora Goodman, Elizabeth Hunter, Ellen Roxburgh, Himmelfarb, and Hurtle Duffield are all profoundly conscious of the presence in their lives of some 'infinitely gentle, infinitely suffering thing', often associated with the memory of a lost father or husband, and they set out on a quest for it which often lasts a lifetime.

By definition, therefore, they are explorers, intent upon exploring the interior. Their goal is White's own, 'an overreach- ing grandeur . . . whose essence is contained less in what is said than in the silences. In patterns on water. A gust of wind. A flower opening',[31] a goal which is not to be earned but is sheer gift. It also challenges conventional notions of right and wrong, of happiness and unhappiness, and of success and failure. Elizabeth Hunter, for instance, is in many respects morally unattractive, ruthless, self-absorbed, and often unloving. What makes her memorable, however, is her acceptance of herself and the revaluation which follows from this. In this sense, she begins to be a successful human being when she comes to terms with her failures. Similarly, with happiness, when Laura falls mysteriously ill, sharing Voss's final agony in the desert, Mr and Mrs Bonner begin to realize that what they had thought to be happiness was an illusion: 'their whole lives had been a process of illusion'. 'Oases of affection had made the desert endurable, till now the fierce heat of unreason began to wither any such refuge',[32] as Laura's suffering paradoxically gives them an insight 'into an intensity in which pain and joy are one'. Here 'the sceptical, utilitarian spirit' gives way before a sense of life which is essentially religious: White's vision of man is not Promethean but of man as 'God with a spear in his side'.[33]

This vision of man has something to do with White's darkly pessimistic reading of contemporary history but also with his feeling for the land itself, the 'country of the bones', which, as he told John Hetherington, has become part of him 'by reason of generation of my ancestors'. Unlike most Australians he is aware of the convict origins and of the sufferings of the Aborigines and of generations of migrants forced into the cramp of conformity. *A Fringe of Leaves*, for instance, makes a great deal not only of our convict origins but also of its legacy of moral infection. Paradoxically, however, it is this sense of Australia as a 'land of whips and thorns'[34] which leads him to see Australia as the equivalent of the dream of America as the place of resurrection, where people enter into a new and freer mode of existence, since for him, as for Sartre, the life that is properly human lives on the far side of despair.

Extreme as this may seem, at least it avoids the middling standards which, as de Tocqueville predicted, tend to prevail in the New World. A sense of contingency is always revolutionary since it undercuts confidence in the status quo: White is revolutionary in this sense. But although he came out strongly in support of the Whitlam experiment, the change he looks for cannot be brought about by political, social, or economic measures. It is a 'change from right to wrong which has nothing to do with category' but involved uniting 'all those who have a capacity for living . . . [and opposing] them to the destroyers'.[35] This unification and this opposition are both crucial: Theodora Goodman and Moraitis, Voss and Laura, Hurtle Duffield and Rhoda, the four Riders in the Chariot, Stan Parker and Doll Quigley, all recognize in one another fellow inhabitants of this new country, the land of vision which is in one sense yet to be created and in another already in existence 'every moment that we live and breathe, and love, and suffer and die',[36] as Laura declares at the end of *Voss*.

To some this vision of Australia will seem fantastic and even perverse. Nevertheless, despite its satiric exaggeration, the evidence White assembles indicates that all is not well in Australia. No society can afford to dispense with its dark, unconscious side as Australian society has done. Its loss, as Jung argues, is 'always and everywhere . . . a moral catastrophe'.[37]

In attempting to provide some metaphysical basis for life in Australia and to create the imaginative forms to express it, White may be establishing the conditions for a more properly human culture, recalling it to the archaic world view that conceives the cosmos as one great organic whole, a series of interlocking analogies involving invisible realities and centring upon the human body and the embodied human consciousness. In this view, knowledge is less a matter of calculation than of intuition, body is the means by which spirit expresses itself, and consciousness the instrument upon which the universe can play its 'final, if also fatal' music.[38] So the physical world becomes a means of illumination, as it does for Eddie Twyborn newly returned to Australia, for instance:

[Riding across the paddocks] loss of faith in himself was replaced by an affinity with the landscape surrounding him. It happened very gradually, in spite of a sadistic wind, the sour grass, deformed trees, rocks crouching like great animals petrified by time. A black wagtail swivelling on a grey-green fence post might have been confusing an intruder had he not been one who knew the password.[39]

In contrast with a society so objective that people themselves tend to become objects, in this subjective world everything is personal, and silence itself a mode of communication since it is in silence that it is possible to listen to the primary language of the world. The password Eddie refers to is memory since the ability to respond to this language belongs to childhood or to so-called primitive cultures in which consciousness of self and of the external world have not yet been sharply separated.

In this way, we return to the question the New World poses, 'who am I?' the crucial question, White implies, for Australian society, since all of his heroes and heroines wrestle with it. The answer they find lies not in the flight from history and from physical reality he indicts in the people of Sarsaparilla but in a new sense of time and space. Taking possession of the past both personally and on the larger historical scale, accepting the full range of an existence suspended 'inter stellas et faeces' and taking responsibility for it, his visionaries make their Australia 'the country of the future'. White's position is thus a radical one, prophetic and even oracular since he does not so much reflect upon Australian society as prophecy against it, calling, like Lawrence, for 'some sort of new show, a new recognition of the life-mystery'.

It is at least possible that he may be right.

Part IV
Conclusion

14. National Identity

John Carroll

What can we conclude by the 1980s, the time of the bicentennial of the first white settlement, about the state of Australian national identity? I shall not bother to summarize the findings of this book; the reader may do that for himself. What I do think worth doing is to look at the Australian problem in terms of the four domains in which other nations have generally staked out their sense of what they are, what they stand for, where they have come from, and where they are going. These are the domains of the great individuals, the typical individuals and their character traits, national rites, and the works of artistic vision that have imprinted themselves on a people's sense of itself.

Before beginning my theme I should say that I shall not concern myself with the long-term future of Australian culture. Predictions about such things usually turn out to be silly, the complexities of history far outwitting the dullness of the human mind. My own long-term view, for what it is worth, is that the twenty-first century will be marked on this continent by some cross-breed of our adapted Anglo-Saxon culture with Asian, and predominantly Chinese, culture—whether our descendants choose this or not. If this works well it will result in a unique and splendid mixture of British institutions and the best of British political and moral culture with the superior refinement and depth of the great Chinese traditions. But I am dreaming.

Great Individuals

A town or a city has many different aspects. It has its own use of space, width, and patterning of streets, style and placing of gardens, type, height and street-scaping of buildings. It has its own light, its own climate, its own smells and sounds. It has a number of recurring models of house and public building. It also has some unique buildings, ones of oddity or distinction that give it a special tone. These are not noticed by many of the inhabitants much of the time, but they contribute unconsciously to everyone's sense of the character of where he lives. Visitors are more likely to see the town in terms of its distinctive build-ings. Now national identity or character works in a somewhat analogous manner. Different groups in the population see different things and take different things as important; more-over, there are many different things to see. But if one could stand back one would make out a bounded form, and one would be able to distinguish its different features. The inhabitants, although little conscious of any of this, do take their cultural identity for granted, and live in unconscious acceptance of it, dependent on the full implicit form of its structure. In this town of the mind let us first consider the few distinguished buildings.

I noted in Chapter 9 that Australia lacks the pantheon of heroes normal in other countries. The Cromwells, Nelsons, Napoleons, and Lincolns who save their nation in a moment of great trial, or who lead their people on to great deeds, do not have a place in Australian mythology. This is not altogether due to a benign history pretty much free from testing moments of civil war, invasion, or imperial adventure. After all Gallipoli is remembered precisely because it was the first moment that the nation's manhood was under fire, and many men died heroic-ally for their country. But the Anzac tradition has not fostered great individual heroes. This is not for want of a candidate. General Sir John Monash, Australian commander for the latter part of the war, is widely regarded now as the one leader of high calibre on the Franco—British side. His own nation has not been interested in identifying with him.

In the other area that one would expect some contribution to a national mythology, that of foundation, the same holds. Neither the first settlement in Sydney Cove nor the formation of the Commonwealth in 1901 has fluttered the imagination. The Americans have their first pioneers, the Pilgrim Fathers and many others, and they have Benjamin Franklin and Thomas Jefferson. Australia has no one. Not even Alfred Deakin, one of the key figures in Federation, the second Prime Minister, a man of principle, vision, great oratorical and literary skills, and a man with interesting spiritual yearnings—a worthy candidate to form a legend—not even he has received the weakest call.

Many say that given time Sir Robert Menzies will be canonized. I doubt it. There was no crisis during his long reign; he was never called upon to save the nation in any way whatsoever. Moreover, he retired and died of old age, which leaves him with none of the qualifications that made of Abraham Lincoln his nation's most untouchable hero.

Of course there is Ned Kelly. Most Australians, when asked, cite him as the nation's hero. But few of them know much about him; nor do they care. He is prominent because of the lack of anyone else to point to when sociologists and journalists ask their simplistic questions. What he stands for is far too narrow to serve more than a very small minority of the population as an inspirational figure.

Typical Individuals and Character Traits

Enough has been said already in this book to deflate the bushman, and his egalitarian-mateship traits, as the representative of what is typically Australian. I wish to propose an alternative character trait, one that is unique in its full form to this country, and one that is far less dependent for its existence than egalitarian-mateship on general developments that have taken place in all Western countries. I refer to scepticism. Australian scepticism has two strains, one dark and deeply pessimistic, without the dignity and idealism of tragedy; the other is more epicurean, carrying a jocular light-hearted irreverence towards life.

The dark strain of scepticism is embodied in the theme of failure in Australian culture. It has no more evocative representation than in what is arguably the finest short story in Australian literature, Henry Lawson's 'Water them Geraniums'. The story is set in a remote bush environment, unyielding to the toil of the pioneer farmer. Nature is persecuting, and even the women, the sole bearers of moral courage for Lawson, finally decline—get 'past carin' as the theme of the second half of the story puts it. The machinery rusts, the horses creak, 10-year-old girls have lined, worried faces, and the women are proud but with 'the pride that lies down in the end and turns its face to the wall and dies'. There are the makings of high tragedy here, of man fighting for survival against an inexorably cruel fate as embodied in the harshness of the landscape. But the men are not heroes; Joe Wilson, the narrator and central character, shows little inclination to battle the weight of the elements set against him. He does not have the spine of an Oedipus or a Lear. Rather he and his kind are abject, frightened, pathetic creatures who turn to drink, or 'shoot through'—run off leaving their families to make do on their own. In Lawson's bleak vision these men in the end destroy their women, and therewith virtue itself, and then eventually commit suicide or go mad. There is no triumph over hardship, no dignity won through struggle, simply unmitigated dismal failure. Behind the story runs a bitter scepticism about the human condition.

There have been other significant literary embodiments of the failure theme since Lawson. George Johnston's highly successful middle-brow novel, *My Brother Jack* (1964), traces the failure of the egalitarian-mateship ideal. More recently David Williamson's play, *Don's Party* (1971), examines the sense of failure in two contemporary suburban middle-class couples, and the vicious resentments that it generates. In Johnston's case failure results from the interference of fate in the form of an accident causing physical injury, and from the unavailability of work in the modern city suitable to the aspirations of the egalitarian hero. In Williamson's case there is no explicit cause of failure: it is rather human nastiness and incompatibility, and the vicissitudes and futility of modern aspirations that are to blame.

The more epicurean scepticism has its finest rendition in Jack Hibberd's one-man play, *A Stretch of the Imagination* (1972). Monk O'Neill, the hero, lives the last day of his long life as a wilfully, almost manically anarchic display of self-assertion. He reminisces about the major events in his life: his travels, his three marriages, his romances, the death of his brother, his withdrawal to live as a hermit in the bush, the time he was threatened with a visit, and above all his own physical decline. He entertains himself with a raw, self-caressing monologue, delighting in irreverence towards the ideals of his youth, women, human attachment, and anything that might intrude upon his solitary kingdom. He mocks himself with his own masochism: he cut down the one tree on his hill, although he loves trees and has worked ever since to fertilize a replacement. His last friend was his dog: he shot his dog. His vision is acutely pessimistic; the life he recounts is composed of a sequence of encounters with his fellow humans in which he invariably ends up beaten, abused, or abandoned. Yet he tells his story with such relish, re-enacting each episode then ruminating on it with his own peculiar vernacular philosophizing, that his narcissism is compelling. He is a substantial, likeable figure, and his life gains a sense of fulfilled completion.

One of the richest sources of scepticism was the literature produced during World War I. The mateship ethic gains one of its injections of emotive tonic from Gallipoli: a brotherhood of equals fighting heroically side by side against formidable odds. But what is striking about the literature from the trenches is the light-hearted sceptical wit with which life under the constant threat of death was conducted. *The Anzac Book* (1916), written and illustrated by the soldiers at Gallipoli, has as typical of its style a dialogue that ends '"D . . . it . . . shut up, Bill," says his mate. "You're always growling . . . you'll want flowers on your grave next."' George Johnston repeats a story from World War II that struck him as typifying Australian humour: at one bend on the Kokoda Trail in New Guinea the skeletal hand and forearm of some hastily buried Japanese soldier had become exposed and it stuck out of the track up which the Australian infantry was laboriously climbing. Every Australian as he passed would seize the grisly claw and give it a shake, enviously saying, 'Good on you sport'.

One of scepticism's offshoots in the Australian case is a talent for satire. The theatre that played the most innovative role in the advance of Australian drama in the late 1960s and early 1970s, the Pram Factory in Melbourne, created a company whose speciality was a fast, irreverent vaudeville style of clowning. None of the major Australian companies can put on tragedy convincingly. Australia's one internationally recognized one-man performer, Barry Humphries, is the nation's leading sceptic (and, incidentally, most perceptive sociologist). Moreover, domestically, the most able of the television personalities, ones who created a highly distinctive style of their own, Graham Kennedy and Norman Gunston, both had as their stock-in-trade a buoyant impish irreverence. Kennedy made his name by focussing his variety show, 'In Melbourne Tonight', on the sending up of the products he was meant to be advertising. Gunston's scepticism works through the innocence of a boy from simple origins inadvertently turning the self-importance and ambition of the famous into traits that make them look ridiculous.

Scepticism is not reserved for the exceptional cases such as heroes in literature and television stars. There is a general mood of scepticism that pervades Australian attitudes to religion, politics, and indeed all ultimate values. It constrasts notably with that blend of idealism and sentimentality, of violence and a passion for justice that has had such an influence over American culture.

This generic scepticism has a number of attractive consequences. It means that Australians are less likely to take fanatics seriously, and therefore the nation is unlikely ever to be swept along by extremist politics. It means that the leading political figure is not idealized to the degree that many American presidents have been celebrated as virtue incarnate: it is difficult to imagine an equivalent to the Kennedy cult taking root in Australia. Similarly the momentous evangelical revival in the United States that marked the 1970s had no echo in Australia.

Moreover, to take a more general cultural index, the stock Western, with its idealized hero and its happy ending, is alien to the mature Australian sensibility. Australian art has been more down-to-earth, readier to confront failure and death, less in need of softening arbitrary or bleak events with sentimental music or glamorized images of compassion and community. There is something much too uncompromising in the harshness of 'Water them Geraniums', the film *Wake in Fright*, or *Don's Party* for them to have been products of America. The darkest themes in American fiction, as in the novels of Hawthorne, Melville, and Faulkner, are always offset by the fortitude of the tragic hero, his gains in inner strength, or transcendental recognition.

Australian scepticism equally has its negative consequences. Political idealism has been the exception in Australian history. There is not a convinced belief that mundane institutions and this-worldly activity can be radically transformed for the better, that idealistic passion can be translated into social progress. Australians are more indifferent than Americans to their political institutions; they are less likely to become indignant about injustice or inefficiency. They were quite happy to have the same Prime Minister for sixteen years as long as he offered them stability and moderation, and did not become too obviously self-important. Indeed, Menzies had to retire in 1966 to end his reign.

Scepticism means that there are no grand visions of the past, the present, or the future. It means that when there is poetry it draws its rhythms from the struggles and victories of everyday reality, and not from great and exceptional events. By association there is another unattractive consequence: an indifference to excellence. Scepticism reinforces that element in the egalitarian temper that distrusts difference, ambition, and achievement. It was not untypical when Nellie Melba returned to Australia at the height of her international celebrity that rumours should have started circulating about her having become a drunkard.

The roots of Australian scepticism are much more difficult to pinpoint than those of egalitarianism. Traces can be read both of the British capacity for ironical understatement and the Irish debunking of worldly pretension and success. Bill Wannon, in his *A Treasury of Australian Humour*, finds the origins of the mainstream of the humour in the jests and street ballads of London, Glasgow, and Dublin in the latter part of the eighteenth century. But there is at least a prima facie case for finding here a uniquely antipodean species, and in addition one that has crossed successfully from the bush to the city.

Whether this scepticism will survive is another question. The most potent cultural force operating today in Australia, as in all other Western countries, is that of consumerism. There is no need to detail its dominance over the styles and practices of modern living. The new materialism has successfully replaced the patriarchal bias of British, Puritan cultural forms, and has ensured that if the egalitarian-mateship ethic survives, it does so among families drinking beer and wine around a suburban garden barbecue.

In the face of the modern tide surging towards uniformity, however, the native scepticism may have shown some resistance. It is true that Lawson's characters are no more than echoes from the past, the hardship and sombreness of scratching a subsistence living in the wild bush having given way to the comfort of consumer affluence. Moreover, very few take the path of Monk O'Neill, in retreat from humanity. But scepticism did somehow enter the blood, making Australia an extraordinarily secular society, and Australians extremely doubtful about the pursuit of any holy grail, extremely casual in their approach to things.

We should not over-emphasize the inheritance from the past. Consumerism breeds its own scepticism, which would have reinforced while somewhat redirecting the generic trait in the local culture. In the first place, consumerism's own material values truly command only those in physical need: advanced industrial economies, as they have become more successful in satisfying physical need, and providing circuses to counter boredom, have undermined their own ultimate consumer values, of more quantity and more choice. The law of diminishing marginal returns in pleasure applies acutely beyond a certain level of affluence. Consumerism thus creates a scepticism about its own driving values.

In response the indigenous Australian scepticism has served to accentuate the distance of the average individual from consumer values. Australians have believed less than Americans in the virtues of a successful career and its material rewards, and they have generally been less carried away by the introduction of new appliances on the market. In short they have been less enthused by visions of the materialist utopia, while at the same time remaining largely indifferent to other possible paths to salvation.

Consumerism breeds scepticism at another level. The attainment of relative physical comfort with a high degree of individual mobility and choice seems to lessen the allure of metaphysical goals, whether religious, aesthetic, or political. The longing for the infinite is subdued by abundance. The opulent breast of consumerism nourishes a general scepticism about charged beliefs and grand ambitions. At its most dismal the modern mode of scepticism is given voice in the play, *Don's Party*.

The scepticism nourished by a consumer style of life is in danger of becoming lethargic, rather in the manner of the obese man who two hours after his latest feast thinks to himself as he stirs slightly in his deep armchair that over-eating is bad for him, but then recognizes as he sighs with repletion that he will continue in his gluttony, for he has little else to absorb him, and certainly not to the degree of driving him out into the cold on a night like this—eating at least brings him some pleasure. The scepticism of Monk O'Neill and even Joe Wilson is by contrast dynamic, displaying a seriousness about the human predicament: both men keep up the eternal struggle to accommodate the realities of living to the grand expectations fostered by human ideals, consoling themselves with their scepticism for their inability to narrow the distance. When they become resigned, there still remains a resistance to how things have turned out. They are not in danger of becoming lethargic; they are not comfortable. It will be a loss if the typical Australian sheds his bitterly irreverent or Monkish skin and emerges as a full-blooded consumer.

A recent example of Australian scepticism at its best shows that the great tradition is alive and well, and reminds us of the pitilessly stark yet impish vitality of this native trait. Michael Leunig, in the *Age* of 14 January 1981, presented six cartoon sketches of 'People to Ignore in the Eighties', one of which was 'Rev. David Slope, Anglican Priest, 37, doesn't believe in Jesus anymore but needs the job. Cynical. Burnt out. Unfriendly. Watches Tattslotto draw religiously.' This says it all.

Rites

The third domain in which nations stake out their identity consists of events and rituals, repeated periodically, that are enshrined in great symbolic and emotional significance. In pre-modern societies such events are religious, devoted to praising or propitiating the gods. By contrast, in secular societies they typically celebrate moments of national achievement, such as foundation, independence, or victory in great battles. They can also take the form of sporting contests, for example the ancient Olympic Games, or cultural festivals.

New nations, like new organizations, have great difficulty establishing rites that carry much authority, for such things depend in part on time—on tradition. Nevertheless Australia has developed some commanding rituals, or rather two, that have attracted to themselves an elaborate mythology and carefully prescribed rules of practice. They are prepared for and eagerly anticipated weeks in advance. They are talked about incessantly to the point of monopolizing conversation in the days immediately preceding them. Moreover, they draw in most of a population that for the rest of the year has extremely diverse and incompatible interests. I refer to the Melbourne Cup and the Victorian Football League Grand Final. If this seems a Melbourne-centred view of Australian culture it is because of the odd fact that the other state capitals have not generated national events. To be sure every state has its football final, but none of them touches the Melbourne rite in the religious intensity of the talk, decor, and ritualized behaviour that surround the event, or in the monopoly it holds over the imagination of the people. There is something of the grand drama and ethos of *The Iliad* in Australian Rules Football at its best. One of the many characteristics of the Melbourne Cup is that it attracts all classes of society, who dress for it, parade at it, and drink to it, all in their own deliberate and confident ways.

There is a second rank of rites that are significant in Australia, but of lesser sway. Test-match cricket, and especially when played against the traditional rival, England, can still arouse much of the nation, and has evolved in the ethos of the game, the wit of the crowd, and the genial reminiscing of the commentators, a sense of deep and rich tradition. In the 1970s, the vulgarity of Mr Packer seriously damaged the ritual, preparing the way for a new generation of yahoo spectators, totally ignorant of the lore of the game. We can only hope that this is a passing phase. The worst sign is a new breed of utilitarian commentator, who is replacing the jocular scepticism of the Keith Millers and Lindsay Hassets, with their wise and urbane tales of past glory. The best sign was the nation-wide outcry, and ensuing moral debate, that followed on Captain Greg Chappell's dishonourable ordering of an underarm delivery to defeat New Zealand in February 1981. Chappell's decision, within the rules, was a natural consequence of Mr Packer's commercialization of cricket as entertainment for colour television. The intensity of the protest, and the refinement of moral argument from some of the commentators (especially Alan McGilvray) is a sign that cricket may withstand the sale of its manners, and retain its place as a rite that instructs the young in how to behave with honour.

The Arts Festival in Adelaide and the Moomba Festival in Melbourne have both developed their own style and momentum. It is too early to tell whether they will consolidate themselves as commanding rituals. Unfortunately, the one celebration of past glory that ever took hold in Australia, Anzac

Day, is on the wane. The dawn service, the morning march, and the noon service are still deeply moving to watch, but they are in the process of crossing the line from living legend to museum event: already sociology and history students, tourists and journalists, outnumber the genuine witnesses to the march. By the way, it is the whole truth in Melbourne that the term 'living legend' is in everyday usage and refers to a great footballer, Jack Dyer. As a footnote we should note that 'Australia Day' is unique for its nullity, and the surest thing of the decade is that the Bicentennial in 1988 will be a complete flop, at best attracting half a dozen puzzled Japanese and American tourists, and our own clucking media, recycling yet again the mumbo-jumbo of Professor Manning Clark.

None of the attempts to transplant European rites has succeeded. Let us just consider the main example. Christmas, although originally a religious festival, still retains much of its traditional richness in twentieth-century secular Europe. But in Australia it has never worked, except as an excuse for the whole extended family gathering together once a year. This is in large part because of the climate: European Christmas, with its green trees, log fires, candles, and carols, depends on winter, providing a moment of cosy and warming colour in the midst of the drab inwardness that the unremitting cold enforces. The glaring heat of the Australian summer, and the hedonism it induces, cancels the need that a secular Christmas festival serves. And no antipodean adaptation has emerged to lift the mind above the body sweating over turkey and Christmas pudding.

Our rites are sporting ones, and so they shall remain until there is either a religious revival or some national military or political crisis. Sporting rites, however, can never be more than half-hearted, for they do not tap any of the metaphysical or transcendental yearnings and terrors that truly move men. They do not connect us with the infinite and the eternal, with the great questions of human existence. As a result they are a rickety basis on which to build any sense of identity. The nation was right in the late 1920s when it tried again to make something out of the Anzacs.

Artistic Vision

Homer's *Iliad* provided the Greeks of the fifth century B.C. with a range of heroes and events that told them about their significant past, of its great men and what they did, and it taught them how to behave in the present—at least ideally. The stories of the Old Testament have played a similar role for Jews and Christians. The plays of Shakespeare have contributed, although more obliquely, to the Englishman's sense of his nation and its traditions, explicitly in the portraits of kings such as Henry V and Richard III, implicitly in the morals drawn about human character and destiny in *Julius Caesar*, *Othello*, and most of the other plays. Putting the same point differently, our sense of Russia will always have as a staple part the images of Anna Karenina and Mitya Karamazov, Uncle Vanya and Eisenstein's Ivan the Terrible.

The great artists are those who tell us the deeper truths about our condition, ones that we had at best glimpsed dimly. Such truth is in part universal, laying bare the human experience pretty much irrespective of particular culture or time. Another part tells the truth about a specific country, its society and its people, getting at their more fundamental character. Once told and we never see things quite the same again. In the Australian case I have already suggested that Lawson's Joe Wilson has revealed something about men and women under trial in the harsh and relentless bush. The theme is put even more brutally in Barbara Baynton's story, 'Squeaker's Mate', brilliantly turned into a film by David Baker. When this film was shown as a short at the Rivoli Cinema in Melbourne, its portrait of a man's savage hatred for his wife, and his weakness to the point of total immorality, so hit a nerve in the normally urbane and civil upper middle-class audience that seats were slashed. The film had to be taken off after two days. Another side of the same truth is told by Shirley Hazzard, in her novel *The Transit of Venus*:

To appear without gloves, or in any other way to suggest the flesh, to so much as show unguarded love, was to be pitchforked into brutish, bottomless Australia, all the way back to primitive man. Refinement was a frail construction continually dashed by waves of raw, reminding humanity.

Australia has most to learn about itself from its one truly great writer, Patrick White. As Veronica Brady has reminded us, at last there is a vision of Australian man that is powerful, deeply disturbing, that does not derive from European models, and that we shall not get out of our gizzards for many decades. In Sarasparilla, in Voss's journey of the mind, in the brothers Brown, in the chariot, and in many other places, White has intimated various fragments of the truth. Serious students of Australian culture should in the 1980s spend most of their time reading and re-reading Patrick White.

There were a few moments of greatness in the films of the 1970s. *Mad Max* stands out as the one film to use the landscape in a starkly original and compelling way, choosing the Mallee as the background for shooting a futuristic nightmare of gratuitous violence. Peter Weir's erratic film, *The Last Wave*, had haunting moments—of torrential rain and of the psychic power of Aboriginal rites—which showed up in an unnerving way the spiritual poverty of the modern West. The film *Wake in Fright* (directed by a Canadian) was a masterly study of the breakdown of a weak, civilized man under the pressure of the outback, and it provided the great and exemplary character of Doc Tydon. *Breaker Morant* caught something of the nation's need to find its own moral code through the trials of a dubious yet savage war directed by a corrupt Britain. Finally, the television series, *Water Under the Bridge* (1980), stuck uncompromisingly to its guns, updating Lawson and Baynton, in a remorseless unveiling of timid men and punishing women. It was really a film, being far too good for television, as its low ratings showed.

Painting is the artistic medium that might have been expected to play the key role in getting at the truth about Australia, the land in which the sheer power of nature ensures that the visual sense will dominate. And indeed Australian painting has been celebrated here and abroad. My own view is that none of our painters has told us anything of importance. All their work is feeble next to the real Australian desert, the contained yet lyrical harmonies of Sydney harbour, the awesome grandeur of Port Campbell and Wilson's Promontory. Australian painting made a hit in London because Englishmen did not know the reality. From the Heidelberg School onwards, the bush itself—the view of Mt Buffalo from the Buckland Valley—has been far more memorable than the painters' mimicry. Australia has not produced a Cezanne, who gave a new dimension to his native Provence. I do not even mention sculpture: to sculpt in this country is totally presumptuous, given for one the inimitable and infinite beauty of rock formations and textures from the oceans to the desert heart.

There is to my mind one Australian contributor to the visual arts with greatness of vision. That is the contemporary cartoonist, Michael Leunig. It may be significant that Leunig is a poet rather than someone distinguished for his drawing, both in the words he attaches and in the combination of his images. He is not a sceptic, but a metaphysician who preaches, in the words of one of his characters, Vasco Pyjama, 'vague wonder' in the midst of what he experiences as the deep sadness and aimlessness of modern life. If Leunig reminds one of anyone, it is Kafka.

The photography in most films, whatever its technical virtuosity, has failed for the same reason that the painters have failed. The film of *Picnic at Hanging Rock* is visually dull compared with the uncanny and mysterious, wild beauty of the rock itself. Even Patrick White, in *Voss*, leaves a far more memorable picture of domesticated nature in Sydney than he does of the interior. It may be that nature is so powerful in Australia that man, so puny by contrast, should stick to wailing his humility, and recognize that only the gods are fit to walk here. We should take note of Robyn Davidson's story of herself, a tertiary educated, upper middle-class product of the 1960s, a little bored with her aimiable but conventional city life, setting about to ride camels from Alice Springs to the west coast across the Gibson Desert. With striking honesty and insight she tells of her struggles, which turn out to be with herself and other humans, and hardly at all with the nature that we would imagine constituting her giant adversary. As in *Voss*, the interior does not really come to life in her book: it remains like the unknowable God, the all-encompassing context. In a way she fails in her quest for revelation, for she is not embraced by the desert heavens: but she has asked, she has tried, she has endured, and she has learnt something about men, and especially herself.

Drought, bushfire, blasting heat, hurricane, and the sheer monumental vastness of nature, of oceans, cliffs, deserts, mountains, and the sky itself—much larger and brighter than in Europe—will always make man feel a nobody on this continent. This is our greatest asset in an age in which man has the vanity of believing that he can do anything, that nothing in nature can check him, that his technology and his medicine will protect him from any threat. Australians are lucky that in spite of their fearlessness of God, they must submit to a nature with many of the implacable and punitive powers of their lost divinity.

There is one event in our history fit to become a national myth. It complements the native scepticism as a signpost of identity. Its truth is about our relationship to our continent. I speak of the death of Harold Holt in Cheviot Bay, Portsea, on 17 December 1967. There is a unique, an awesome and humbling truth, but one of which we might be proud, about having had a Prime Minister walk into the surf, swim strongly between rocks towards a deep rock pool which he always enjoyed, find himself in a vicious undertow, swim confidently with it, and be ripped out to sea never to be seen again. A friend who watched helplessly from the shore later said: 'He was like a leaf being taken out. It was so quick and so final.' All the Portsea life-savers to enter the sea in the search that afternoon did so in fear: it was so ferocious, with 5 metre waves breaking over the reef. Divers searching for him had to be recalled repeatedly because of the seas, the sudden cloud-bursts, and the strong winds.

Mr Holt was no amateur swimmer but a spear-fisherman of long experience. Just before going in to the surf on that Sunday morning he told his worried companions that he knew this beach like the back of his hand. Presumably he knew that it was a dangerous morning to go swimming in this notoriously dangerous stretch of water. From his own comments on his passion for spear-fishing, and his love of the Portsea ocean coast, and especially Cheviot Bay, we can presume that he felt a need for the cleansing power of the surf, for being alone in the vast cavern of the ocean deep, at the mercy of, in harmony with, the eternal swell of nature. He had just arrived from Canberra: presumably here was his release from the strains of office, the tedium of administration, the weighing responsibility of political leadership. Presumably he felt the need to take the risk. There was a certain celebration in this act, the greatest of all tributes: the last sight of him was of his silver hair in the broken water as he appeared to be swimming strongly with the current. His death portends far more than Voss's analogous end. In the martyrology of our country—and martyrs are always the leading heroes—Harold Holt has a far more important place than the squalid, unoriginal, and irrelevant Ned Kelly, and not the less for his having been, as Prime Minister, an amiable and undistinguished figure.

1. The Bushman Legend

1. Russel Ward, *The Australian Legend*, 2nd edn, Oxford University Press, Melbourne, 1965.
2. Ibid., p. v.
3. Ibid., pp. 1–2.
4. Ibid., p. 99.
5. Ibid., quoted on p. 107.
6. Ibid., p. 162.
7. Ibid., Vance Palmer quote, p. 207.

2. The Pioneer Legend

1. Taken from *The Song of the Manly Man and other Verses*, London 1908.
2. Robert Caldwell, *The Pioneers and other Poems*, Adelaide, 1898.
3. The *Argus*, 2 September 1890.
4. *Mt Alexander Mail*, 20 March 1903.
5. This study is chiefly confined to these three colonies and states.
6. Old Colonists Association, *An Account of the Celebration of the Jubilee Year of South Australia* (1886), Adelaide 1887; G. Serle, *The Rush to be Rich*, Melbourne, 1971, p. 236.
7. M. Aveling, A History of the Australian Natives Association 1871–1900, Ph.D. thesis, Monash University, 1970, pp. 103, 108; *National Australian*, March 1886, p. 1, April 1886, pp. 13, 17, July

1886, p. 13, September 1886, pp. 7–9; *The Australian*, March 1887, p. 10, March 1888, p. 9.

8. 21 May 1898; 11 June 1898.

9. T. T. Reed (ed.), *The Poetical Works of Henry Kendall*, Adelaide, 1966, pp. 198, 378, 438–9.

10. *The Collected Verse of A. B. Paterson*, Sydney, 1921, pp. 132–6. The poem first appeared in book form in *Rio Grande's Last Race and Other Verses*, Sydney, 1902.

11. Colin Roderick (ed.), *Henry Lawson, Autobiographical and Other Writing*, Sydney, 1972, pp. 6–8.

12. Colin Roderick (ed.), *Henry Lawson, Collected Verse*, vol. 1, Sydney, 1967, p. 56.

13. Colin Roderick (ed.), *Henry Lawson, Short Stories and Sketches 1888–1922*, Sydney, 1972, pp. 24–5.

14. Lawson, *Collected Verse*, pp. 361–3.

15. 'Crime in the Bush', *Autobiographical and Other Writings*, pp. 32–6.

16. *The Collected Verse of G. Essex Evans*, Sydney, 1928, pp. 2–3, 89–91.

17. A. A. Phillips, *The Australian Tradition*, Melbourne, 1958, pp. 43–8.

18. Lawson, *Collected Verse*, pp. 400–01.

19. Lawson, *Short Stories and Sketches*, p. 544.

20. Ibid., pp. 107–09, 390, 731.

21. Ibid., pp. 431–2.

22. In his contrived contest with Paterson over the nature of bush life, Lawson mocked the view that 'the bush was better in the "good old droving days" ', *Collected Verse*, p. 214, but he shared Paterson's romanticism more often than not.

23. *Collected Verse of A. B. Paterson*, pp. 41–3.

24. *Empire*, vol. 2, no. 4, May 1854; G. Serle, *The Golden Age*, Melbourne, 1963, p. 133.

25. The *Bulletin*, 21 January 1888, reprinted in Ian Turner, *The Australian Dream*, Melbourne, 1968, pp. 226–34. Barry Andrews, *Price Wariung* (William Astley), Boston, 1976, pp. 99–101.

26. Lawson, *Collected Verse*, p. 75.

27. The *Age*, 16 August 1905.

28. Kay Daniels *et al.* (eds), *Women in Australia. An Annotated Guide to Records*, Canberra, 1977, pp. xxvii–xxviii.

29. James Collier, *The Pastoral Age In Australasia*, London, 1911, pp. 2–5.

30. Stephen Roberts, *The Pastoral Age in Australia*, Melbourne, 1964, pp. 1–2.

31. W. K. Hancock, *Australia*, Brisbane, 1961, p. 2.

32. *The Passionate Heart*, Sydney, 1918. See also Miles Franklin and Dymphna Cusack, *Pioneers on Parade*, Sydney, 1939, whose plot turns on the convict origins of a pioneer family.

33. The *Argus*, 29 September 1909. Victorian Bush Nursing Association, *Report of the Central Council*, Melbourne, 1918, p. 3.

34. *Collected Verse of G. Essex Evans*, pp. 252–3.

35. *School Paper*, Grades III and IV, April 1924.

36. Victorian Education Department, *Education Gazette and Teachers' Aid*, 18 February 1916, p. 30.

37. See B. Wannan (ed.), *Pioneers: verse, ballad, picture*, Melbourne, 1975.

38. *The Australasian Pioneers' Club Rules*, Sydney, 1910. The Club was founded following a meeting on 2 May 1910 convened by Mr Douglas Hope Johnstone, a direct descendant of Lieutenant George Johnstone who arrived with the First Fleet. Travers Burrows, *The Genesis of the Pioneers' Assocation of South Australia*, Adelaide, 1946.

39. Russel Ward, *The Australian Legend*, Melbourne, 1958, p. 211.

40. Henry Lawson, *Short Stories and Sketches*, pp. 41–2, 63, 103–4, 269, 275, 321–3, 417, 502, 507, 585; *Collected Verse*, pp. 115–19.

41. 'The Australian legend', *Meanjin*, September 1962, pp. 366–9.

3. Ned Kelly

1. The writer would like to express his gratitude to Alan Davies, Graham Little, Roger Joyce, and Mark Considine for their detailed comments.

2. The quote is from Colin F. Cave, 'Introduction', Colin F. Cave (ed.), *Ned Kelly Man and Myth*, Cassell, 1968, p. 1. See also, John McQuilton, *The Kelly Outbreak 1878–1880: The Geographical Dimension of Social Banditry*, Melbourne University Press, 1979, p. 2.

3. This account of the Fitzpatrick affair is based on the following sources: Second Progress Report of the Royal Commission of Enquiry into the Circumstances of the Kelly Outbreak, the Present

State and Organization of the Police Force, etc., pp. ix–x. Police Commission Minutes of Evidence taken before Royal Commission on the Police Force of Victoria, 1881, Facsimile Reprint, 1968, Q. 12801–12994, Q. 2275, p. 702, Q. 2278. Charles White, *History of Australian Bushranging*, vol. 2, Lloyd O'Neill, 1970, p. 263. The *Ovens and Murray Advertizer*, 21 May, 10 October, 15 October 1878.

4. The conversations at Stringybark Creek are recorded in the Deposition of Thomas McIntyre, 7 August 1880. The description of the shootings are based on ibid. and McIntyre's verbal report of 28 October 1878 to Superintendent Sadlier as recorded in John Sadlier, *Recollections of a Victorian Police Officer*, Penguin Colonial Facsimiles, 1973, pp. 187–8. Also, Ian Jones, 'The Years Ned Kelly Went Straight', *Walkabout*, July 1962, p. 16.

5. Max Brown, *Australian Son, The Story of Ned Kelly*, Georgian House, 1956, p. 77. Deposition of James Gloster, 9 August 1880. Statement by Mr McDougall quoted in the *Argus*, 12 December 1878. Second Progress Report, p. x. John Malony, *I am Ned Kelly*, Allen Lane, 1980, p. 149. McQuilton, *The Kelly Outbreak, 1848–1880*, pp. 101, 111. Mrs Robert Scott, 'It's the Kellys!' *Nautilus*, October 1958, p. 19. Geoffrey Serle, *The Rush to be Rich: A History of the Colony of Victoria, 1883–1889*, Melbourne University Press, 1974, p. 11.

6. Brown, *Australian Son*, p. 96. The Cameron Letter reprinted in Brown, *Australian Son* and Charles Osborne, *Ned Kelly*, Anthony Blond, 1970. The italics appear in the original.

7. Heinz Kohut, *The Analysis of the Self: A Systematic Approach to the Psychoanalytic Treatment of Narcissistic Personality Disorders*, International Universities Press, 1974, pp. 108–9. The *Argus*, 12, 13 February 1879. McQuilton, *The Kelly Outbreak, 1878–1880*, p. 119. Malony, *I am Ned Kelly*, p. 170. Douglas Stewart, *Ned Kelly*, Angus and Robertson, 1972, p. 14. Ian Jones and Glen Tomasetti, 'Kelly —The Folk-Hero', Cave (ed.), *Ned Kelly, Man and Myth*, p. 90. E. J. Hobsbawm, *Primitive Rebels: Studies in Archaic Forms of Social Movement in the 19th and 20th Centuries*, Manchester University Press, 1974, p. 18. Brown, *Australian Son*, pp. 142, 272.

8. The Jerilderie Letter, Public Record Office, Victoria and reprinted in Brown, *Australian Son*.

9. Jones and Tomasetti, 'Kelly—The Folk-Hero', pp. 80–1. Weston Bate, 'Kelly and His Times', Cave (ed.), *Ned Kelly, Man and Myth*,

p. 54. Hobsbawm, *Primitive Rebels*, p. 15. Police Commission Minutes of Evidence, Q. 1282, Q. 755, Q. 1498, Q. 1500, Q. 1501, Q. 7607, Q. 17597, Q. 1503, Q. 1505, Q. 1506, Q. 8263, Q. 7291, Q. 7292, p. 674. Stewart, *Ned Kelly*, p. 64. Second Progress Report, pp. xx, xxi, xxv, xxvii, xxviii. Brown, *Australian Son*, pp. 177–8.

10. Louis Waller, 'Regina v. Edward Kelly', Cave (ed.), *Kelly, Man and Myth*, pp. 113, 114, 119, 124. The *Argus*, 30 October 1880. Brown, *Australian Son*, p. 263.

11. McQuilton, *The Kelly Outbreak, 1878–1880*, p. 27, 163, 173. Heinz Kohut, 'Creativeness, Charisma, Group Psychology Reflections on the Self-Analysis of Freud', Paul H. Ornstein (ed.), *The Search for the Self: Selected Writings of Heinz Kohut: 1950–1978,* International Universities Press, 1978, Vol. 2, p. 823, *passim*. Christine Olden, 'About the Fascinating Effect of the Narcissistic Personality', *American Imago*, vol. 2, no. 4, 1941, p. 354, *passim*. E. J. Hobsbawm, *Bandits*, Weidenfeld and Nicolson, 1969, pp. 112, 114. Malony, *I am Ned Kelly*, p. 249.

5. The Conditions of Early Settlement

1. Russel Ward, 'The Australian Legend re-visited,' *Historical Studies*, vol. 18, 1978, pp. 172, 175, 177, 183.

2. Alan Frost, *Convicts and Empire: A Naval Question 1776–1811*, Oxford University Press, 1980.

3. P. G. Fidlon and R. J. Ryan (eds), *The Journal of Arthur Bowes Smyth: Surgeon, Lady Penrhyn 1787–1789*, Australian Documents Library, 1979, p. 47.

4. Phillip to Grenville, 20 June 1790, Public Record Office, CO 201/5:146; to Sydney, 11 November 1791, Dixson MS Q 162:31 (my emphasis).

5. W. C. Wentworth, *Statistical, Historical, and Political Description of the Colony of New South Wales*, G. and W. B. Whittaker, 1819, pp. 46–8.

6. Watkin Tench, *Sydney's First Four Years*, L. F. Fitzhardinge (ed.), Library of Australian History in association with the Royal Australian Historical Society, 1979, p. 264.

7. Quoted in Elizabeth Macarthur to Eliza Kingdon, 23 August 1794, in S. M. Onslow (ed.), *The Macarthurs of Camden*, Rigby, 1973 [1914]), p. 45.

8. King to Hobart, 9 May 1803 and 1 March 1804, *Historical Records of Australia*, vol. iv, pp. 122, 461. 469. 480.

9. Hazel King, citing from Elizabeth Macarthur to Eliza Kingdon, March 1816, in *Elizabeth Macarthur and Her World*, Sydney University Press, 1980, p. 74.

10. François-Maurice Lepailleur, *Land of a Thousand Sorrows*, F. M. Greenwood (trans. and ed.), Melbourne University Press, 1980, pp. 13, 18, 30, 46, 78.

11. Quoted in C. M. H. Clark, *Select Documents in Australian History 1788–1850*, Angus and Robertson, 1950, Vol. I, 200–01.

12. Quoted in Cecil Hadgraft, *Australian Literature*, Heinemann, 1960, p. 6.

13. Phillip to Sydney, 15 May 1788, *Historical Records of New South Wales*, vol. I, no. ii, p. 128.

14. See Alan Frost, 'Eighteenth Century Perceptions of "the Romantic", New Zealand, and Tahiti,' *The New Zealand Journal of History*, vol. 5, 1971, pp. 185–90; and H. B. Proudfoot, 'Botany Bay, Kew, and the Picturesque,' *Journal of the RAHS*, vol. 65, 1979, pp. 30–45.

15. Roger Therry, *Reminiscences of Thirty Years' Residence in New South Wales and Victoria*, Sampson Low, Son, and Co. 1863, p. 35.

16. Mrs Charles Meredith, *Notes and Sketches of New South Wales during a Residence in the Colony from 1839–1844* [1844], Ure Smith in association with the National Trust of Australia, 1973, p. 34.

17. Quoted in R. M. Crawford, *Australia*, 4th ed., Hutchinson, 1979, p. 78.

18. Quoted in J. W. C. Cumes, *Their Chastity was not too Rigid*, Longman Cheshire/Reed, 1979, p. 37.

19. George Bennett, *Wanderings in New South Wales*, Richard Bentley, 1834, vol. I, p. 96.

20. White to Skill, 17 April 1790, *Historical Records of New South Wales*, vol. I, no. ii, p. 333.

21. Elizabeth Macarthur to Eliza Kingdon, 1 September 1795, in Onslow (ed.) *The Macarthurs of Camden*, pp. 46–7.

22. Quoted in *Australian Dictionary of Biography*, vol. II, pp. 583–4.

23. Quoted in John Ritchie (ed.), *The Evidence to the Bigge Reports*, Heinemann, 1971, vol. II, p. 41.

24. J. T. Bigge, *Report . . . on the State of Agriculture and Trade in the Colony of New South Wales* [1823], Libraries Board of South Australia, 1966, p. 82.

25. James to William Henty, August 1828, quoted in Marnie Bassett, *The Hentys: An Australian Colonial Tapestry*, Melbourne University Press, 1962, pp. 34–6.

26. Quoted in Ritchie, vol. II, pp. 25–6.

27. Gipps to Stanley, 3 April 1844, *Historical Records of Australia*, vol. xxiii, p. 510.

6. The Nomadic Tribes of Urban Britain

For the sake of brevity detailed references to documents and most secondary sources used in this chapter have been omitted. Full references will be found in *Historical Studies*, no. 71, October 1978.

1. Eris O'Brien, *The Foundations of Australia, 1786–1800*, London, 1937.

2. G. A. Wood, 'Convicts', *Journal and Proceedings of the Royal Australian Historical Society*, vol. 8, 1922.

3. M. Clark, 'The Origins of the Convicts Transported to Eastern Australia, 1787–1852', *Historical Studies ANZ*, vol. 7, nos 26 and 27, May and November 1956.

4. L. L. Robson, *The Convict Settlers of Australia*, Melbourne, 1965.

5. A. G. L. Shaw, *Convicts and the Colonies*, London, 1966.

6. M. Clark, 'The Origins of the Convicts . . .', p. 316.

7. The theoretical perspective underlying this paper has drawn upon the work of Sigmund Freud, Melanie Klein, John Dollard, Erik H. Erikson, Peter L. Berger and T. Luckmann, and David M. Rafky. It is summarized in the original article in *Historical Studies*, no. 71, October 1978.

8. Since our original article was written, Lawrence Stone has presented an interesting and controversial view of the evolution of patterns of 'family' in differing levels of English society in *The Family, Sex and Marriage in England 1500–1800*, Harper and Row, London, 1977.

9. In the Black Country between 1839 and 1855, David Philips found that workers in 'unskilled' and labouring categories were substantially over-represented.

10. Eileen Yeo shares this view of Mayhew's qualitative data, and praises his sympathetic understanding and capacity to discern sub-cultures and the feelings of those who differed from his own norms and values.

11. The Ragged School movement started about 1840.

12. In Lancashire such cases were regarded as extreme.

13. E. P. Thompson has suggested that the facade of worthy respectability which characterized Mayhew's father who was 'a substantial London solicitor' masked a feared and sadistic domestic tyrant, and that despite Mayhew's rebellious and Bohemian leanings, he was dependent financially on his father through his twenties and thirties. Thus the images of wayward youth as victims of domestic tyranny or neglect had personal salience.

14. Anderson felt that in Lancashire, the mother provided an important focus of family life, and that strong bonds existed between her and the children, even though adolescents might leave home to get away from a brutal or tyrannical father. On the other hand, a mother's inability to defend her children from paternal brutality whether through fear or apathy would do little to strengthen the basis of trust between mother and child. Alternatively, the female victim of male aggression and social degradation might in turn become an oppressive, unreliable or withdrawn parent.

15. There are reports of criminal associations between kin outside London also.

16. Delineation of the 'frame' within which definition of situations takes place is most relevant here and is treated theoretically by E. Goffman.

17. In working-class districts of Lancashire, neighbours or relatives were often called upon to 'care for' children of working mothers.

18. Social problems associated with excessive consumption of spirits (especially gin) were given prominence by social investigators in both the eighteenth and nineteenth centuries.

19. Moreover, during the summer months, many metropolitan refuges were closed, compelling habitués to seek alternative shelter. Seasonal habits of the first class thieves and pickpockets known as the 'swell mob' differed from those of less able and less industrious petty pilferers, tricksters, beggars, and trampers.

20. In this context incest was perceived as a problem.

21. Patronizing attitudes were fiercely resented and the abhorrence of 'tracts' which prevailed among the lowest rungs of urban society owed much to their patronizing tone and reactionary political stance.

22. It is worth bearing in mind that attention has been concentrated on the lives of metropolitan criminals and those who made London their base. On the basis of findings for the Black Country in the period 1835–55, D. Philips estimated that only 10 per cent of indictable offences in that region were committed by professional thieves; 'the great majority were committed by people who were not full-time criminals. . . .'

23. Fears concerning the character and influence of large lodging houses were not confined to the London scene. Anderson recounts that in Lancashire they were regarded as being hotbeds of promiscuity and anti-social values, housing in the main vagrants, prostitutes and thieves.

24. Note, for example, Jonathon Wild's notorious combined operations both as private thief-taker and as manager of several gangs in the early eighteenth century.

25. Much used in psychoanalysis, this concept refers to an individual's mental energy which is attached to an object, image or idea.

7. Sydney and the Bush

For more detailed footnoting the reader is referred to the original version of this chapter in *Historical Studies*, no. 71, October 1978.

1. Lawson to G. Robertson, 21 January 1917 as quoted in Colin Roderick (ed.), *Henry Lawson, Collected Verse*, vol. 1, 1885–1950, Sydney, 1967, p. 423.

2. Russel Ward, *The Australian Legend*, Melbourne, 1958, *passim*.

3. N. D. Harper, 'The Rural and Urban Frontiers', *Historical Studies*, vol. 10, no. 40, May 1963, p. 421; M. Roe, 'The Australian Legend', *Meanjin*, vol. 21, 1962, p. 364.

4. G. Serle, *From Deserts the Prophets Come*, Melbourne, 1973, p. 58.

5. 'The Status of Literature in New South Wales II, How the Publishers Look at It', *Centennial Magazine*, vol. 2, no. 2, September 1889, p. 92.

6. Fred. H. Bathurst, 'Reporters and their Work', ibid., vol. 2, no. 7, February, 1890, pp. 498–502.

7. Select Committee on Common Lodging Houses, N.S.W. *Votes and Proceedings*, vol. 6, 1876, pp. 2–9; Report of the Royal Commission on Chinese Gambling and Immorality and charges of bribery against members of the police force, ibid., vol. 7, 1891–92, pp. 20, 26, and Appendix Table 3, pp. 487 ff; John Wolforth, 'Residential Concentration of Non-British Minorities in 19th Century Sydney', *Australian Geographical Studies*, vol. 12, no. 2, October 1974, pp. 207–18.

8. On the general characteristics of the 'zone-in-transition' see E. W. Burgess, 'The Growth of the City: An Introduction to a Research Project', R. E. Park, E. W. Burgess, and R. D. McKenzie (eds), *The City*, Chicago, 1925, pp. 54–56.

9. 'Titus Salt', 'The Row in Our Boarding House', *Bulletin*, 19 December 1891.

10. 'Faces in the Street', *Bulletin* 28 July 1888 (my emphasis).

11. On Lawson's childhood see D. Prout, *Henry Lawson, The Grey Dreamer*, Adelaide, 1963 and 'A Fragment of Autobiography', in Colin Roderick (ed.), *Autobiographical and Other Writings, 1887–1922*, Sydney, 1972, esp. p. 175.

12. 'A Christmas Story', *Dawn*, December 1889.

13. 22 April 1888, George Black Papers, Mitchell Library.

14. *Dawn*, 5 November 1889.

15. 'Army of the Rear', *Bulletin* 12 May 1888.

16. Sylvia Lawson, 'J. F. Archibald,' *Australian Dictionary of Biography*, vol. 3, pp. 43–8.

17. 'With Dickens' (1900), *Collected Verse*, vol. 1, p. 389; J. le Gay Brereton, *Knocking Round*, Sydney, 1930, p. 5.

18. G. R. Sims, *My Life. Sixty Years Recollections of Bohemian London*, London, 1917, pp. 111, 135–7, 332; *Dagonet Ballads*, London, 1881, *Bulletin* 12 February 1887, 6 July 1889.

19. James Thomson, *The City of Dreadful Night*, 2nd ed., London, 1894.

20. Henry Lawson, 'Straight Talk', *Albany Observer*, 1890 in his *Autobiographical and Other Writings, 1887–1922*, p. 11.

21. Ibid., p. 9. Compare C. Semmler, *The Banjo of the Bush*, 2nd ed., Sydney, 1974, ch. 4–6.

22. 'Clancy of the Overflow', 1889.

23. E. J. Brady 'Personalia', Brady Papers, M. L. 'Lights of Labour', Brady Papers, A.N.L., *Sydney Harbour*, Sydney 1903, p. 32.

24. E. J. Brady, 'The Intelligentsia' in 'History of the Labour Party', A.N.L., Poems of E. J. Brady, c. 1887–1912, La Trobe Library Manuscripts.

25. 'Personalia'.

26. C. Roderick, 'Henry Lawson: The Middle Years, 1893–6', *Royal Australian Historical Society, Journal and Proceedings*, vol. 53, part 2, June 1967, pp. 103–4, 114–9.

27. Ibid., p. 39.

28. 'The Beating of the Drums', *Australian Workman*, 4 April 1891.

29. 'The Man Outside', *Bulletin*, 24 September 1892, *Henry Lawson, by his Mates*, Sydney, 1931, p. 134.

30. E. J. Brady, 'Lights of Labour', 'The Wage-Writer', *Bulletin*, 26 November 1892.

31. *Bull Ant*, 21 August 1890, *Rhymes from the Mines*, Sydney, 1896.

32. *Bulletin*, 1 June 1901, reprinted in *Dawnward?*, Sydney, 1903.

33. C. Mann (ed.), *The Stories of Henry Lawson*, First series, Sydney, 1964, p. 191.

34. A. G. Stephens, 'Henry Lawson', *Art in Australia*, Sydney, 1922, reprinted in C. Roderick (ed.), *Henry Lawson Criticism 1894–1971*, Sydney, 1972, p. 217.

35. 'Borderland' (later re-titled 'Up the Country'), *Bulletin*, 9 July 1892.

36. B. Nesbitt, 'Literary Nationalism and the 1890s', *Australian Literary Studies*, vol. 5, no. 1, May 1971, pp. 3–17.

37. V. Palmer, *A. G. Stephens: His Life and Works*, Melbourne, 1941, pp. 235–6.

38. W. D. Flinn to G. Black, 14 January 1892, Black Papers.

39. G. A. Taylor, *Those were the Days*, Sydney, 1918, *Henry Lawson, by his Mates*, p. 63.

8. Mateship in Country Towns

1. I would like to thank Rae Ball, Jill Gooch, and Eleanor Hodges for their valuable assistance in the preparation of this chapter, and Emma Morrison for providing a number of ideas.

9. Mateship and Egalitarianism

1. This chapter is an elaboration of part of an essay of mine, 'An Outline of Australian Culture', first published in *Quadrant*,

October 1978, and reprinted in my book, *Sceptical Sociology*, Routledge & Kegan Paul, London, 1980.

2. One important institution that was not derived from a British precedent was the Conciliation and Arbitration Commission. The obvious case of a significantly adapted institution is federal Parliament, the establishment of which took elements from the United States example: a written Constitution and a Senate.

3. Nineteenth-century Melbourne, in particular, benefited from the Scottish influence. For instance, it was hardly more than a small town when in 1854 its university was founded—four years earlier Melbourne's population was a mere 23 000.

4. Geoffrey Serle, *The Golden Age*, Melbourne University Press, 1963, p. 374. Serle provides a detailed discussion of migration to Victoria in this period, and speculates on levels of disillusionment (pp. 372–6).

5. W. K. Hancock in his profoundly influential study, *Australia*, Benn, London, 1930, advised all Australians to read Tocqueville's *Democracy in America* in order to make comparisons (p. 269). However, Hancock himself did not see the crucial relevance of Tocqueville, who knew that democracies would pursue in the end the equality of enjoyment rather than the equality of opportunity (Hancock, pp. 183, 269–70).

6. John Carroll: *Puritan, Paranoid, Remissive: a Sociology of Modern Culture*, Routledge & Kegan Paul, London, 1977.

10. Australian Drama

1. This group of playwrights includes Louis Nowra, Steve J. Spears, and Stephen Sewell, as well as writers with other cultural backgrounds like Roger Pulvers and John Lee. It is not possible in a discussion of this scope to offer anything like a general survey of Australian drama, and the reader who seeks a less selective account of plays, playwrights, and social influences in recent years should consult Leslie Rees's *A History of Australian Drama*, vol. II, Angus and Robertson, Sydney, 1978, or my own *After 'The Doll'. Australian Drama Since 1955*, Edward Arnold, Melbourne, 1979.

2. See, for example, some of the exchanges in Alan Seymour's *The One Day of the Year* (1960). The phenomenon of sliding registers gives some naturalistic licence even to Jack Hibberd's very electric monologuist Monk O'Neil in *A Stretch of the Imagination* (1971).

3. Louis Nowra, 'On this Use of Language', *Theatre Australia*, vol. I, no. 4, November/December, 1976, p. 11.

4. A fuller account of this development may be found in my article, 'Jokers and Losers: Some Themes in Recent Australian Plays', in *Canadian Drama* (Commonwealth Drama Issue), vol. 6, no. 1, Spring 1980, pp. 43–55.

11. Film

1. A revealing account of these difficulties is provided by David Stratton, *The Lost New Wave*, Angus and Robertson, 1980, pp. 98–105.

2. 'Australian Films and Fantasies', *Meanjin Quarterly*, vol. 38, no. 2, July 1979, p. 193.

3. Richard Thompson has provided a valuable guide to what he calls the 'red-neck film' in *Film Comment*, vol. 16, no. 4, July/August 1980, p. 34.

12. Painting an Australian Identity

1. M.O.M.A. 1977, *Fred Williams Catalogue*, introduction by William S. Lieberman.

2. Patrick McCaughey, *Fred Williams*, Bay Books, 1980, p. 120.

3. George Johnston, *Clean Straw for Nothing*, Collins 1969, p. 183.

4. Albert Tucker, 'Art, Myth and Society', *Angry Penguins*, no. 4, 1943.

5. Sidney Nolan, review of Max Harris, 'The Vegetative Eye, *Angry Penguins*, 'Ern Malley Issue' Autumn 1944, p. 104.

6. Nolan's wartime letters, quoted by Jaynie Anderson, 'The Early Work of Sidney Nolan 1939–49', *Meanjin*, September 1967, p. 318.

7. Ibid., p. 317.

8. Ibid., p. 318.

9. Charles Spencer published virtually identical interviews in *Studio*, November 1964, and *Art and Australia*, September 1965.

13. Patrick White's Australia

1. Jean-Paul Satre, *Politics and Literature*, Calder & Boyars, 1973.

2. Patrick White, *The Solid Mandala*, Eyre & Spottiswood, 1966, p. 41.

3. Patrick White, *The Tree of Man*, Penguin, p. 212.

4. Quentin Anderson, *The Imperial Self*, Vintage Books, 1971, pp. 3–5.

5. A. G. Stephens, in Ian Turner (ed.), *The Australian Dream*, Sun Books, 1968, p. x.

6. In John Hetherington, *Forty-Two Faces*, Cheshire, 1962, p. 144.

7. Patrick White, *Happy Valley*, Hanap, 1939, p. 116.

8. Ibid., p. 115.

9. Patrick White, *Voss*, Penguin, 1960, p. 446.

10. Ibid., p. 29.

11. Ibid., p. 349.

12. Patrick White, *Riders in the Chariot*, Penguin, p. 486.

13. Patrick White, *The Eye of the Storm*, Penguin, 1975, p. 273.

14. White, *The Tree of Man*, p. 474.

15. Ibid., p. 476.

16. Ibid., p. 42.

17. White, *Riders in the Chariot*, p. 198.

18. I have argued the influence of Simone Weil on White in 'The Novelist and the Reign of Necessity' in R. Shepherd and K. Singh (eds), *Patrick White: A Critical Symposium*, Flinders University, 1978, pp. 108–16.

19. White, *The Tree of Man*, pp. 399–400.

20. White, *Riders in the Chariot*, p. 208.

21. Patrick White, *The Vivisector,* Cape, 1970, p. 170.

22. White, *The Solid Mandala*, p. 303.

23. Paul Ricoeur, *The Symbolism of Evil*, Beacon Press, 1967, pp. 100–01.

24. White, *Riders in the Chariot*, p. 44.

25. Ibid., p. 407.

26. Ibid., p. 248.

27. Sören Keirkegaard, *Fear and Trembling, the Sickness Unto Death*, Anchor Books, 1954, p. 154.

28. White, *Voss*, p. 446.

29. White, *The Vivisector*, p. 29.

30. Ibid., p. 20.

31. Patrick White, 'Flaws in the Glass', *Bulletin Centenary Issue*, 29 January 1980, p. 151.

32. White, *Voss*, pp. 357–8.

33. Ibid., p. 297.

34. Patrick White, *A Fringe of Leaves*, Penguin, 1977.

35. Patrick White, *The Living and the Dead*, Penguin, 1967, p. 240.

36. White, *Voss*, p. 446.

37. C. G. Jung, in Richard Ellmann and Charles Feidelson (eds), *The Modern Tradition*, Oxford University Press, 1965, p. 653.

38. Patrick White, *The Aunt's Story*, Eyre & Spottiswoode, p. 298.

39. Patrick White, *The Twyborn Affair*, Cape, 1979.

Veronica Brady is Senior Lecturer in English at the University of Western Australia, a member of the Loreto Order, and author of *The Future People* (1969), *The Mystics* (1973), and *Australian Literature and the Question of God* (1981).

John Carroll is Reader in Sociology at La Trobe University, and author of *Puritan, Paranoid, Remissive: a Sociology of Modern Culture* (1977) and *Sceptical Sociology* (1980).

Jack Clancy is Senior Lecturer in Media Studies at the Royal Melbourne Institute of Technology.

Graeme Davison is Senior Lecturer in History at the University of Melbourne, author of *The Rise and Fall of Marvellous Melbourne* (1978), and editor of *Melbourne on Foot* (1980).

Kenneth Dempsey is Senior Lecturer in Sociology at La Trobe University, and author of *Power and Politics in the Local Church*, (in press).

Mary Eagle is a freelance writer on the arts.

Peter Fitzpatrick is Senior Lecturer in English at Monash University and author of *After 'The Doll'. Australian Drama since 1955* (1979).

Alan Frost is Senior Lecturer in History at La Trobe University, and author of *Convicts and Empire: A Naval Question 1776–1811* (1980).

Bill Gammage is Senior Lecturer in History at the University of Adelaide, and author of *The Broken Years* (1974) and *An Australian in World War I* (1976).

241

J. B. Hirst is Senior Lecturer in History at La Trobe University, author of *Adelaide and the Country 1870–1917* (1974), and editor of the journal *Historical Studies*.

Eleanor Hodges is a graduate student in Sociology.

Angus McIntyre is Lecturer in Politics at La Trobe University.

C. B. Schedvin is Professor of Economic History at the University of Melbourne, author of *Australia and the Great Depression* (1970), co-author of *War Economy 1942–1945* (1977), and co-editor of *Urbanization in Australia: The Nineteenth Century* (1974) and *Australian Capital Cities: Historical Essays* (1978).

M. B. Schedvin is a graduate student in Political Science.